The Best
AMERICAN
SHORT
STORIES
1984

GUEST EDITORS OF
The Best American Short Stories

1978 Ted Solotaroff
1979 Joyce Carol Oates
1980 Stanley Elkin
1981 Hortense Calisher
1982 John Gardner
1983 Anne Tyler
1984 John Updike

The *Best* AMERICAN SHORT STORIES 1984

Selected from
U.S. and Canadian Magazines
by John Updike
with Shannon Ravenel

With an Introduction by John Updike

 1984

Houghton Mifflin Company Boston

Shannon Ravenel is grateful to David Weems,
who gave valuable consultation on science fiction
and science fantasy.

ISSN 0067-6233
ISBN 0-395-35413-7
ISBN 0-395-36512-0 (pbk.)

Printed in the United States of America

V 10 9 8 7 6 5 4 3 2 1

"The Final Proof of Fate and Circumstance" by Lee K. Abbott. First published in
The Georgia Review. Copyright © 1983 by Lee K. Abbott. Reprinted by permission
of the author.

"The Naked Lady" by Madison Smartt Bell. First published in *The Crescent Review.*
Copyright © 1983 by Madison Smartt Bell. Reprinted by permission of the author.

"Unknown Feathers" by Dianne Benedict. First published in *MSS.* Copyright ©
1982 by Dianne Benedict. Reprinted by permission of the author.

"In the Red Room" by Paul Bowles. First published in *Antaeus.* Copyright © 1981
by Paul Bowles. Reprinted by permission of the author.

"The Cure" by Mary Ward Brown. First published in *Ascent.* Copyright © 1983
by *Ascent* Corporation. Reprinted by permission of the editor.

"Gent" by Rick DeMarinis. First published in *CutBank.* Copyright © 1983 by Rick
DeMarinis. Reprinted by permission of the author.

"A Father's Story" by Andre Dubus. First published in *Black Warrior Review.*
Copyright © 1983 by Andre Dubus. Reprinted by permission of the author.

"Lena" by Mavis Gallant. First published in *The New Yorker.* Copyright © 1983 by
Mavis Gallant. Reprinted by permission of the author.

"Inexorable Progress" by Mary Hood. First published in *The Georgia Review.*
Copyright © 1983 by Mary Hood. Reprinted by permission of the author.

"The Artificial Moonlight" by Donald Justice. First published in *Antaeus.* Copyright © 1983 by Donald Justice. Reprinted by permission of the author.

"Morrison's Reaction" by Stephen Kirk. First published in *The Greensboro Review.*
Copyright © 1983 by Stephen Kirk. Reprinted by permission of the author.

Contents

Publisher's Note

The *Best American Short Stories* series was started in 1915 under the editorship of Edward J. O'Brien. Its title reflects the optimism of a time when people assumed that an objective "best" could be identified, even in fields not measurable in physical terms.

Martha Foley took over as editor of the series in 1942 when Mr. O'Brien was killed in World War II. With her husband, Whit Burnett, she had edited *Story* magazine since 1931, and in later years she taught creative writing at Columbia School of Journalism. When Miss Foley died in 1977, at the age of eighty, she was at work on what would have been her thirty-seventh volume of *The Best American Short Stories*.

Beginning with the 1978 edition, Houghton Mifflin introduced a new editorial arrangement for the anthology. Inviting a different writer or critic to edit each new annual volume would provide a variety of viewpoints to enliven the series and broaden its scope. *Best American Short Stories* has thus become a series of informed but differing opinions that gains credibility from its very diversity.

Also beginning with the 1978 volume, the guest editors have worked with the annual editor, Shannon Ravenel, who during each calendar year reads as many qualifying short stories as she can get hold of, makes a preliminary selection of 120 stories for the guest editor's consideration, and selects the "100 Other Distinguished Short Stories of the Year," a listing that has always been an important feature of these volumes.

The stories chosen for this year's anthology were originally published in magazines issued between January 1983 and January 1984. The qualifications for selection are: (1) original publication in nationally distributed American or Canadian periodicals; (2) publication in English by writers who are American or Canadian; and (3) publication *as* short stories (novel excerpts are not knowingly considered by the editors). A list of the magazines consulted by Ms. Ravenel appears at the back of this volume. Other publications wishing to make sure that their contributors are considered for the series should include Ms. Ravenel on their subscription list (P.O. Box 3176, University City, Missouri 63130).

Introduction

GIRDING MY LOINS for this editorial task, I read the collection of fifty years ago, *The Best Short Stories 1934*. It came out when I was two, and its contents were written in my infancy and perhaps conceived before I was. It contained thirty stories, selected single-handedly by Edward J. O'Brien, who also managed, from his address on Banbury Road in Oxford, to edit an annual British counterpart as well. Some of the authors whose works he reprinted in 1934 are still well remembered — William Faulkner most emphatically so. Indeed, against the general impression that Faulkner was an unappreciated author until his last years may be set the fact that throughout the thirties and forties, an annual *Best* without a Faulkner story in it was more the exception than the rule. Also represented in 1934 were Erskine Caldwell, Morley Callaghan, Langston Hughes, and Allen Tate (with an odd sad tale as stilted as his poetry). Some others of the honored names ring fainter bells — Manuel Komroff; Marquis Childs; Vincent Sheean; William March, author of *The Bad Seed;* Alvah C. Bessie, of the blacklisted "Hollywood Ten"; and both Whit Burnett and Martha Foley, who together took over the editorship of this series when O'Brien died (and who are one of two married couples present in the collection, since Tate's wife, Caroline Gordon, also has a story among the thirty). A good third of the writers in that year's *Best* were quite unknown to me, though they had produced some of the collection's gems, for example, Eugene Joffe's "Siege of Love" and Alexander Godin's "My Dead Brother Comes to America."

Perusal of the volume's index of "Distinctive Short Stories in American Magazines" reveals that O'Brien could have reprinted, but chose not to, "The Red Pony," by John Steinbeck, and "A Clean, Well-Lighted Place," by Ernest Hemingway, along with works by Sherwood Anderson, Gertrude Stein, Conrad Aiken, and Thomas Wolfe.

A number of the stories he did select struck this belated reader as, really, atrociously written, in a hard-breathing, toss-it-all-in style of portentous flashbacks and parenthetical urgencies more fashionable then (see Faulkner and Wolfe) than now. Zestful formal experimentation coexisted in 1934 with tame, Tarkingtonish stories of domestic misadventure. One entry (Louis Mamet's "The Pension," reprinted from *The Anvil*) was virtually a play, a little piece of agitprop set in a heartless factory of murderously defective machines. But vernacular monologue, with its dramatic ironies and verbal humor, was a popular form, and rural scenes predominate, redolent of a raw poverty more shocking, perhaps, now than then. "Bad time now in America," a bankrupt immigrant tells an out-of-work stranger on a park bench. Bums and bumming were commonplace in 1934; a policeman kicks a body in Lincoln Square, and to his chagrin discovers it to be a dead body, a starved man wearing religious medals, a Roman Catholic like himself ("The Sacred Thing," by Paul Ryan). Two of the stories (Alvah Bessie's "No Final Word" and Alan Marshall's "Death and Transfiguration") harrowingly portray birth-labor under primitive conditions; in one, the mother dies, and in the other, the infant.

The Best Short Stories 1934 reflects a harsh world, but not a hopeless or narrow one. No doubt thanks in part to O'Brien's selecting hand, there is a vigorous ethnic and geographical variety: two of the stories have black heroines, another (*not* by Saroyan) concerns an Armenian community in California. The sandy coast of Florida, waiting for its boom, and the clammy marshes and decayed villages of New Hampshire's meager coast are evoked with a specificity that puts us squarely there. Western desert rats and southern gentry, New York jazz musicians and strong silent women of the prairie are conjured up, and there is no interchangeability of milieu or persona. Less homogenous than today's America, that of 1934 feels more consciously democratic, in the range of types and accents that authors felt empowered to bring to life. Hollywood movies of the time, of course, also embody this hopeful richness of types, each distinct to the point of caricature and functioning within the bounds of an assigned social "place," yet all nevertheless embraced by the egalitarian myth, available to one another's admiration and use, a certain shared American energy winning each a vote at least in the imagination of artists. In a nation still composed of more or less closed and insular regions, classes, and immigrant groups, a writer arising anywhere had something to deliver — a report to the nation at large as to conditions in Asheville, or upper Michigan, or Mississippi, or Harlem, or Fresno. Even now, the Hispanic and Chinese Americans are just beginning to check in (Richard Rodriguez, Maxine Hong Kingston).

Yet it must be admitted that many of *The Best Short Stories 1934* could appear in this present selection with scarcely a jarring note and that a surprising number of this year's stories are rural or small-town in locale. Surprising, that is, because many more Americans live in cities or their suburbs than elsewhere, and the most influential short-story writers of the last decades — J. D. Salinger in the fifties, Donald Barthelme in the sixties, Ann Beattie in the seventies — were all urban sensibilities. Yet urbanity, and the exhilarations of big-city life, seemed in notable recession in the short fiction of 1983, and the charms of southern aunts and country-flavored reminiscence in notable resurgence. Perhaps Americans no longer trust and adore their cities; or perhaps most writers now live on campuses, where bucolic appearances are artificially preserved. Or the short story could be a basically conservative form. A thirties painting or a thirties automobile looks more dated than a thirties story. Like women's skirts, short prose fiction can only go up and down so much, and this season we are somewhere between the racy Barthelme mini and the wide-swinging Harold Brodkey maxi with its heavy folds and multiple pleats.

All of nine of *The Best Short Stories 1934* came from *Story* magazine, now long defunct. Two more came from *The American Mercury*, one from *Scribner's Magazine*, and two from *Vanity Fair*, which has recently been rendered, for a time at least, de-defunct. Some of the magazines represented — *Harper's, The Atlantic Monthly, Prairie Schooner, The Yale Review, Commonweal* — are still with us, in revised formats. Conspicuously absent from O'Brien's sources is *The New Yorker,* though the magazine was nine years old in 1934 and had turned the corner into solvency and fashionability. Arthur Kober and John O'Hara have a few *New Yorker* contributions listed in the index of also-rans, marked mostly with one star (the minimum in O'Brien's rather fussy rating system), and that's about it for the publication that has come to dominate the short-fiction market and (with the exception of John Gardner's volume) recent *Best* collections. In 1948 — the inverse of our year and the one, of course, in which Orwell wrote *1984* — *The New Yorker,* with three stories to still-functioning *Story's* two, does not loom overwhelmingly; but two of the three are classics that lent their titles to memorable books: "The Enormous Radio," by John Cheever, and "The Second Tree from the Corner," by E. B. White. Since 1980 the guest editors of this series have picked nearly half of their *Best* from *The New Yorker;* with some determination I have held my own quota to five, or one quarter.

Fifty years, in sum, have seen the number of general magazines that publish fiction greatly shrink, and the field of weekly national magazines that print fiction shrink to one. I wonder, could any young writer now support himself or herself and a family, as I did in my twenties, by selling six or so short stories a year? The magazines that pay significant (four-figure) amounts for short fiction cannot presently be more than a dozen, and of those perhaps four (*The New Yorker, The Atlantic Monthly, Esquire,* and *Playboy*) are open to what we might call artistic experimentation. For Faulkner, short stories were bread and butter; for Scott Fitzgerald, in the palmy days of the old *Post,* they were an avenue to glamour such as now awaits rock stars. Now, for the bright young graduates that pour out of the Iowa Writers' Workshop and its sister institutions, publishing short stories is a kind of accreditation, a certificate of worthiness to teach the so-called art of fiction. The popular market for fiction has shriveled while the academic importance of "creative writing" has swelled; academic quarterlies, operating under one form of subsidy or another, absorb some of the excess. The suspicion persists that short fiction, like poetry since Kipling and

Bridges, has gone from being a popular to a fine art, an art preserved in a kind of floating museum made up of many little superfluous magazines. The populist flavor of *Best Short Stories 1934* — the sense of a pluralistic people trying to explain themselves to themselves — is not likely to be tasted by a reader of *Best American Short Stories 1984* in the murky year 2034.

Enough of the past and the future. The present facts are these: Shannon Ravenel, that St. Louis saint of scrutiny, sifted out of 1428 eligible stories published in 539 issues of 141 different periodicals a mere 120, which she forwarded to me and which I then sifted, shuffled, and squeezed to make these twenty. Nineteen, actually: I have added on my own Mavis Gallant's "Lena," because in the course of my year's casual reading I had especially liked it and because I thought a volume describing itself as "Selected from U.S. and Canadian Magazines" should contain at least one story by a Canadian. Who better to welcome from the north than the annually amazing Ms. Gallant, whose talent, exercised for many years in Parisian exile, is as versatile and witty as it is somber and empathetic?

Ms. Ravenel's batch contained two stories by me and one by my mother, Linda Grace Hoyer; I instantly disqualified myself as an interested party and set all three aside. Of what remained, I had hoped that perhaps half could be dismissed at a skimming glance; but in fact almost every one of the stories compelled a reading through to the end. I made three piles — in order of eventual size, "Yes," "Maybe," and "No." I leaned away from candidates that seemed to be fragments of novels or parts of a greater whole, and also from stories that seemed to be thinly disguised memoirs, even when they were as elegant and illuminating as those by Jamaica Kincaid and Andrea Lee. I asked that something feel invented, that there be something free-standing and, if seemingly remembered, yet willfully distorted about the stories considered, whether written in the first or the third person. Even so, so many of the stories I ended up choosing were composed in the first person that I considered deviating from the traditional alphabetical-by-author order in order to distribute them, lest one many-headed ego seem to be chanting this book. But in the end the alphabetical order seemed as

good as any, and to have the advantage of being patently arbi-
trary. Even the anthologist's lowly art must have that sacred
pinch of the accidental, of the *given*. Had I arranged these myself, for instance, I might have put side by side Ms. Gallant's
"Lena" and Norman Rush's "Bruns" — both character portraits
in exotic settings — to point up, a bit pedantically, the sex-
reversal of author and narrator in each. In an age when an
unbridgeable chasm and a permanent state of war are often
said to loom between the sexes, it is gratifying to observe how
easily Ms. Gallant, here and elsewhere, assumes the dry, wry,
faintly harried voice of a woman-baffled male, and to observe
how Mr. Rush's anthropologist, curiously, *because* she speaks in
such a relaxed, brusque, unsentimental, "mannish" manner, is
somehow all the more persuasively female and fit to wear the
large breasts she casually admits to.

Making a selection like this turns out to be a kind of Ror-
schach test, pulling our secret proclivities from us. I was drawn
to stories about funerals and passed over a number about baseball. I would rather read about sleazy people than genteel ones.
My tolerance for, in print, violence and nature description is
rather high. I like those relatively rare stories that are about
people at work, such as a dentist (see pp. 140–49) or the young
woman who, in Mary Morris's "Copies" (admired but not chosen
for inclusion here), winds up happily pinned between one of
her boyfriends and the flashing, throbbing, pulsing body of a
color Xerox Model 2200. In a way, I want — perhaps we all
want — facts, words I can picture. I want stories to startle and
engage me within the first few sentences, and in their middle to
widen or deepen or sharpen my knowledge of human activity,
and to end by giving me a sensation of completed statement.
The ending is where the reader discovers whether he has been
reading the same story the writer thought he was writing. Two
chains of impression have been running in rough parallel; the
ending — "the soft shock at the bottom of the story, the gasp of
the dimly unfolding wings of finished symmetry" (to quote another story just barely excluded from this collection, "The
Dealer's Yard," by Sharon Sheehe Stark) — confirms or dis-
solves the imagined partnership. The ending of James Salter's
"Foreign Shores," for instance, returns us not to poor passive

Truus, our ostensible heroine, but to Gloria, and we realize that the story has been about her, her failures of the heart, all along. And the ending of Jeanne Schinto's "Caddies' Day," which ends this book, lifts a grubby and inconsequential-seeming scene from the underworld of childhood into timeless significance: the caddies' casual brutality and the little heroine's stubborn adherence to the menacing shack (a stickiness like that of the ants and bottles so insistently mentioned) add up to a celebration of — we venture to guess — our prepubescent pest's eventual sexuality. To explain, as I have just done, one's sensation of rightness slightly suffocates it; the *echt* ending is finer than analysis, an inner release, as Aristotle said, of tensions aroused. A narrative is like a room on whose walls a number of false doors have been painted; while within the narrative, we have many apparent choices of exit, but when the author leads us to one particular door, we know it is the right one *because it opens.* Wright Morris's splendid "Glimpse into Another Country" shows a set of rather confusing events amiably experienced by an elderly man whose actions are themselves confused, yet at the end, when another addled person affords him recognition and lifts her hand to wave, the gesture is identified and welcomed as "assurance," and we remember that at the outset he had headed to New York for "something in the way of assurance"; we realize, furthermore, that a great deal of what might appear to be our random, inefficient, and extravagant human activity is in fact a quest for reassurance. "You're okay, right, girlie? Right?" the heroine of "Caddies" is complimented, having stoically endured her little trial. And the family of protagonists in Susan Minot's "Thorofare," having bravely executed, in seven individual styles, their bizarre ritual of disposal, feel "something lofty" in their departing procession. The good ending dismisses us with a touch of ceremony, and throws a backward light of significance over the story just read. It *makes* it, as they say, or unmakes it — a weak beginning is forgettable, but the end of a story bulks in the reader's mind like the giant foot in a foreshortened photograph.

The ending of Lee K. Abbott's "The Final Proof of Fate and Circumstance" troubled me, as having somehow too many words, and the particular disconcerting word *fellow* arriving out of the blue; but I decided that this is Mr. Abbott's blue, and that this attempt at rendering in words a father-son rapport wraps up well enough so delicate and grappling a reformulation of heroic stoicism and comradely love, in a southern atmosphere where grown men refer to their father as "my daddy." Sexual love and its distress of the social order is the common theme of fiction; the more elusive matter of comradeship, within a family or social circle, is a relatively low-octane fuel that comfortably propels the compact form of the short story. Mr. Abbott deals with a son's love for his father; Andre Dubus's "A Father's Story" tells of a father's for his daughter. Ms. Minot shows a family assembled to scatter a mother's ashes; Mary Ward Brown's "The Cure" assembles three daughters at a mother's deathbed. Jonathan Penner's "Things To Be Thrown Away" reveals itself, in the end, to be about the helpless love of brother for brother. Paul Bowles's "In the Red Room" presents, at a level of understatement almost beneath thermal detection, that original hotspot, the Oedipal triangle, and Donald Justice's "The Artificial Moonlight" almost as coolly sketches that tenuous but tenacious erotic web, the group of young adult friends. In this case the friends' total history becomes a demonstration of the stunning work of time, as, like wind erosion, it slowly carves lives into unforeseeable shapes.

Time, that immense invisible in our midst, is part of the substance of narrative, as it is of music; from the standpoint of our subjectivity, death is time's ultimate fruit, and perhaps I need not be embarrassed or surprised that so many of these stories deal with death — deaths in the family, more or less close, and deaths as experienced or longed for by the subjects of Dianne Benedict's "Unknown Feathers" and Mary Hood's "Inexorable Progress." Also there were Molly Giles's "Rough Translations," whose heroine, Ramona, tries in vain to plan a good-taste funeral for herself, and Amy Hempel's "In the Cemetery Where Al Jolson Is Buried," wherein one young woman confronts another, just as young, dying in the hospital. In our heavily paved and sanitized world, death is an astounding visitor, a piece of nature that will not quite go away. Paradoxically, the merciful machinery of modern science does everything to prolong and give financial importance to dying. Several of the *Best* stories of fifty years ago dramatized how difficult it was to come into the world; a more contemporary theme seems to be how difficult it is to leave it. The heroines of "The Cure" and "Inexorable Progress" and Cynthia Ozick's "Rosa" are all burdened with life; euthanasia and gerontology figure in the eighties short story as distinctively as live-in lovers, Little League, shopping malls, television, and rickety extended families of stepparents and stepsiblings.

Equable distribution of theme, milieu, or authors by sex or degree of fame was not one of my conscious concerns; I tried to enter each microcosm as it rotated into view and to single out those that somehow, in addition to beginning energetically and ending intelligibly, gave me a sense of deep entry, of entry into life somewhat below the surface of dialogue and description; this nebulous sense of deep entry corresponds to the sensation we get in looking at some representational paintings that render not merely the colors and contours but the heft and internal cohesion of actual objects, which therefore exist on the canvas not as tinted flat shapes but as palpables posed in atmosphere. Skill alone cannot produce this extra fidelity to the real; it needs passion. Nor is it a matter of literal realism; Kafka has it more abundantly than Zola. In this collection, "Unknown Feathers" takes us into the center of a real dying, though it is hard to know how many of the events — the wife chopping the bed legs, the nun climbing the tree — are hallucinations. Joyce Carol Oates quickly and forcefully introduces the reader into the nervous systems of her heroines but does not always bother to tie up loose ends in the "real" world that frames their tensions; in "Nairobi" we do not know exactly what Ginny has been doing with her life up to now or why Oliver needs to have a presentable companion at his meeting. We do know, however, that we are experiencing an act of prostitution, performed with the not-quite-invulnerable inner distancing whereby the prostitute preserves her dignity. The atmosphere, as in Robbe-Grillet's mechanical renderings of circumstance, is fear; the tentative "puckish kiss" at the end is pathetic. The reassurance delivered in this instance — "You were lovely up there" — is in its dismissive past tense a cold far cry from "You're okay, right, girlie?"

The inner spaces that a good short story lets us enter are the

old apartments of religion. People in fiction are not only, as
E. M. Forster pointed out in his *Aspects of the Novel*, more sensitive than people one meets; they are more religious. Religion
and fiction both aver, with Kierkegaard, that "subjectivity is
truth"; each claims importance for the ephemeral sensations of
consciousness that material science must regard as accidents, as
epiphenomena. Fictional technique and the craft of suspense
are affected: without a transcendental ethics, of what significance are our decisions? It pleased me to hear, in "A Father's
Story," the grave, responsible voice of a convinced Roman Catholic, quite free of the impishness and hysteria that so often
attend this faith's manifestations in twentieth-century fiction.
With no unnatural stretching, a supernatural dialogue emerges
from a tawdry dilemma, an automotive mishap and its coverup.
Lena, in Mavis Gallant's more satiric world, is also a faithful
Catholic, but entirely, one feels, to suit her earthly purposes and
vanity. "Inexorable Progress" begins in church, and "Bruns"
ends with an act of sacrifice, a saintly feat ghastly and even sadly
comic in its modern context. Not just Christianity haunts these
imagined spaces: Paul Bowles describes, with an eerie indirec-
tion and softness of tone, a blood-soaked private shrine; Susan
Minot, a rite of water and bone and air; and Cynthia Ozick, a
private religion involving rapturous and lengthy communica-
tion with one of the dead. And surely there is something numi-
nous about the serpent ("This old snake just comes and goes
when the spirit moves him") that makes itself at home in the
untidy hovel of Madison Smartt Bell's "The Naked Lady."

Bell's story is the strangest in this selection, but I liked it the
instant I read it, for its delicate misspellings and cheerful voice
— a descendant of those vernacular voices that used to tell so
many stories in this country, from Mark Twain to Ring Lardner,
from John O'Hara to Eudora Welty. Bell's two heroes are no
more sociologically placeable than a pair of Beckett clowns; but
their fire in the cave of being seems securely lit, and we rejoice
to see their slow upward progress, like that of our remote ances-
tors. Ozick's "Rosa" is at the opposite pole — an exercise in several high styles, loosely translated from the Polish and the
Yiddish, as well as a very funny rendering of a star-crossed
courtship among feisty oldsters. It should be read, ideally, as a

sequel to her much bleaker and shorter story "The Shawl," which appeared in *The Best American Short Stories 1981*. In a few minimal pages, "The Shawl" told of the infant Magda's death by electrocution on a concentration-camp fence, of the shawl that the then-fourteen-year-old Stella steals and with which Rosa, rather than be shot for screaming, stifled herself. In these hellish circumstances Rosa voted for life, and she votes again for life here, in the gaudier hell of a broiling Florida populated by lascivious homosexuals, potential muggers, and garrulous retirees from the garment industry.

> In the street a neon dusk was already blinking. Gritty mixture of heat and toiling dust. Cars shot by like large bees. It was too early for headlights: in the lower sky two strange competing lamps — a scarlet sun, round and brilliant as a blooded egg yolk; a silk-white moon, gray-veined with mountain ranges. These hung simultaneously at either end of the long road. The whole day's burning struck upward like a moving weight from the sidewalk. Rosa's nostrils and lungs were cautious: burning molasses air.

Such gorgeous prose, abrupt in rhythm and replete with metaphor, we have already had from Bellow and Malamud, Fuchs and Elkin; in a woman's hands it becomes even more highly colored, more outrageously figured. So much clotted brilliance is thinned enough to flow by injected dialogue of laconic veracity:

> "I got my own troubles," Rosa said.
> "Unload on me."

One has to love Ms. Ozick for daring a bravura style in an age when many short-story writers are as tight-lipped as cardplayers on a losing streak — in faithful reflection, no doubt, of the *Weltgeist*, the post-Vietnam cool, cautious and anti-inflationary. Experience itself, in an age when so much is reported and exposed, has been cheapened. In the stories of, say, Bobbie Ann Mason and Frederick Barthelme, the people seem to be glancing away from television at the events of their own lives with the same barely amused, channel-changing diffidence. So one is grateful to Lee K. Abbott for his own bravura style and his willingness to stand up for filial love, and to Lowry Pei, whose "The Cold Room" melts into an old-fashioned love story — guy meets girl, guy dumps other girl, guy maybe gets right girl. One sits up when Stephen Kirk, showing an alarming intimacy with dental procedures, in "Morrison's Reaction," turns a three-hour appointment into a battle as strenuous and gruesome as Beowulf's long tug on Grendel's arm. One smiles, if wistfully, when, in Rick DeMarinis's "Gent," a twelve-year-old boy comes to see that his own mother is trouble — what they used to call a hot number. This story, incidentally, was one of many told from the standpoint of children (often with baroque titles such as "The Man Who Gave Brother Double Pneumonia" and "Frankenstein Meets the Ant People") but one of the few that seemed to me to catch childhood without hyperbole or condescension and to indicate with precision the links of dependence and imperception that connect it to the adult world. Our information about each other remains, in the midst of a sophistication glut, wonderfully faulty, and for this reason we read short stories. Each is a glimpse into another country: an occasion for surprise, an excuse for wisdom, and an argument for charity.

JOHN UPDIKE

The Best
AMERICAN
SHORT
STORIES
1984

LEE K. ABBOTT

The Final Proof of Fate and Circumstance

(FROM THE GEORGIA REVIEW)

HE LIKED TO BEGIN his story with death, saying it was an uncommonly dark night near El Paso with an uncommon fog, thick and all the more frightful because it was unexpected, like ice or a parade of gray elephants tramping across the desert from horizon to horizon, each moody and terribly violent. He was driving on the War Road, two lanes that came up on the south side of what was then the Proving Grounds, narrow and without shoulders, barbed-wire fences alongside, an Emergency Call Box every two miles, on one side the Franklin Mountains, on the other an endless spectacle of waste; his car, as I now imagine it, must have been a DeSoto or a Chrysler, heavy with chrome and a grill like a ten-thousand-pound smile, a car carefully polished to a high shine, free of road dirt and bug filth, its inside a statement about what a person can do with cheesecloth and patience and affection. "A kind of palace in there," he'd always say. "Hell, I could live out of the back seat." He was twenty-eight then, he said, and he came around that corner, taking that long, stomach-settling dip with authority, driving the next several yards like a man free of fret or second thought, gripping that large black steering wheel like a man with purpose and the means to achieve it, like a man intimate with his several selves, scared of little and tolerant of much. I imagine him sitting high, chin upturned, eyes squinty with attentiveness, face alight with a dozen gleams from the dashboard, humming a measure of, say, "Tonight We Love" by Bobby Worth, singing a word of romance now and then, the merry parts of the music as familiar to him as a certain road sign or oncoming dry arroyo. "I'd just come from Fort Bliss," he said. "I'd played in a golf tournament that day. Whipped Mr. Tommy Bolt, Jr. Old Automatic, that's me. Show up, take home the big one." He was full of a thousand human satisfactions, he said — namely, worth and comforts and renewals. He could hear his clubs rattling in the trunk; he could hear the wind rushing past, warm and dry, and the tires hissing; and he was thinking to himself that it was a fine world to be from, a world of many rewards and light pleasures; a world, from the vantage point of a victory on the golf course, with heft and sense to it, a world in which a person such as himself — an Army lieutenant such as himself, lean and leaderly — could look forward to the lofty and the utmost, the hindmost for those without muscle or brain enough to spot the gladsome among the smuts; yes, it was a fine world, sure and large enough for a man with finer features than most, a grown-up man with old but now lost Fort Worth money behind him, and a daddy with political knowledge, and a momma of substance and high habit, and a youth that had in it such things as regular vacations to Miami Beach, plus a six-week course in the correct carving of fowl and fish, plus a boarding school and even enough tragedy, like a sister drowning and never being recovered, to give a glimpse of, say, woe — which is surely the kind of shape you'd like your own daddy's character to have when he's about to round a no-account corner in the desert, a Ray Austin lyric on his lips, and kill a man.

It was an accident, of course, the state police saying it was a combination of bad luck — what with the victim standing so that his taillight was obscured — and the elements (meaning, mostly, the fog, but including as well, my daddy said, time and crossed paths and human error and bad judgment and a certain fundamental untidiness). But then, shaken and offended and partly remorseful, my daddy was angry, his ears still ringing with crash noises and the body's private alarms. "God damn," he said, wrestling open a door of his automobile, its interior dusty and strewn with stuffings from the glove box, a Texaco road map still floating in the air like a kite, a rear floormat folded like a tea towel over the front seat, a thump-thump-thump coming from here and there and there and there. It was light enough for him to see the other vehicle, the quarter-moon a dim milky spot, the fog itself swirling and seemingly lit from a thousand directions — half dreamland, half spook-house. "There was a smell, too," he told me, his hands fluttering near his face. A smell like scorched rubber and industrial oils, plus grease and disturbed soils. His trunk had flown open, his clubs — "Spaldings, Taylor, the finest!" — flung about like pick-up sticks. His thoughts, airy and affirming an instant before, were full of soreness and ache; for a moment before he climbed back to the road he watched one of his wheels spinning, on his face the twitches and lines real sorrow makes, that wheel, though useless, still going round and round, its hubcap scratched and dented. He was aware, he'd say every time he came to this part, of everything — splintered glass and ordinary night sounds and a stiffness deep in his back and a trouser leg torn at the knee and a fruitlike tenderness to his own cheek pulp. "I felt myself good," he said, showing me again how he'd probed and prodded and squeezed, muttering to himself, "Ribs and necks and hips," that old thighbone-hipbone song the foremost thing on his mind. He said his brain was mostly in his ears and his heart beat like someone was banging at it with a claw hammer, and there was a weakness in the belly, he remembered, which in another, less stalwart sort might have been called nausea but which in this man, he told himself as he struggled to the roadway, was nothing less than the true discomfort that comes when Good Feeling is so swiftly overcome by Bad.

At first he couldn't find the body. He said he walked up and down the road, both sides, yelling and peering into the fog, all the time growing angrier with himself, remembering the sudden appearance of that other automobile stopped more on the road than off, the panic that mashed him in the chest, the thud, the heart-flop. "I found the car about fifty yards away," he said, his voice full of miracle and distance as if every time he told the story — and, in particular, the parts that go from bad to worse — it was not he who approached the smashed Chevrolet coupe but another, an alien, a thing of curiosity and alert eyeballs, somebody innocent of the heartbreak humankind could make for itself. The rear of that Chevy, my daddy said, was well and thoroughly crunched, trunk lid twisted, fenders crumpled, its glowing brake light dangling, both doors sprung open as if whatever had been inside had left in a flurry of arm- and leg-work. My daddy paced around that automobile many times, looking inside and underneath and on top and nearabout, impatient and anxious, then cold and sweaty both. "I was a mess," he said. "I was thinking about Mr. Tommy Bolt and the duty officer at the BOQ and my mother and just every little thing." He was crying, too, he said, not sniveling and whimpering but important adult tears that he kept wiping away as he widened his circle around the Chevy, snot dribbling down his chin, because he was wholly afraid that, scurrying through the scrubgrowth and mesquite and prickly cactus and tanglesome weeds, he was going to find that body, itself crumpled, hurled into some unlikely and unwelcome position — sitting, say, or doing a handstand against a bush — or that he was going to step on it, find himself frozen with dread, his new GI shoes smack in the middle of an ooze that used to be chest or happy man's brain. "I kept telling myself Army things," he said one time. "Buck up. Don't be afraid. Do your duty. I told myself to be calm, methodical. Hope for the best, I said." And so, of course, when he was hoping so hard his teeth hurt and his neck throbbed and his lungs felt like fire, he found it, bounced against a concrete culvert, legs crossed at the ankles, arms folded at the belt, with neither scratch nor bump nor knot nor runny wound, its face a long and quiet discourse on peace or sleep.

"At first, I didn't think he was dead," my daddy told me. He scrambled over to the body, said *get up*, said *are you hurt*, said *can you talk, wake up, mister*. His name was Valentine ("Can you believe that name, Taylor?" Daddy would say. "Morris E. Valentine!") and my daddy put his mouth next to the man's earhole and hollered and grabbed a hand — "It wasn't at all cold" — and shook it and listened against the man's nose for breaths or a gurgle and felt the neck for a pulse. Then, he said, there wasn't anything to do next but look at Mr. Valentine's eyes, which were open in something like surprise or marvel and which were as inert and blank and glassy, my daddy said, as two lumps of coal that had lain for ten million years in darkness. It was then, my daddy said, that he felt the peacefulness come over him like a shadow on a sunny day — a tranquillity, huge and fitting, like (he said) the sort you feel at the end of fine drama when, with all the deeds done and the ruin dealt out fairly, you go off to eat and drink some; yup, he said one night, like the end of the War Road itself, a place of dust and fog and uprooted flora and fuzzy lights where you discover, as the state police did, a live man and a dead one, the first laughing in a frenzy of horror, the second still and as removed from life as you are from your ancestral fishes, his last thought — evidently a serious one — still plain on his dumb, awful face.

He told me this story again today, the two of us sitting in his back yard, partly in the shade of an upright willow, him in a racy Florida shirt and baggy Bermudas, me in a Slammin' Sammy Snead golf hat and swim trunks. It was hooch, he said, that brought out the raconteur in him, Oso Negro being the fittest of liquors for picking over the past. Lord, he must've gone through a hundred stories this afternoon, all the edge out of his voice, his eyes fixed on the country club's fourteenth fairway which runs behind the house. He told one about my mother meeting Fidel Castro. It was a story, he said, that featured comedy in large doses and not a little wistfulness. It had oomph and running hither and hoopla when none was expected. "Far as I could tell," he said, "he was just a hairy man with a gun. Plus rabble-rousers." He told another about Panama and the officers' club and the Geists, Maizie and Al, and a Memphis industrialist named T. Moncure Youtees. It was a story that started bad, went some distance in the company of foolishness and youthful huggermugger and ended not with sadness but with mirth. He told about Korea and moosey-maids and sloth and whole families of yellow folk living in squalor and supply problems and peril and cold and, a time later, of having Mr. Sam Jones of the Boston Celtics in his platoon. "You haven't known beauty," he said, smiling, "till you see that man dribble. Jesus, it was superior, Taylor." He told one about some reservists in Montana or Idaho — one of those barren, ascetic places — and a training exercise called Operation Hot Foot which involved, as I recall, scrambling this way and that, eyes peeled for the Red Team, a thousand accountants and farmboys and family men in night-time camouflage, and a nearsighted colonel named Krebs who took my daddy bird watching. My daddy said that from his position on a bluff he could see people in green scampering and diving and waving in something approaching terror, but that he and Krebs were looking through binoculars for nest or telltale feather, listening intently for warble or tweet or chirp, the colonel doing his best, with nose and lipwork, to imitate that sort of fear or hunger or passion a rare flying thing might find appealing. "It was lovely," my daddy said, the two of them putting over two hundred miles on the jeep in search of Gray's wing-notch swallow or something that had been absent from the planet, Daddy suspected, for an eon. There were trees and buttes and colors from Mr. Disney and a kind of austerity, extreme and eternal, that naturally put you in mind of the Higher Plane.

For another hour he went on, his stories addressing what he called the fine, events in which the hero, using luck and igno-rance, managed to avoid the base and its slick companion, the wanton. I heard about a cousin, A. T. LeDuc, who had it, let it slip away, and got it back when least deserved. I learned the two things any dog knows: Can I eat it, or will it eat me? I learned something about people called the Duke and the Earl and the Count and how Mr. Tommy Dorsey looked close up. I was touched — not weepy, like my wife Nadine gets when I tell her a little about my Kappa Alpha days at TCU or how I came out looking like a dope when I had gone in imagining myself a prince. To be true, I was in that warm place few get to these days, that place where your own daddy — that figure who whomped you and scolded you and who had nothing civil to say about the New York Yankees or General Eisenhower, and who expressed himself at length on the subjects of hair and fit read-ing matter and how a gentleman shines his shoes — yes, that place where your own daddy admits to being a whole hell of a lot like you, which is sometimes confused and often weak; that place, made habitable by age and self-absorption and fatigue, that says much about those heretofore pantywaist emotions like pity and fear.

Then, about four o'clock, while the two of us stood against his cinder-block fence, watching a fivesome of country-club ladies drag their carts up the fairway, the sun hot enough to satisfy even Mr. Wordsworth, my daddy said he had a new story, one which he'd fussed over in his brain a million times but one which, on account of this or that or another thing, he'd never told anyone. Not my momma, Elaine. Not my uncle Lyman. Not his sisters, Faith and Caroline. His hand was on my forearm, squeezing hard, and I could see by his eyes, which were watery and inflamed by something I now know as purpose, and by his wrinkled, dark forehead and by his knotted neck muscles — by all these things, I knew this story would not feature the fanciful or foreign — not bird, nor military mess-up, nor escapade, nor enterprise in melancholy; it would be, I suspected while he stared at me as though I were no more related to him than that brick or that rabbit-shaped cloud, about mystery, about the odd union of innocence and loss, which sometimes passes for wisdom, and about the downward trend of human desires. There was to be a moral, too; and it was to be, like most morals, modern and brave and tragic.

This was to be, I should know, another death story, this one related to Valentine's the way one flower — a jonquil, say — is related to another, like a morning glory, the differences between them obvious, certain, and important; and it was to feature a man named X, my daddy said; a man, I realized instantly, who was my father himself, slipped free of the story now by time and memory and fortunate circumstance. X was married now, my daddy said, to a fine woman and he had equally fine children, among them a youth about my own age, but X had been married before and it would serve no purpose, I was to know, for the current to know about the former, the past being a thing of regret and error. I understood, I said, understanding further that this woman — my daddy's first wife! — was going to die again as she had died before.

She was a French woman, my daddy said, name of Annette D'Kopman, and X met her in September 1952 at the 4th Army Golf Tournament in San Antonio, their meeting being the product of happenstance and X's first-round victory over the

professional you now know as Mr. Orville Moody. "X was thirty-
one then," my daddy said, filling his glass with more rum, "the
kind of guy who took his celebrating seriously." I listened
closely, trying to pick out those notes in his voice you might call
mournful or misty. There were none, I'm pleased to say, just a
voice heavy with curiosity and puzzlement. "This Annette person was a guest of some mucky-muck," my daddy was saying,
and when X saw her, he suspected it was love. I knew that
emotion, I thought, it having been produced in me the first time
I saw Nadine. I recalled it as a steady knocking in the heart-spot
and a brain alive with a dozen thoughts. This Annette, my
daddy said, was not particularly gorgeous, but she had, according to X, knuckles that he described as wondrous, plus delicate
arches and close pores and deep sockets and a method of getting
from hither to yon with style enough to make you choke or ache
in several body parts. So, X and Annette were married the next
week, the attraction being mutual, a Mexican JP saying plenty,
for twenty dollars, about protection and trust and parting after
a long life of satisfactions, among the latter being health and
offspring and daily enjoyments.

As he talked, my daddy's face had hope in it, and some pride,
as though he were with her again, thirty years from the present
moil, squabbling again (as he said) about food with unlikely and
foreign vegetables in it, or ways of tending to the lower needs
of the flesh. X and Annette lived at Fort Sam Houston, him the
supply officer for the second detachment, she a reward to come
home to. "It wasn't all happy times," Daddy was saying, there
being shares of blue spirits and hurt feelings and misunder-
standings as nasty as any X had since had with his present wife.
"There was drinking," he said, "and once X smacked her. Plus,
there was hugging and driving to Corpus Christi and evenings
with folks at the officers' club and swimming." I imagined them
together and — watching him now slumped in his chair, the sun
a burning disc over his shoulder — I saw them as an earlier
version of Nadine and me: ordinary and doing very well to keep
a healthful distance from things mean and hurtful. The lust
part, he said, wore off, of course, the thing left behind being
close enough to please even the picky and stupid. Then she
died.

I remember thinking that this was the hard part, the part
wherein X was entitled to go crazy and do a hundred destructive
acts, maybe grow moody and sullen, utter an insulting phrase
or two, certainly drink immoderately. I was wrong, my daddy
said. For it was a death so unexpected, like one in a fairy tale,
that there was only time for an "Aaaarrrggghhh!" and seventy
hours of sweaty, dreamless sleep. "X didn't feel rack or nothing," my daddy said. "Not empty, not needful, nor abused by
any dark forces." X was a blank — shock, a physician called it
— more rock than mortal beset with any of the familiar hard-
ships. "X did his job," Daddy said, "gave his orders, went and
came, went and came." X watched TV, his favorite being Mr.
Garry Moore's "I've Got a Secret," read a little in the lives of
others, ate at normal hours, looked as steadfast as your ordinary
citizen, one in whom there was now a scorched and tender spot
commonly associated with sentiment and hope. Colonel Buck
Wade made the funeral arrangements — civilian, of course —
talking patiently with X, offering a shoulder and experience
and such. "X kept wondering when he'd grieve," Daddy said.
Everyone looked for the signs: outburst of the shameful sort,
tactless remark, weariness in the eyes and carriage, etc. But
there was only numbness, as if X were no more sentient than a
clock or Annette herself.

"Now comes the sad part," my daddy said, which was not the
ceremony, X having been an Episcopalian, or the burial because
X never got that far. Oh, there was a service, X in his pressed
blues, brass catching the light like sparkles, the minister, a Dr.
Hammond Ellis, trying through the sweep and purl of learned-
ness itself to put the finest face on a vulgar event, reading one
phrase about deeds and forgiveness and another about the af-
terworld and its light comforts, each statement swollen with a
succor or a joy, yet words so foreign with knowledge and accep-
tance that X sat rigid, his back braced against a pew, his pals
unable to see anything in his eyes except emptiness. No, the
sadness didn't come then — not with prayer, not with the sniffling of someone to X's left, not at the sight of the casket itself
being toted outside. The sadness came, my daddy said, in the
company of the driver of the family car in which X rode alone.
"The driver was a kid," my daddy said, "twenty, maybe younger,

name of Monroe." Whose face, Daddy said, reflected a thousand conflicting thoughts — of delight and of money and of nookie and of swelter like today's. Monroe, I was to know, was the squatty sort, the kind who's always touchy about his height, with eyeballs that didn't say anything about his inner life, and chewed nails and a thin tie and the wrong brown shoes for a business otherwise associated with black, and an inflamed spot on his neck that could have been a pimple or ingrown hair. "Stop," X said, and Monroe stared at him in the mirror. "What —?" Monroe was startled. "I said stop." They were about halfway to the gravesite, funeral coach in front, a line of cars with their lights on in back. "Stop here. Do it now." X was pointing to a row of storefronts in Picacho Street — laundry, a barber's, a Zale's jewelry.

My daddy said he didn't know why Monroe so quickly obeyed X, but I know now that Monroe was just responding to that note in my daddy's voice that tells you to leave off what you're doing — be it playing canasta, eating Oreos with your mouth open, or mumbling in the favorite parts of "Gunsmoke" — and take up politeness and order and respectfulness. It's a note that encourages you toward the best and most responsible in yourself, and it had in it a hint of the awful things that await if you do not. So the Cadillac pulled over, Monroe babbling "Uh-uh-uh," and X jumped out, saying, "Thank you, Monroe, you may go on now." It was here that I got stuck trying to explain it to Nadine, trying to show that funeral coach already well up the street, Monroe having a difficult time getting his car in gear while behind him, stopped, a line of headlamps stretching well back, a few doors opening, the folks nearest startled and wild-eyed and looking to each other for help, and X, his hat set aright, already beginning a march down the sidewalk, heels clicking, shoulders squared, a figure of precision and care and true strength. I told Nadine, as my daddy told me, about the cars creeping past, someone calling out, Colonel Buck Wade stopping and ordering, then shouting for X to get in. X didn't hear, my daddy said. Wade was laughable, his mouth working in panic, an arm waving, his wife tugging at his sleeve, himself almost as improbable as that odd bird my daddy and another colonel had spent a day hunting years ago.

"X didn't know where he was going," my daddy said. To be true, he was feeling the sunlight and the heavy air and hearing, as if with another's ears, honks and shouts, but X said he felt moved and, yes, driven, being drawn away from something, not forward to another. The sadness was on him then, my daddy said, and this afternoon I saw it again in his face, a thing as permanent as the shape of your lips or your natural tendency to be silly. X went into an ice-cream parlor, and here I see him facing a glass-fronted counter of tutti-frutti and chocolate chip and daiquiri ice, and behind it a teenage girl with no more on her mind than how to serve this one then another and another until she could go home. X ordered vanilla, my daddy said, eating by the spoonful, deliberately and slowly, as if the rest of his life — a long thing he felt he deserved — depended on this moment. It was the best ice cream X ever ate, my daddy said, and for three cones he thought of nothing, not bleakness, not happiness, not shape, nor beauty, nor thwarts, nor common distress — not anything the brain turns toward out of tribulation. It was then, my daddy said, that X realized something — about the counter girl, the ice cream itself, Colonel Buck Wade, even the children and the new wife he would have one day, and the hundreds of years still to pass — and this insight came to X with such force and speed that he felt lightheaded and partially blind, the walls tipping and closing on him, the floor rising and spinning, that mountain of sundae crashing over his shoulders and neck; he was going to pass out, X knew, and he wondered what others might say, knowing that his last thought — like Mr. Valentine's in one story — was long and complex and featured, among its parts, a scene of hope followed by misfortune and doom.

When Nadine asked me an hour ago what the moral was, I said, "Everything is fragile." We were in the kitchen, drinking Buckhorn, she in her pj's; and I tried, though somewhat afflicted by drink and a little breathless, to explain, setting the scene and rambling, mentioning ancient times and sorrows and pride in another. It was bad. I put everything in — the way of sitting, how the air smelled when my daddy went inside, gestures that had significance, what my own flesh was doing. But I was wrong.

Completely wrong. For I left out the part where I, sunburned but shivering, wandered through X's house, one time feeling weepy, another feeling foolish and much aged.

The part I left out shows me going into his kitchen, reading the note my momma wrote when she went to Dallas to visit my aunt Dolly; and it shows me standing in every room, as alien in that place as a sneak thief, touching their bric-a-brac and my daddy's tarnished golf trophies, sitting on the edge of the sofa or the green, shiny lounger, opening the medicine cabinet in the guest bathroom, curiosity in me as strong as the lesser states of mind. It's the part that has all the truth in it — and what I'll tell Nadine in the morning. I'll describe how I finally entered my daddy's room and stood over his bed, listening to him snore, the covers clenched at his chest, saying to myself, as he did long ago, headbone and chinbone and legbone and armbone. Yes, when I tell it I'll put in the part wherein a fellow such as me invites a fellow such as him out to do a thing — I'm not sure what — that involves effort and sacrifice and leads, in an hour or a day, to that throb and swell fellows such as you call triumph.

MADISON SMARTT BELL

The Naked Lady

(FROM THE CRESCENT REVIEW)

For Alan Lequire

THIS IS A THING that happened before Monroe started maken the heads, while he was still maken the naked ladies.

Monroe went to the college and it made him crazy for a while like it has done to many a one.

He about lost his mind on this college girl he had. She was just a little old bit of a thing and she talked like she had bugs in her mouth and she was just nothen but trouble. I never would of messed with her myself.

When she thown him over we had us a party to take his mind off it. Monroe had these rooms in a empty mill down by the railroad yard. He used to make his scultures there and we was both liven there too at the time.

We spent all the money on whiskey and beer and everbody we known come over. When it got late Monroe appeared to drop a stitch and went to thowin bottles at the walls. This caused some people to leave but some other ones stayed on to help him I think.

I had a bad case of drunk myself. A little before sunrise I crawled off and didn't wake up till up in the afternoon. I had a sweat from sleepin with clothes on. First thing I seen when I opened my eyes was this big old rat setten on the floor side the mattress. He had a look on his face like he was wonderen would it be safe if he come over and took a bite out of my leg.

It was the worst rats in that place you ever saw. I never saw nothin to match em for bold. If you chunked somethin at em they would just back off a ways and look at you mean. Monroe had him this tin sink which was full of plaster from the scultures and ever night these old rats would mess in it. In the mornin you could see they had left tracks goen places you wouldnt of believed somethin would go.

We had this twenty two pistol we used to shoot em up with but it wasnt a whole lot of good. You could hit one of these rats square with a twenty two and he would go off with it in him and just get meaner. About the only way to kill one was if you hit him spang in the head and that needs you to be a better shot than I am most of the time.

We did try a box of them exploden twenty twos like what that boy shot the president with. They would take a rat apart if you hit him but if you didnt they would bounce around the room and bust up the scultures and so on.

It happened I had put this pistol in my pocket before I went to bed so Monroe couldnt get up to nothin silly with it. I taken it out slow and thew down on this rat that was looken me over. Hit him in the hindquarter and he went off and clamb a pipe with one leg draggen.

I sat up and saw the fluorescents was on in the next room thew the door. When I went in there Monroe was messen around one of his sculture stands.

Did you get one, he said.

Winged him, I said.

That aint worth much, Monroe said. He off somewhere now plotten your doom.

I believe the noise hurt my head more'n the slug hurt that rat, I said. Is it any whiskey left that you know of.

Let me know if you find some, Monroe said. So I went to looken around. The place was nothin but trash and it was glass all over the floor.

I might of felt worse some time but I dont just remember when it was, I said.

They's coffee, Monroe said.

I went in the other room and found a half of a pint of Heaven Hill between the mattress and the wall where I must of hid it before I tapped out. Pretty slick for drunk as I was. I taken it in to the coffee pot and mixed half and half with some milk in it for the sake of my stomach.

Leave me some, Monroe said. I hadnt said a word, he must of smelt it. He tipped the bottle and took half what was left.

The hell, I said. What you maken anyway?

Naked lady, Monroe said.

I taken a look and it was this shape of a woman setten on a mess of clay. Monroe made a number of these things at the time. Some he kept and the rest he thown out. Never could tell the difference myself.

Thats all right, I said.

No it aint, Monroe said. Soon's I made her mouth she started in asken me for stuff. She wants new clothes and she wants a new car and she wants some jewry and a pair of Italian shoes.

And if I make her that stuff, Monroe said, I know she's just goen to take it out looken for some other fool. I'll set here all day maken stuff I dont care for and she'll be out just riden and riden.

Dont make her no clothes and she cant leave, I said.

She'll whine if I do that, Monroe said. The whole time you was asleep she been fussen about our relationship.

You know the worst thing, Monroe said. If I just even thought about maken another naked lady I know she would purely raise hell.

Why dont you just make her a naked man and forget it, I said.

Why dont I do this? Monroe said. He whopped the naked lady with his fist and she turned into a flat clay pancake, which Monroe put in a plastic bag to keep soft. He could hit a good lick when he wanted. I hear this is common among scultures.

Dont you feel like doen somethin, Monroe said.

I aint got the least dime, I said.

I got a couple dollars, he said. Lets go see if it might be any gas in the truck.

They was some. We had this old truck that wasnt too bad except it was slow to start. When we once got it goen we drove over to this pool hall in Antioch where nobody didnt know us. We stayed awhile and taught some fellers that was there how to play rotation and five in the side and some other games that Monroe was good at. When this was over with we had money and I thought we might go over to the Ringside and watch the fights. This was a bar with a ring in the middle so you could set there and drink and watch people get hurt.

We got in early enough to take seats right under the ropes. They was an exhibition but it wasnt much and Monroe started in on this little girl that was setten by herself at the next table.

Hey there Juicy Fruit, he said, come on over here and get somethin real good.

I wouldnt, I told him, haven just thought of what was obvious. Then this big old hairy thing came out from the back and sat down at her table. I known him from a poster out front. He was champion of some kind of karate and had come all the way up from Atlanta just to beat somebody to death and I didnt think he would care if it was Monroe. I got Monroe out of there. I was some annoyed with him because I would have admired to see them fights if I could do it without bein in one myself.

So Monroe said he wanted to hear music and we went some places where they had that. He kept after the girls but they wasnt any trouble beyond what we could handle. After while these places closed and we found us a little railroad bar down on Lower Broad.

It wasnt nobody there but the pitifulest band you ever heard and six bikers, the big fat ugly kind. They wasnt the Hell's Angels but I believe they would have done until some come along. I would of left if it was just me.

Monroe played pool with one and lost. It wouldnt of happened if he hadnt been drunk. He did have a better eye than me which may be why he is a sculture and I am a second rate pool player.

How come all the fat boys in this joint got on black leather jackets? Monroe hollered out. Could that be a new way to lose weight?

The one he had played with come bellyen over. These boys like to look you up and down beforehand to see if you might faint. But Monroe hooked this one side of the head and he went down like a steer in the slaughterhouse. This didnt make me as happy as it might of because it was five of em left and the one that was down I thought apt to get up shortly.

I shoved Monroe out the door and told him to go start the truck. The band had done left already. I thown a chair and I thown some other stuff that was layen around and I ducked out myself.

The truck wasnt started yet and they was close behind. It was this old four ten I had under the seat that somebody had sawed a foot off the barrel. I taken it and shot the sidewalk in front of these boys. The pattern was wide on account of the barrel bein short like it was and I believe some of it must of hit all of em. It was a pump and took three shells and I kept two back in case I needed em for serious. But Monroe got the truck goen and we left out of there.

I was some mad at Monroe. Never said a word to him till he parked outside the mill. It was a nice moon up and thowin shadows in the cab when the headlights went out. I turned the shotgun across the seat and laid it into Monroe's ribs.

What you up to? he said.

You might want to die, I said, but I dont believe I want to go with you. I pumped the gun to where you could hear the shell fallen in the chamber.

If that's what you want just tell me now and I'll save us both some trouble.

It aint what I want, Monroe said.

I taken the gun off him.

I dont know what I do want, Monroe said.

Go up ther and make a naked lady and you feel better, I told him.

He was messen with clay when I went to sleep but that aint what he done. He set up a mirror and done a head of himself instead. I taken a look at the thing in the mornin and it was a fair likeness. It looked like it was thinkin about all the foolish things Monroe had got up to in his life so far.

That same day he done one of me that was so real it even looked like it had a hangover. Ugly too but that aint Monroe's fault.

He is makin money with it now.

How we finally fixed them rats was we brought on a snake. Monroe was the one to have the idea. It was a good-sized one and when it had just et a rat it was as big around as your arm. It didnt eat more than about one a week but it appeared to cause the rest of em to lay low.

You might say it was as bad to have snakes around as rats but at least it was only one of the snake.

The only thing was when it turned cold the old snake wanted to get in the bed with you. Snakes aint naturally warm like we are and this is how come people think they are slimy which is not the truth when you once get used to one.

This old snake just comes and goes when the spirit moves him. I aint seen him in a while but I expect he must be still around.

DIANNE BENEDICT

Unknown Feathers

(FROM MSS)

HE WOKE IN THE NIGHT in the room she had put him in when they found out he was not going to get well. He saw a pool of moonlight in one corner and the long gauze curtains flapping out the open window like ghosts waving. He knew from the color of the shadows that it was near the morning. He looked past the foot of the bed and saw that the door was open into the hall, and that the top part of the stairs was caught in a square of moonlight crossed with thin black bars. Into this moonlight appeared his wife, coming barefooted up the stairs in her cotton slip. The black bars glided over her face and breast, and then she was in the room, standing in front of his chifforobe, which had the door hanging open and all the drawers pulled out. He watched her take his shirts down, with the hangers still in them, and all his trousers, and the brass ring holding his neckties. She took down also his two suits, the lightweight gray one and the brown wool one, which had hung there, unworn, for over twenty years. She held these clothes against her, lifting them high to keep them from dragging, and went to the top of the stairs. There she paused, then descended sideways, looking carefully to see where to put her feet.

He drew himself up on his elbow and gazed about the room. It looked bare and strange. His fiddle was missing from the oak bench beside his bed. Gone, as well, were all his catalogues, and the bell that she had given him to summon her. He reached out and felt along the windowsill for his pipe and scraper, but they were gone, too. He lay back and stared at the ceiling, studying a water-mark there, shaped like a crab, with which, over the past two months, he had grown very familiar.

After a few moments, his wife returned. This time she brought with her an old slat basket into which she gathered all his unwashed clothes that he'd thrown in a heap on the chair, and the belongings he'd collected on the shelf over the wash-stand, including his many bottles of medicine.

"What have you done with my fiddle?" he asked her. "And my catalogues?"

She turned and stared at him, then came and stood beside him.

"I've reached the end of it," she said. "You have got to call the county people to come get you. I can't keep you any more."

She pulled his blanket back until she had uncovered the small dog, which had curled itself into a ball against his leg. The dog raised its head sleepily and looked around the room. She lifted it by the skin of its neck and put it into the basket under the clothes. Then she went down the stairs. He got out of the bed and followed her.

Twice he had to rest on the stairs, braced against the wall until his head cleared. When he reached the landing at the bottom, he caught sight of himself in the old silver-spotted mirror which had hung there since he was a young man, newly married. He hardly recognized himself. He looked much older than his fifty years, and his eyes were large and dark and sunk into his head. He drew back from the specter of this, startled, as though from the face of an animal. Then he forced himself to look again, steadily, and this time was content that he'd kept himself shaven and clean. He was glad that he had been careful with his large mustache, which had remained glossy and reddish and full of vigor.

He had not been downstairs in many weeks, and everything looked smaller there, crowded, and not as clean as he remembered it. When he entered the kitchen, he found his wife waiting for him by the back door, holding the dog against her breast. She lifted the latch and went out, and then stood on the steps, keeping the screen door open for him. He came down beside her on the steps and took the dog out of her hands.

"The keys are in the truck," she said. "It's been too long and I can't take no more of it."

She went back up into the house and closed the wooden door.

He turned on the steps and regarded the horizon, which was a diffuse, silver-colored haze bearing in its center the white edge of the sun. Nearby, in the dark yard, he saw the bed they had always used for sleeping in the open on warm nights. Spreading over it, just as he remembered, was the big pear tree. This tree was caught in the first light, and crowded to the tip of every branch with buds.

Two weeks later, at around the same hour, he lay asleep under the flowering tree in the old iron bed. He lay exposed, in his suit of sweat-stained underwear, his long legs tangled in a brown blanket. He had grown a coarse beard, and his hair looked as stiff and unruly as a horsebrush. His pale, sorrowing face was troubled by some dream that was bothering him.

The night had ceased its deep sounding and turned toward the morning. With the coming of the light, the full moon, hovering in the northern quarter, had grown as thin and insignificant as a piece of old cheesecloth.

In the countryside, the animals slept on. The coyotes were flung out on mounds of husks under the cactus. The old boar havalenas, fallen like stones in the open, ground their tusks. The little armadillos slept curled around roots underground.

In the henhouse, the hens quaked and teetered in deep sleep behind the dusty panes; the calf slept in the barn, next to the cow, who slept tied to the wall; and the two mares, sisters, slept with their faces touching. Even the metal-blue milkpails slept in a row, dreaming, in a slant of shadow by the bin of oats.

The man slept on his side, his hands pressed together between his thighs. All night he'd been calling to his wife for water, and she hadn't brought it. Now he slept heavily in a stupor of thirst and exhaustion. Against his chest slept the small, hairless dog, which was about the size of a teapot.

Suddenly the back door of the house was flung open, and his wife rushed barefoot down the steps, carrying an iron pot full of water. She was a small middle-aged woman with wiry arms and cropped hair the color of gunpowder. She wore a long-tailed khaki shirt, which flapped around her like a brown bird taking flight.

She ran full speed across the yard, clutching the pot, and

when she reached the man in his bed, she drenched him with the water.

He sat up, gasping, his arms held away from his sides, and the small dog leapt to the ground and began running in a circle, carrying on pitifully, as if it had been struck by lightning.

The woman held the pot upside down and shook out the last drops. Then she crossed the yard and went back into the house.

The man got out of bed and picked up the dog and scraped the water off it, holding it under the armpits. It continued to cry piercingly, the way an animal cries when it is certain it has been killed. He shook it, then hugged it to him, then put his hand over its face, but nothing would console it. Finally he dropped it to the ground and stood at the foot of the bed, shaking.

"Mrs. Hart," he shouted at the house. "Mrs. Hart, I say. Can you hear me?"

There was no answer.

"I am leaving here today, Mrs. Hart. I am going to call the county people to come get me. Can you hear me?" The large white face of a horse, with dark eyes, appeared in a window of the barn.

"But first off you can expect a caller. For I aim to come calling on you, Mrs. Hart. I aim to enter the house today. And the county people can enter with me as witness."

The man put his hand on the bed railing to steady himself.

"What have you done with my fiddle?" he shouted. "And my catalogues!"

Again there was no answer, only his own voice coming back at him from out of the rangeland.

"I will not be held accountable for what happens now! Not after you violated my personal belongings! Do you hear me?"

"Hear me? Hear me?" came the echo from the countryside.

"That, Ma'am, is where you went too far!"

"Too far. Too far."

He sat on the foot of the bed, hugging himself, shivering.

"No food this whole time," he said, "and now she's stopped bringing the water."

He studied the small dog, which lay on its side, whimpering, glassy-eyed, as if it had lost all sense of this world.

"Soon's she hears a man's about to croak, she gets possessed to see if she can murder him."

He ran his hands roughly through his hair, shedding a shower of drops.

"Goes overboard with it."

He moved backward onto the bed and lay down, drawing his legs up. He lay with his back to the house, staring at the countryside. Every few seconds a bout of violent shivering racked him. Beside him, on the hard ground, the small dog grew quiet and drifted into a stupor.

In the barn window, the mare moved over to make room for her sister. The two of them lifted their chins over the sill, and watched the man with deep interest, as if something new and unusual were about to happen to him.

Woody Hart woke to the sound of his wife taking an axe to a leg of his bed. He lay rigid, feeling a thud hit the bed every few seconds, aware that this had been going on for quite some time. He rolled over with an arm up, expecting to see the axe raised, but no one was there. He eased over to the edge and peered down and there was the small dog lying in the dust, looking stunned. After a second, the dog came alive and sat up, measuring the distance up onto the bed with a keen eye. Then it hove back on its haunches and shot through the air like a slung stone. It hit the side of the bed hard, and fell back into the dust.

"Fool dog has drove out his brains thataway long as I can recall," Woody said. "Doesn't never seem to learn."

He stretched out his hand to the dog, and it got to its feet, shaking, and began to prance about weakly. It came to him and sniffed the length of each of his fingers, then climbed into his palm, lifting its feet in carefully one at a time.

Woody put the dog inside his shirt next to his ribs and lay back. He looked through the branches of the pear tree and felt himself being drawn upward through the clusters of blossoms into the sky, which had flung itself over the earth like a bolt of blue cloth. He heard, far away, the calling of geese. "What month is this?" he said, listening to the geese coming, and soon they were close overhead, descending swiftly, and he counted them as they went by, five geese, of an unknown feather, all faintly dappled and brown, like rooks.

"Headed for the sinkhole, likely," he said.

He watched the geese drift down into the mesquites near the bend in the road. He pictured them settling into the crater of water, scummy and green, in its beach of pocked mud.

"Is it the month of geese?" he said. "By damn, what geese are those?"

He heard the door up at the house open and close, and he turned and called out through the bars of his bed, "Mrs. Hart, are you aware that the summertime is over, and it's into the time now of the migration of the birds?"

He watched his wife go into the shed and come out with a harness, and he called out, "It's getting on too late in the *year* to be turning the sod." She paid no attention to him. She went on into the barn. After a few minutes, she came back out, leading the mule. The mule plodded in his harness, the loose straps trailing behind him.

"You take that animal out in the heat of the day," Woody said, "and come evening you'll be towing him home by the hind feet."

His wife drew the mule up in front of the shed and harnessed him to the plow and crossed with him between the trough and the windmill.

"Is it or is it not the fall of the year?" Woody Hart shouted.

But she was gone. He knew that she was headed around the shed, and would urge the mule into the wide plot bordered on three sides by prickly-pear so dense that it was like a sea of turtles. He pictured the mule throwing his weight forward against the collar, and saw the woman's small sinewy arms, brown as saddle leather, steadying the blade in the cut.

A memory came to him then of his wife, maybe three, maybe four years ago, bringing his fiddle to him over a field of busted sod. He was mending fence. He looked up and saw her coming toward him over the rough furrows. He remembered how she had looked in her cotton dress, her feet bare, the fiddle held high in one hand and the bow held high in the other, and he said, "I recollect now why she brought that fiddle *out* there." He laughed a low laugh, and the small dog, roused up by this, shuffled against him.

"She never was up to no good, that one," Woody said.

He recalled, as if it were only the day before, the deep light of that evening and the shadow of the fence stretching further and further over the field. He remembered lifting the fiddle to his chest and drawing whispers out of it as she undid her buttons and slipped out of her garments, one by one.

Afterwards, she had gone back across the field alone, bare and sleek as a child who's been playing in the river.

"Wished I had that fiddle now," he said. "Maybe she'd feed me."

He reached inside his shirt and put his hand over the small dog. With its globular belly and thin feet, it felt like a warm, dry frog. He traced, with his fingers, the pea-sized cowlick on its breast.

"Wished I had that fiddle now," he said.

He dozed, and woke, and dozed again.

He dreamed that it was night, and he was standing in the middle of the yard in the moonlight, and he looked up and saw his fiddle, with the bow beside it, lying on the roof of the house. In that moment, he caught sight of his wife standing at the window, wrapped all around with the long gauze curtains. He raised both fists and shouted to her that he was coming in, that it was no earthly use to bolt the door, but before he had taken very many steps forward, the house broke into flame at all of its seams, like something made out of paper, and sank by slow degrees toward the ground.

He woke, trembling and weak, blinded by the sun which blazed at him through the branches. He turned onto his side and studied the house. The tarpaper roof, littered with broken shingles, was set upon in that moment by sparrows falling on it like a shower of leaves.

Then he caught sight of something which interested him.

It was a length of fishwire, wrapped around a branch over his head, hanging down maybe two or three feet with a cork on the end of it.

He took the dog out of his shirt and set it in a twist of the blanket. Then he eased up, took hold of the wire and hauled it free. When he did this the limb snapped back, showering him with petals, and making him feel dizzy and frail. After a moment he crawled to the head of the bed and tied the fishwire tautly between two bars of the railing. He strummed on it, and it gave out a good sound that was a little like an acorn dropping down inside an old piano. He plucked on the wire rhythmically, pressing it up against the rail in different locations with his thumb, and this made a sound like eaveswater dripping into a barrel.

"Dogged if it ain't a regular sound," he said.

He played on, searching out the notes, until soon he was into some of his old tunes. He lost track of the time, propped against the head of the bed, making his music, singing with an increasingly full heart. The small dog crept up by slow degrees, and turned itself around deftly on his belly, and slept.

After a while, Woody became aware of someone on the road down near the sinkhole. He looked over and saw a group of women approaching. He counted five of them. He thought at first they were gypsies, but when they got closer he decided they must be the nuns from the old people's home in Twin Rivers, coming around on their yearly drive for bottles and rags. They were dressed in brown habits with the hoods thrown back, and seemed very relaxed and happy, looking about them as if vastly pleased to be out in this great wilderness of cactus and thorny mesquite.

As they passed through the gate, he saw that one of them had a light-haired child by the hand, a slightly built boy, not yet of school age.

They filed into the yard, smiling and waving to him, and the lead nun called out, "That was very fine music, Mr. Hart," and the others nodded and said, "Yes, indeed," and "Truly." They all came on toward him, looking tired and happy, as if they had reached the end of a long journey. They walked barefoot through the dust of the track, and when they were closer he saw that they wore, under their coarse habits, garments of fine white cloth which flashed at their wrists and ankles as they walked.

As they approached, he was overcome by shame regarding his state of attire.

"Mrs. Hart is in the sorghum field out back of the shed," he said, trying, with this information, to fend them off before they got any nearer, but they came on toward him.

"My, what a fine place to lie you have there, Mr. Hart," the lead nun said. "Do you mind if we rest here with you for a space of time?"

She had come right up to his bed by then, and she upended his bucket — which, to his profound relief, was empty at that moment — and settled herself on it, and then they had all arrived. They milled around him, making him feel dizzy and frail. They moved in and out of his line of vision, speaking in low voices, and it was something to do with an air they had, slightly, of taking charge of him, that afforded him a small sense of relief. He felt like an ailing turtle overtaken by a school of energetic fish.

Two of the nuns went behind him at the head of the bed. Another crossed over to the base of the tree and pulled herself onto one of the lower limbs.

"I wouldn't put no weight on them branches," Woody said, but the nun rolled her sleeves to the elbow and climbed from one limb to another until she had reached a place high up. As she settled herself there, she was struck and lit up by the sun, and Woody looked closely, shielding his eyes with his hand, and saw that the light-haired child had made his way up there too, and was sitting on the branch beside her. The boy looked down through the branches, swinging his feet, and the sight of him sitting there, rocking back and forth with a pleased look, reminded Woody that two years ago there was a deck of planks with a roof over it in that very place in the tree. He hadn't thought about that deck in a long while. He remembered putting it together out of the boards and tin lining of an old trough which had leaked so badly that no amount of repair could make it right.

Thinking back on this deck in the tree, he felt the chills from earlier that morning creep in on him again. He drew up his blanket and turned onto his side.

Beside the bed, the lead nun spoke to one of the others in a low voice and all the sounds — the voices of the women, the wind in the leaves, the heavy tread nearby of the two mares moving in the stall — began to drone, as if everything were happening in a huge, windy chamber.

Woody drew the blanket closer around him and looked far out into the countryside. There he saw a tired orange light approaching under a haze of dust which had lifted and covered the sun.

He remembered how strange that deck of planks had looked, like something that had fallen down into the tree from another planet.

"Sawed off the limb, by damn, and brought it down," he said.

He reached out his hand to the two nuns beside the bed. "Not too long ago there was a child on the way," he said, "and I put a deck up for it. I put a deck up in the tree for it to play in. But it was born dead."

He lay back on his pillow, watching the branch split the last inch, after the sawing, watching the deck descend swiftly, all of a piece, with an explosion of leaves and branches, to the ground.

He studied the deep orange light that was moving swiftly toward him across the cedars. It slipped heavily over him, and lit up the yard, and the slow blades on the windmill, and the roof of the house — like a wing on a long journey. The dust, which had come up heavily out of the rangeland, was filtering like smoke over the sun, and all he could think on was the sight of that branch falling, and falling, and his wife weeping — a high, weak sound with no heart left in it. It made him tired to hear it.

On that day, two years ago, the dust had defeated him. He'd been out in the eastern sector that whole morning, shearing, and by noon was full of wool grease and thorns. He was working with his friend, John, who had his sheep there, too, and the three hands from town that they were hiring by the day. They'd gone through no more than half the bunch they'd brought in, but the dust had begun to blow, and it was the middle of that kind of white-heat drought that can drive a man to the staggers and raise up for him, in the faraway stretches, whole cities of celestial light — and so at midday they turned out into the pens the ones that were left and put the rest of it off into the cool of the following morning.

By the time he arrived home, the dust was a wall around him, out of which the thorn trees and the outbuildings loomed suddenly and came toward him like shapes in a dream. In the barn, his horse pulled out of the loosened saddle and whirled in the stall, squealing with raw temper, maddened by the dust which drifted through every crack and could not be gotten away from.

He wrapped his head in his jacket and felt his way along the paddock fence through the dervish sand, and when he had climbed the steps and pulled open the back door against the wind, and latched it behind him, the house was deeply and strangely quiet. He recalled that his wife had gone out on foot early that morning to look for a lamb of hers, a dark one that she'd been raising, that had gotten out of the barn. The worry came over him that she'd gotten lost, herself. He called to her, and looked around the kitchen for some sign of her, but could not tell, even, what was laid out on the table, for the room was filling with dust and had grown very dark in the last hour. He went to the pump and tried for a long time to draw water, though there was hardly a cupful left in the bucket to prime with. Finally he pulled open his shirt and went up the stairs to the basin in the bedroom. The small portion of water there was laid over thickly with dust, but he cupped it in his hands, and raised it to his face. Then he heard, downstairs, a single muffled cry which he knew, without need for any questioning, was his wife gone into labor with the child.

He descended the stairs two at a time and found her lying on her side on the bare mattress in the spare room. She was holding the bed railing, and her face was streaked with dust and tears. She had thrown the covers off onto the floor, and nearby was the cradle laid over with a long gauze cloth. The air in the room was very deep with the dust.

He slipped his hands under her, thinking to carry her directly to the truck, but she rolled away and began to breathe rapidly, with a little cry for each breath. Then she drew a long shuddering breath, and held it, and in the deep silence before she breathed again, he watched a stain bloom and spread swiftly on the mattress under her.

"It's now! It's now!" she said, drawing breath rapidly, and then the deep breaths came again, and then the silence. This time she gripped his sleeve in one hand, staring at him with eyes that could not see, and lifted up slowly with the strain.

He unfastened her trousers and hauled them off her and rolled her over, and she let out her breath in a long high wail.

Her legs looked very small and white, and now he could spread them open and crawl up and kneel between them, and this time when she fell silent and bore down, he looked and saw the bulge of the child's head, a taut oval spreading wider, and inside the oval of patch of blue scalp with hair.

"Push, push," he said. "Yes! Push!" but she let go of the air, and lay back, gasping, and the child's head was drawn back up into her body.

He reached past her legs and took hold of both her hands. "It's going to come right now, oh, now," she said, drawing the deep breath. "Yes, it's coming now," he said, "it's coming. Push. Push," he said, bearing down with her, and this time, in the long silence, it was as if they were rocking together in a small craft, and holding onto her was like pulling on the oars. Then the oval bloomed over the head once more, and the image came to him of the sheep getting turned out of the wool, one after the other — of the wool-mat laying back first at the neck, then off the shoulders, then lifting away from the flanks, and the sheep emerging white and clean and without blemish, as though getting born into a new life. His wife shuddered violently and called out, "I'm falling. Oh, Woody, don't let go of me," and all this while the child was sliding out slowly, with great dignity.

It was blue as a hyacinth, folded, glistening. It was smooth as if it were made out of marble. It lay quivering on the bed, already filming with the dust.

"Don't let go of me," his wife said.

"It's got to breathe," he said.

"I'm falling, Woody, don't let go!"

"It's got to cry," he said, and he took the child up by the feet and shook it, but it didn't cry.

"Is it the child?" she said.

"Jesus, God," he said. "You can't help me." And he laid the child face down and knelt over it and pressed on it heavily to make it suck air; but though he worked at this tirelessly — forgetting his wife, and the dust, and the house shuddering in the hot wind, and the vast tracts of land upon which, by now, most of his sheep lay dying in the heat — though he kneaded and pulled on the small body, the child remained still. Finally he stopped. His wife had raised herself up on her elbow, and was watching, and she reached out to touch the child, but he pushed her hand away, and brought out his knife, and severed the cord.

"The child is dead," he said.

"No, listen," she said, holding onto his arm, "I want to have it."

"The child is dead," he said.

He pulled the long cloth off the cradle, and wound the child up in it tightly, solid and white. He took this bundle out of the room and laid it on the dough-board in the kitchen. Then he backed off, and stood in the doorway, watching. The white cloth was soon laid over by a fine powdering of dust, like flour.

He was brought out of his reverie by the sound of the plow dragging, and he looked back through the bars of the bed and saw his wife coming in from the field. She halted the mule in front of the shed and leaned on his shoulder. She had a hand-kerchief knotted around her head, against the sweat, and was all over one color from the dust. The mule stood with his head down, the plow still bound to him by the harness.

"Couple of jackstraws," Woody said. "Either one moves, the other'll drop."

His wife unstrapped the plow, and led the mule into the barn.

After that the light began to deepen and evening came on slowly. Woody wondered what had happened to the day. Over his head, the tree began to shimmer, and he looked up and saw that the nun and the child had decked every branch, even the small twigs, with crystal glass. It had become very quiet, and the wind, which was dying down, stirred the tree and beat the pieces of glass against each other like chimes. Gradually the sun descended into deepening layers of color out over the farthest reaches of the cedars, and Woody lay still on his pillow, listening to the chimes and watching the shadow of his bed lengthening into the yard like a giant crab.

When he spoke, it felt as if the words came from him like a river moving slowly.

"Why has she brought me no water?" he said.

"Did you call to her for water?" someone said, and he turned and saw the lead nun standing beside him. Her voice had the sound of someone calling up out of a well.

"Yes, I called for water. I called for water plenty!"

"Well, she finally brought it to you, didn't she?" she said.

By then he could hear other voices. He saw light flickering, like the noon sun through the foliage, and then the nuns were leaning close over him and he felt a great wind blowing past as if they had pulled his bed into a tunnel, and then he slept.

He woke, and it was night. The full moon, crossed with short rags of clouds, cast a light over the countryside that was like a white sea with the waves halted.

Something moved nearby, and he looked closely into the shadow of the tree and saw his wife standing there, wrapped in a blanket. She gazed at him with eyes full of dark feeling. He moved over to make a place for her in the bed, and her blanket opened like a husk, and she came out of it bare and frail in the moonlight. Her little white breasts looked childish and exposed, and her limbs reminded him, as they always had, of those of a half-grown boy. She came in beside him, slipping one leg under him, and crossing the other over him, and eased herself close up into the hollow under his arm.

Then they lay still, taking in the night sounds. He heard the frogs lamenting by the sinkhole, and the crickets' wall of song, and, raining steadily down on everything, the massive hollow booming of the stars.

He watched, over their heads, the tree sailing through the night sky swiftly, with strong purpose. It bore the full moon with it, netted in its branches like a chalice, or a giant moth.

When he woke the next morning, his wife lay curled against him, cold as a stone. He took her by the shoulder and shook her, but she would not waken. He drew away from her and gazed down at her. Her hair was stiff with dust and chaff; the skin over her nose was raw from the sun, and her lips were blistered. He reached beyond her for the blanket and worked it under her so that he could wrap her in it tightly and safely. Then he saw, standing upright in the crotch of the tree, the bottle of sleeping tablets they'd given him at the hospital, and half of them gone.

"Did you think to get rid of me thataway?" he said to her

angrily. He stared for a long while at her gaunt and sorrowing face and at the tear streaks running from her closed eyes into her hair.

After that, he lay without moving beside her as the hours passed and the heat of the day intensified. The shade from the tree was scant in the buffeting white waves of heat. He lay beside his wife under the noon sun, wondering what it would be like to have a thunderstorm roll up overhead and drench him, and sometimes it felt to him, indeed, as if water of some kind were very close; but then he would hear the dog whine and feel it licking the salt sweat from his hand, and he would recall that they were now into some dry portion of the summer, and that there would be many days still ahead without rain.

He picked up the dog and set it on the ground beside the bed, hoping maybe it would relieve itself and then go and find water, but it only stood weakly, looking down at its own shadow lying between its four feet like a little puddle.

"Go on over and sit up on the step there, buddy," Woody said, forgetting that his wife lay wrapped securely beside him. "Maybe she'll take notice of you."

He thought he heard the sound of the pump handle then, and he looked over at the house and was surprised to see that the five nuns had come calling on them again. They were approaching in a group.

"Don't take one more step in my direction without bringing water," he called out, and the lead nun raised her hand and answered, "Indeed, Mr. Hart, that's exactly what we had on our minds. We were thinking maybe you'd like to go down with us to the river."

He laughed at this, thinking of the blistered land with its few sinkholes of water. "What river is that?" he asked, and she said, "The one we passed on our way here."

Then they were surrounding him on all sides and lifting him easily until he was on his feet beside the bed.

"Now, hold on here," he said. "I believe this is something has got to be talked over first with Mrs. Hart," but they had slipped their arms around him by then, and the lead nun pointed down the road and said, "It's only just a short distance over the rise, Mr. Hart. Did you think it was in some faraway country?"

They moved with him slowly forward, and he wondered what rise she could be referring to, for the land was as flat as a griddle. He looked ahead and caught sight of the light-haired child standing at the gate, looking back and waiting.

"If we're going out into the pasturage," Woody said, "she'd want to know," but they bore him steadily on across the yard and through the gate, and when they passed over into the open country he looked ahead a short distance and saw the child standing in the dust of the road, motioning to them to come faster.

"I wouldn't let him wander far," Woody said, and then he felt the road lifting them and they started slowly up a long grade. When they reached the top, he looked down at the river, vast and slow-moving, with the light on it almost too bright to be looked at, and now he remembered it well, with its little copse of willows, and its swaying grasses. He saw brightness strike and spread swiftly where the wind scuffed the water.

"It looks like a good place to lie down right there under them willow trees," he said.

They went through the tall grass slowly, with the child running ahead of them, leaving a wake of silver in the green.

"She should know to come here," Woody said. "Could one of you run tell her? She's probably still out in the field behind the shed."

They gathered close around him, then, in the shade under the willows. He felt himself being eased down, and he thought he saw the child going naked into the water. "Time to bathe him," the lead nun said, and he thought at first she meant the boy; but then they were bending nearer, and they had taken off their coarse brown robes. As the water rose around them, the rays striking off them blazed brighter and brighter, until all he could see was their faces in the wide slow river of light.

PAUL BOWLES

In the Red Room

(FROM ANTAEUS)

WHEN I HAD A HOUSE in Sri Lanka, my parents came out one winter to see me. Originally I had felt some qualms about encouraging their visit. Any one of several things — the constant heat, the unaccustomed food and drinking water, even the presence of a leprosy clinic a quarter of a mile from the house — might easily have an adverse effect on them in one way or another. But I had underestimated their resilience; they made a greater show of adaptability than I had thought possible, and seemed entirely content with everything. They claimed not to mind the lack of running water in the bathrooms, and regularly praised the curries prepared by Appuhamy, the resident cook. Both of them being in their seventies, they were not tempted by the more distant or inaccessible points of interest. It was enough for them to stay around the house reading, sleeping, taking twilight dips in the ocean, and going on short trips along the coast by hired car. If the driver stopped unexpectedly at a shrine to sacrifice a coconut, they were delighted, and if they came upon a group of elephants lumbering along the road, the car had to be parked some distance up ahead, so that they could watch them approach and file past. They had no interest in taking photographs, and this spared me what is perhaps the most taxing duty of a cicerone: the repeated waits while the ritual between man and machine is observed. They were ideal guests.

Colombo, where all the people I knew lived, was less than a hundred miles away. Several times we went up for weekends, which I arranged with friends by telephone beforehand. There we had tea on the wide verandas of certain houses in Cinnamon Gardens, and sat at dinners with professors from the university, Protestant ministers, and assorted members of the government. (Many of the Sinhalese found it strange that I should call my parents by their first names, Dodd and Hannah; several of them inquired if I were actually their son or had been adopted.) These weekends in the city were hot and exhausting, and they were always happy to get back to the house, where they could change into comfortable clothing.

One Sunday not long before they were due to return to America, we decided to take in the horse races at Gintota, where there are also some botanical gardens that Hannah wanted to see. I engaged rooms at the New Oriental in Galle and we had lunch there before setting out.

As usual, the events were late in starting. It was the spectators, in any case, who were the focus of interest. The phalanx of women in their shot-silk saris moved Hannah to cries of delight. The races themselves were something of a disappointment. As we left the grounds, Dodd said with satisfaction: It'll be good to get back to the hotel and relax.

But we were going to the botanical gardens, Hannah reminded him. I'd like to have just a peek at them.

Dodd was not eager. Those places cover a lot of territory, you know, he said.

We'll just look inside and come out again, she promised.

The hired car took us to the entrance. Dodd was tired, and as a result was having a certain amount of difficulty in walking. The last year or so I find my legs aren't always doing exactly what I want 'em to do, he explained.

You two amble along, Hannah told us. I'll run up ahead and find out if there's anything to see.

We stopped to look up at a clove tree; its powerful odor filled the air like a gas. When we turned to continue our walk, Hannah was no longer in sight. We went on under the high vegetation, around a curve in the path, looked ahead, and still there was no sign of her.

What does your mother think she's doing? The first thing we know she'll be lost.

She's up ahead somewhere.

Soon, at the end of a short lane overhung by twisted lianas, we saw her, partially hidden by the gesticulating figure of a Sinhalese standing next to her.

What's going on? Dodd hastened his steps. Run over there, he told me, and I started ahead, walking fast. Then I saw Hannah's animated smile, and slowed my pace. She and the young man stood in front of a huge bank of brown spider orchids.

Ah! I thought we'd lost you, I said.

Look at these orchids. Aren't they incredible?

Dodd came up, nodded at the young man, and examined the display of flowers. They look to me like skunk cabbage, he declared.

The young man broke into wild laughter. Dodd stared at him.

This young man has been telling me the history of the garden, Hannah began hurriedly. About the opposition to it, and how it finally came to be planted. It's interesting.

The Sinhalese beamed triumphantly. He wore white flannels and a crimson blazer, and his sleek black hair gave off a metallic blue glint in the sunlight.

Ordinarily I steer a determined course away from the anonymous person who tries to engage me in conversation. This time it was too late; encouraged by Hannah, the stranger strolled beside her, back to the main path. Dodd and I exchanged a glance, shrugged, and began to follow along behind.

Somewhere up at the end of the gardens a pavilion had been built under the high rain trees. It had a veranda where a few sarong-draped men reclined in long chairs. The young man stopped walking. Now I invite you to a cold ginger beer.

Oh, Hannah said, at a loss. Well, yes. That would be nice. I'd welcome a chance to sit down.

Dodd peered at his wristwatch. I'll pass up the beer, but I'll sit and watch you.

We sat and looked out at the lush greenness. The young man's conversation leapt from one subject to another; he seemed unable to follow any train of thought further than its inception. I put this down as a bad sign, and tried to tell from the inflections of Hannah's voice whether she found him as disconcerting as I did.

Dodd was not listening. He found the heat of low-country Ceylon oppressive, and it was easy to see that he was tired. Thinking I might cover up the young man's chatter, I turned to Dodd and began to talk about whatever came into my head: the resurgence of mask-making in Ambalangoda, devil-dancing, the high incidence of crime among the fishermen converted to Catholicism. Dodd listened, but did no more than move his head now and then in response.

Suddenly I heard the young man saying to Hannah: I have just the house for you. A godsend to fill your requirements. Very quiet and protected.

She laughed. Mercy, no! We're not looking for a house. We're only going to be here a few weeks more.

I looked hard at her, hoping she would take my glance as a warning against going on and mentioning the place where she was staying. The young man was not paying attention, in any case. Quite all right. You are not buying houses. But you should see this house and tell your friends. A superior investment, no doubt about that. Shall I introduce myself, please? Justus Gonzag, called Sonny by friends.

His smile, which was not a smile at all, gave me an unpleasant physical sensation.

Come anyway. A five-minute walk, guaranteed. He looked searchingly at Hannah. I intend to give you a book of poems. My own. Autographed for you with your name. That will make me very happy.

Oh, Hannah said, a note of dismay in her voice. Then she braced herself and smiled. That would be lovely. But you understand, we can't stay more than a minute.

There was a silence. Dodd inquired plaintively: Can't we go in the car, at least?

Impossible, sir. We are having a very narrow road. Car can't get through. I am arranging in a jiffy. He called out. A waiter came up, and he addressed him in Sinhalese at some length. The man nodded and went inside. Your driver is now bringing your car to this gate. Very close by.

This was going a little too far. I asked him how he thought anyone was going to know which car was ours.

No problem. I was present when you were leaving the Pontiac. Your driver is called Wickramasinghe. Up-country resident, most reliable. Down here people are hopeless.

I disliked him more each time he spoke. You're not from around here? I asked him.

No, no! I'm a Colombo chap. These people are impossible scoundrels. Every one of the blighters has a knife in his belt, guaranteed.

When the waiter brought the check, he signed it with a rapid flourish and stood up. Shall we be going on to the house, then?

No one answered, but all three of us rose and reluctantly moved off with him in the direction of the exit gate. The hired car was there; Mr. Wickramasinghe saluted us from behind the wheel.

The afternoon heat had gone, leaving only a pocket here and there beneath the trees where the air was still. Originally the lane where we were walking had been wide enough to admit a bullock-cart, but the vegetation encroaching on each side had narrowed it to little more than a footpath.

At the end of the lane were two concrete gateposts with no gate between them. We passed through, and went into a large compound bordered on two sides by ruined stables. With the exception of one small ell, the house was entirely hidden by high bushes and flowering trees. As we came to a doorway the young man stopped and turned to us, holding up one finger. No noises here, isn't it? Only birds.

It was the hour when the birds begin to awaken from their daytime lethargy. An indeterminate twittering came from the trees. He lowered his finger and turned back to the door. Mornings they are singing. Now not.

Oh, it's lovely, Hannah told him.

He led us through a series of dark empty rooms. Here the *dhobi* was washing the soiled clothing. This is the kitchen, you see? Ceylon style. Only the charcoal. My father was refusing paraffin and gas both. Even in Colombo.

We huddled in a short corridor while he opened a door, reached in, and flooded the space inside with blinding light. It was a small room, made to seem still smaller by having been given glistening crimson walls and ceiling. Almost all the space was filled by a big bed with a satin coverlet of a slightly darker red. A row of straight-backed chairs stood along one wall. Sit down and be comfy, our host advised us.

We sat, staring at the bed and at the three framed pictures on the wall above its brass-spoked headboard: on the left a girl, in the middle our host, and on the right another young man. The portraits had the imprecision of passport photographs that have been enlarged to many times their original size.

Hannah coughed. She had nothing to say. The room gave off a cloying scent of ancient incense, as in a disused chapel. The feeling of absurdity I got from seeing us sitting there side by side, wedged in between the bed and the wall, was so powerful that it briefly paralyzed my mental processes. For once the young man was being silent; he sat stiffly, looking straight ahead, like someone at the theater.

Finally I had to say something. I turned to our host and asked him if he slept in this room. The question seemed to shock him. Here? he cried, as if the thing were inconceivable. No, no! This house is unoccupied. No one sleeping on the premises. Only a stout chap to watch out at night. Excuse me one moment.

He jumped up and hurried out of the room. We heard his footsteps echo in the corridor and then grow silent. From somewhere in the house there came the sonorous chiming of a grandfather's clock; its comfortable sound made the shiny blood-colored cubicle even more remote and unlikely.

Dodd stirred uncomfortably in his chair; the bed was too close for him to cross his legs. As soon as he comes back, we go, he muttered.

He's looking for the book, I imagine, said Hannah.

We waited a while. Then I said: Look. If he's not back in two minutes, I move we just get up and leave. We can find our way out all right.

Hannah objected, saying it would be unpardonable.

Again we sat in silence, Dodd now shielding his eyes from the glare. When Sonny Gonzag returned, he was carrying a glass of water which he drank standing in the doorway. His expression had altered: he now looked preoccupied, and he was breathing heavily.

We slowly got to our feet, Hannah still looking expectant.

We are going, then? Come. With the empty glass still in his hand he turned off the lights, shut the door behind us, opened another, and led us quickly through a sumptuous room furnished with large divans, coromandel screens and bronze Buddhas. We had no time to do more than glance from side to side as we followed him. As we went out through the front door, he called one peremptory word back into the house, presumably to the caretaker.

There was a wide unkempt lawn on this side, where a few clumps of high areca palms were being slowly strangled by the sheaths of philodendron roots and leaves that encased their trunks. Creepers had spread themselves unpleasantly over the tops of shrubs like the meshes of gigantic cobwebs. I knew that Hannah was thinking of snakes. She kept her eyes on the ground, stepping carefully from flagstone to flagstone as we followed the exterior of the house around to the stables, and thence out into the lane.

The swift twilight had come down. No one seemed disposed to speak. When we reached the car Mr. Wickramasinghe stood beside it.

Cheery-bye, then, and tell your friends to look for Sonny Gonzag when they are coming to Gintota. He offered his hand to Dodd first, then me, finally to Hannah, and turned away.

They were both very quiet on the way back to Galle. The road was narrow and the blinding lights of oncoming cars made them nervous. During dinner we made no mention of the afternoon.

At breakfast, on the veranda swept by the morning breeze, we felt sufficiently removed from the experience to discuss it. Hannah said: I kept waking up in the night and seeing that awful bed.

Dodd groaned.

I said it was like watching television without the sound. You saw everything, but you didn't get what was going on.

The kid was completely non compos mentis. You could see that a mile away, Dodd declared.

Hannah was not listening. It must have been a maid's room. But why would he take us there? I don't know; there's something terribly depressing about the whole thing. It makes me feel a little sick just to think about it. And that bed!

Well, stop thinking about it, then! Dodd told her. I for one am going to put it right out of my mind. He waited. I feel better already. Isn't that the way the Buddhists do it?

The sunny holiday continued for a few weeks more, with longer trips now to the east, to Tissamaharana and the wild elephants in the Yala Preserve. We did not go to Colombo again until it was time for me to put them onto the plane.

The black weather of the monsoons was blowing in from the southwest as we drove up the coast. There was a violent downpour when we arrived in midafternoon at Mount Lavinia and checked into our rooms. The crashing of the waves outside my room was so loud that Dodd had to shut the windows in order to hear what we were saying.

I had taken advantage of the trip to Colombo to arrange a talk with my lawyer, a Telugu-speaking Indian. We were to meet in the bar at the Galleface, some miles up the coast. I'll be back at six, I told Hannah. The rain had abated somewhat when I started out.

Damp winds moved through the lobby of the Galleface, but the smoky air in the bar was stirred only by fans. As I entered, the first person I noticed was Weston of the Chartered Bank. The lawyer had not yet come in, so I stood at the bar with Weston and ordered a whiskey.

Didn't I see you in Gintota at the races last month? With an elderly couple?

I was there with my parents. I didn't notice you.

I couldn't tell. It was too far away. But I saw the same three people later with a local character. What did you think of Sonny Gonzag?

I laughed. He dragged us off to his house.

You know the story, I take it.

I shook my head.

The story, which he recounted with relish, began on the day after Gonzag's wedding, when he stepped into a servant's room and found his bride in bed with the friend who had been best man. How he happened to have a pistol with him was not explained, but he shot them both in the face, and later chopped their bodies into pieces. As Weston remarked: That sort of thing isn't too uncommon, of course. But it was the trial that caused the scandal. Gonzag spent a few weeks in a mental hospital, and was discharged.

You can imagine, said Weston. Political excitement. The poor go to jail for a handful of rice, but the rich can kill with impunity, and that sort of thing. You still see references to the case in the press now and then.

I was thinking of the crimson blazer and the botanical gardens. No. I never heard about it, I said.

He's mad as a hatter, but there he is, free to do whatever he feels like. And all he wants now is to get people into that house and show them the room where the great event took place. The more the merrier as far as he's concerned.

I saw the Indian come into the bar. It's unbelievable, but I believe it, I told Weston.

Then I turned to greet the lawyer, who immediately complained of the stale air in the bar. We sat and talked in the lounge.

I managed to get back to Mount Lavinia in time to bathe before dinner. As I lay in the tepid water, I tried to imagine the reactions of Hannah and Dodd when I told them what I had heard. I myself felt a solid satisfaction at knowing the rest of the story. But being old, they might well brood over it, working it up into an episode so unpleasant in retrospect that it stained the memory of their holiday. I still had not decided whether to tell them or not when I went to their room to take them down to dinner.

We sat as far away from the music as we could get. Hannah had dressed a little more elaborately than usual, and they both were speaking with more than their accustomed animation. I realized that they were happy to be returning to New York. Halfway through the meal they began to review what they considered the highlights of their visit. They mentioned the Temple of the Tooth, the pair of Bengal tiger cubs in Dehiwala which they had petted but regretfully declined to purchase, the Indonesian dinner on Mr. Bultjens's lawn, where the myna bird had hopped over to Hannah and said: "Eat it up," the cobra under the couch at Mrs. de Sylva's tea party.

And that peculiar young man in the *strange* house, Hannah added meditatively.

Which one was that? asked Dodd, frowning as he tried to remember. Then it came to him. Oh, God, he muttered. Your special friend. He turned to me. Your mother certainly can pick 'em.

Outside, the ocean roared. Hannah seemed lost in thought. *I* know what it was like! she exclaimed suddenly. It was like being shown around one of the temples by a *bhikku*. Isn't that what they call them?

Dodd sniffed. Some temple! he chuckled.

No, I'm serious. That room had a particular meaning for him. It was like a sort of shrine.

I looked at her. She had got to the core without needing the details. I felt that, too, I said. Of course, there's no way of knowing.

She smiled. Well, what you don't know won't hurt you.

I had heard her use the expression a hundred times without ever being able to understand what she meant by it, because it seemed so patently untrue. But for once it was apt. I nodded my head and said: That's right.

MARY WARD BROWN

The Cure

(FROM ASCENT)

WHEN ELLA HOGUE continued to grow worse, her daughters all came home. Bee came first from nearby Vilula, then Andretta from Ft. Wayne, and Lucindy from Miami. For two days and two nights they took turns sitting by the bed, waiting for the end. On the third day Ella began to improve. Consciousness came back first, then gradually alertness. Unbelieving, her daughters gathered around her.

Ella looked at them and sighed. "I ain't dead yet?" she said.

"Cose you ain't dead!" Lucindy scolded. "You 'live as anybody. You done got better."

"I don't want to be no better," Ella said, "if I can't get up and do, like everybody else."

She lay beneath a quilt she had pieced and quilted years ago, in a bed given to her by Doll's grandmother. The bed was of solid dark wood, with a high, carved headboard and a cracked foot. White women hunting antiques had wanted to buy it, or swap her something for it, for years. When her daughters arrived, the bedclothes had been dingy, and stale as the inside of the trunk where she kept them. Now the sheets on her bed were aggressively clean. The quilt had been aired in the sun. Ella's old head, tied up in a snowy rag, made the only dent in her pillow.

"You soon *be* up, Mama," Lucindy said positively. "You coming back thisaway!"

"How long you been here, Cindy?" she asked. She was too weak to move.

"I come Tuesday," Lucindy said. "Soon as Bee called up, I told my boss-lady, 'My mama sick in Alabama and I got to *go.*' Then I got on that bus!"

Lucindy was Ella's oldest, born the first year after puberty when Ella was barely fourteen. Her large frame, heavily fleshed through the hips and bust, was boney elsewhere. Zipped and buttoned into a polyester pantsuit, she was like a Christmas stocking half-filled with fruit. Her hair was a vigorous iron-gray, and her aging face was pleasant.

"I'm here too, Mama," said Andretta, who had been in Ft. Wayne so long she talked like a Yankee. A copper-colored replica of Ella at the same age, Andretta leaned down to touch her mother's still, unresponsive hand.

"I see you, Retta," she said, and smiled.

Bee's presence was taken for granted. She was a mixture of her two half sisters, smaller and lighter in color than Lucindy, larger and darker than Andretta. Lucindy and Andretta were both "outside" children, but Bee had been born and raised in wedlock. After Bee there were no more, girls or boys, because Ella's husband had mumps that went down on him.

"What got the matter with me?" she wanted to know.

"You had a little sinking spell, is all," Andretta said. "You over it now."

"I don't know nothing about it . . ."

She turned her face toward the open door. She did not even know what month it was. Clusters of yellow berries were on the chinaberry tree, so it had to be fall. Across the road, mock oranges were green and a few lay on the ground.

A small fire burned in the fireplace. Bee began rattling lids on the stove in the kitchen and soon there were smells of cooking and smoke, but Ella felt no hunger. She felt nothing at all, except the faint presence of life itself.

"Has Doll been here?" she asked.

"Every day," Lucindy said proudly. "She be back after while. She don't know you done come to."

Bee pulled up a chair and sat down by the bed with a cup of hot soup.

"Take a sip of this, Mama," she said, holding out a spoon half-full.

Ella waited, then took a small taste. The soup was chicken with soft rice. When Bee held out the spoon again, she let herself be fed and kept on sipping until the spoon scraped bottom.

Afterward she closed her eyes and rested, listening to the girls tiptoeing around, whispering so as not to disturb her. She felt like dozing off, but first she had to attend to something.

"What time she coming?" she asked.

"Who, Doll?" Bee said. They had sat down around the fire to eat. "Why? You want her?"

"I wants her to get Dr. Dobbs to come work on me," she said, "and get me up from here."

All three women turned to look at her. Bee swallowed the food in her mouth, field peas, sprinkled with hot-pepper sauce, and cornbread.

"Dr. Dobbs *been* retired, Mama," she said carefully. "He ain't doctored on nobody in three-four years. I think he even kinda mindless now."

"Thas all right," Ella said. "I ruther have him mindless than them others. Dr. Dobbs know how to move my bowels and flush out my kidneys, and get me back on my feets."

"He could years ago, Mama, but he can't do nothing now . . . Your bowels can't move, noway, until you eat — and you ain't et till just now."

"Who made that soup?" she asked.

"I did, Mama," said Andretta. "Was it good?"

"It needed mo' salt," she said.

They looked at each other and smiled.

"One of y'all go tell Doll I wants to see her," she said in a clear, strong voice, and all the smiles vanished.

Each time someone knocked on the door, Sally Webb thought it was bad news about Netta (her childhood name for Aunt Ella), who had lived on the farm and worked for Sally's family most of her life. Though she dreaded Ella's passing with all her conscious mind, Sally was dimly aware of a subterranean impatience to get it over and behind her, for things to get back to normal, whatever the cost.

Both Sally's parents and all the other old people, black and white, who had lived on the place were now dead and gone. Ella had hung on, puttering around her house and yard, last not only of her generation but of a whole era.

She never asked for anything. On the contrary, she was always coming up with a jar of jelly, bunch of greens, or sack of something. Still, Sally felt responsible for her, down there alone. When she hadn't seen her out for several days last week, she stopped to find her in bed, slightly disoriented. She had called Bee, who came in a dented old car and took Ella to the doctor. Dr. Cox reserved a bed in the hospital, but once out of his office Ella refused to go. Bee brought her home and came to get Sally.

Ella lay on top of the covers in her old-fashioned Sunday clothes and lace-up, size five shoes.

"Dr. Cox wants you in the hospital, Netta," Sally explained, "where they can get you well. Bee and I don't know what to do for you, like they do."

"Yes'm." She looked off to one side. "I be all right here."

"But Bee needs to get back to work," Sally insisted. "There's nobody to look after you here."

"I don't need nobody," she said. "The Lord be with me."

Sally looked at Bee who looked helplessly back.

"Well, you have to go, Netta," Sally said firmly. "You need medical attention . . . Now I'm going back to call the hospital while Bee packs your things. Bee and I will go with you, and stay as long as you need us."

Ella's face was a mask, stoical and lonely. When tears suddenly stood in her eyes, it was as though a woodcarving started to weep. She turned her head and a tear dropped off on the pillow.

"I wants to die at home, Doll," she said.

So Sally called the cafeteria where Bee worked and told them Bee would have to be out for a while. She talked to Dr. Cox on the phone and went to town for medicine. When Ella continued to grow weaker, Bee came up and called the others. Ella would not know now whether they took her to the hospital or not, but no one suggested it. Sally reported to Dr. Cox each day. Ella's daughters turned her frequently from one side to the other as he instructed, and kept her clean. It seemed a matter of time to the end.

Now it was Lucindy who knocked on the door, but Lucindy was smiling.

"Mama done woke up and et," she said. On the underside of the announcement, like an insect behind a sheer curtain, was a hint of disappointment.

"Well, thank the Lord," Sally said.

"Yes'm, but . . ." Lucindy would not come in the door Sally held open. "Now she want you. She want you to get Dr. Dobbs to come see her."

"Dr. Dobbs! Why, he's senile and alcoholic too, they say."

"That's who she want, though."

"Wait a second . . ." Sally went back for her keys and a sweater.

The moment she saw Ella alive and conscious after days beyond reach, her heart seemed to crowd the walls of her chest. Standing by the bed, she looked down at the slight figure beneath a quilt in which were sewn scraps from her own school dresses.

"You go'n get Dr. Dobbs fuh me?" Ella asked.

"I'll do my best," she said.

Dr. Dobbs sat bolt upright in the front seat of the car, beside his black driver, Elmo. A beard of fat hung down around his face, which was mapped with forking red and purple veins. Pale blue eyes stared out as from the raw white of an egg, in a look of fixed displeasure. He wore a dark suit of lightweight wool, a white shirt, and a striped silk tie. A large stomach pushed out against the buttons of his coat.

Sally was waiting on the porch when they drove up, and she hurried out to the long, black sedan.

"I'm Sally Webb, Dr. Dobbs," she said, when Elmo let down the window. "William and Mary Ann Webb's daughter. I'll ride down to Aunt Ella's with you."

"Get in, young lady," he said. "I wish I could assist you . . ."

"Aunt Ella must be nearly ninety now," Sally said, speaking up from the back seat. "But she thinks you can help her."

He seemed not to hear. Instead he turned his head from one side to the other, looking at a dilapidated cotton gin on the left and a leaning seed house on the right.

"This place looks run-down," he said. Each time he spoke an essence of alcohol filled the car as though sprayed from a bottle. "Well, things have changed since my father's time, Dr. Dobbs," Sally said. "The cattle business is off, and there's nobody to clean up and patch up the way there used to be."

"Where's all the niggers?" he asked.

"Everything is done with machinery now," she said quickly. "Most of the black people have gone."

"Good riddance," he said. "I wish they'd all leave — go back to Africa. Except Bojangles, here . . . Wadn't for him, I'd be up the creek without a paddle."

Sally said nothing.

"What's the name of the old nigger woman?"

"It's Ella Hogue, Dr. Dobbs. Aunt Ella. She cooked for us and was your patient for years. You used to like her pecan pies."

"I don't recall," he said.

At Ella's house, a two-room cabin by the side of the road, Elmo helped the doctor from the car as though midwifing a birth. Once on his feet he was handed a cane, but his balance was yet to come by degrees. Glaring about him, he waited.

"Somebody get my bag," he said at last, then fixed his attention on walking.

At the porch steps he turned himself over to Elmo again, and a new struggle began.

Lucindy, Andretta, and Bee, freshly washed and dressed, stood in the open doorway. For the trip home, Lucindy and Andretta had each brought black outfits for a funeral, and not much else. Now they wore the same clothes, rinsed out and dried overnight, in which they arrived.

"Good morning," the old man said formally. "I'm Dr. Dobbs, and this is my companion, Elmo Green."

There was a ripple of greetings, all ending in "Doctor."

"Where have you got the patient?" he asked.

"Right here, Doctor."

The women backed into a room which had been thoroughly straightened, dusted, and swept. An empty cane-bottomed chair had been placed by the bed. In the middle of the room a hanging light bulb was turned on, and a kerosene lamp on the dresser had been lit. Clean, starched cloths, made of bleached feed sacks edged in coarse lace, covered the tops of the dresser, trunk, and one small table. A low fire burned in the fireplace, its hearth freshly brushed with Ella's sedge broom.

Dr. Dobbs made his way to the bed and propped his cane against the wall.

"Well, my old friend." Holding on to the head of the bed, he leaned down and shook Ella's hand. "How are you?"

"Pretty low, Doctor," Ella said. "Pretty low."

He turned to the onlookers. "If you will step outside now," he said, "I'll examine the patient."

First he moved the chair nearer the bed, so close it touched the mattress sideways, and sat down carefully. Then he picked up Ella's wrist, found her pulse, and took out a heavy gold watch on a chain. Counting with his lips, he watched the second hand jerk around its tiny course. Light played along the watch chain as his stomach rose and fell.

Ella's eyes followed with profound interest as he opened the bag on the floor, took out a stethoscope, and adjusted it in his ears.

"Open your gown, please," he said.

Ella did not recognize the gown they had on her. She could not find the opening.

"Pull it up from the bottom," he said. "You remember how to do that, don't you, Auntie?"

"Doctor!" she said, and laughed in spite of everything.

He placed the metal disk on the left side of her chest and looked away as he listened. He moved the disk and listened several times. He had Ella turn on her side and listened from the back.

He took her blood pressure, squeezing the bulb and waiting, squeezing and waiting. With a light, he looked into her eyes, ears, and nose. He felt the glands in her neck.

Finally he leaned back in the chair and called out, "Elmo!"

Elmo appeared in the doorway. "Sir?"

"I need to stand up," the doctor said.

Elmo came forward to pull him up by the arms like a monstrous baby.

"Now stay there and help me," he said.

Elmo reached beneath the old man's coat and gripped his belt firmly. As though holding a large fish on a line, he stood looking the other way while the doctor palpated Ella's stomach, then pulled down the covers to press her ankles for swelling. He examined her feet, one at a time, flexing them up and down and from side to side.

"Do your corns bother you much?" he asked.

"No sir. Not much," she said. "Just when it rains."

Ella helped him pull the covers up. Elmo let him back into the chair and went out, closing the door behind him.

He rested for a moment.

"What you've got, Auntie," he said, "is the same thing I've got — old age. There ain't but one cure for it."

"Sir?"

He spoke a little louder. "I said I can't cure you — but I can get you back up for a while."

"I knowed you could, Doctor. That's why I sent for you. I don't want to be a burden on nobody."

"That's what we all say . . ." He began putting instruments back in the bag. Leaning over squeezed off his breath and he said no more, though Ella listened and waited. When he took out a prescription pad and began to write, she raised her head from the pillow.

"Doctor, I hope you put down that tonic used to hep me so much," she said.

"Tonic?" He stopped to think. "That was Vinatone, probably. In a sherry base." Suddenly he looked at her with fresh interest. "Hold on. Wait a minute. Now I recall! Ain't you the one used to make that good muscadine wine?"

Ella's eyes gleamed in the lamplight. "Scuppernong too," she said.

"Well, bless my time! It was the best in the country . . ." His eyes opened wider. "Have you got any left?"

"Just call one of my girls, Doctor," she said.

"Hey, girl!" he called out, making his stomach heave. "One of you . . . ladies!"

Bee hurried in, plump and womanly. Her face was serious.

"Bring one of them jugs out the kitchen, Beatrice," Ella said. "And a clean glass."

"Bring two glasses, if you don't mind, Beatrice," the doctor said.

They stood in the yard and waited, until Sally began to feel awkward.

"I'll go on home, Elmo," she said. "Stop and blow at the house when you start back. I'll come talk to Dr. Dobbs and get the prescriptions."

When she had gone, the others sat down on the edge of the porch, two on each side of the steps, their feet on the ground. Elmo took a seat beside Andretta.

"Doll sho favors her mother, don't she?" Lucindy said.

"But she got ways more like her daddy." Andretta's speech had lapsed. It was now almost as southern as the rest.

Bee yawned. A sleepy midday pall had settled over them like a spell in a fairy tale. The air was pure and still. Even the birds were quiet. There was no sound except insects saying their mantras, out of sight in the trees and grass.

"He takes his time, don't he?" Lucindy said, at last.

Andretta looked at her wristwatch. "He been in there forty minutes now," she said.

Bee got up, eased to the door, and peeped through the crack. When she turned away, she was grinning.

"They in there sleep, both of 'em," she said, and sat back down. "He bout to fall out the chair . . ."

"Lawd . . ." said Lucindy.

"Jesus!" said Andretta.

Lucindy turned to Elmo. "What us go'n do, just wait till he wake up?"

"It won't be long," Elmo said. "He soon have to make water, drinkin all that wine."

Bee and Andretta chuckled. Smiles lingered on their faces. but Lucindy was frowning.

"Reckon will he do her any good?" she asked.

"If anybody kin, he will," Elmo said. "He a good doctor, and he ain't forgot his learning. He still reads them books we gets in the mail."

"How long you been with him, Mr. Green?" Andretta asked.

"Three years, last month. I started off just drivin him. Then his wife died and my wife left me, so now I stays with him twenty-four hours a day."

"Is that right?" said Bee, from the other side of the porch.

"He old and fractious," he said, "but he don't mean nothin by it. He ain't even woke, 'cept in the mornin-time. And we got a cook to wait on us, and all. He got plenty money . . ."

"Not changing the subject," Lucindy said, "but what us go'n do now, y'all? She can't stay by herself no longer."

"One of us just have to stay with her," Andretta said. "Or take her home with us."

"And that would kill her in a hurry," Bee said. "She done already cried and told Doll she want to die at home."

"Y'all could hire somebody to stay with her, like me," Elmo teased.

"Chile, we ain't no rich doctors," Lucindy said, and they laughed as though harmonizing, their voices weaving in and out of each other before fading into silence.

Andretta sighed. "I'd never find a job down here, good as the one I've got up there," she said.

"Old as I is, I couldn't find no other job a'tall," Lucindy said. "But if anybody stay, it ought to be me. I'm the oldest. I'm old enough to be y'all's mama, myself."

"I'm the closest, though," said Bee.

Elmo turned to Andretta. "Maybe you ought to relocate yourself, Miss Andretta, and come on back home."

She gave him a sidelong smile. "Why? You go'n still be round?"

"One thing we *ain't* go'n do," Bee said, "is put her in no nursing home like white folks."

There was instant agreement. "Naw!"

"I tell y'all something . . ." Lucindy looked off through bare trees to the wide, impersonal sky. "Old age is *bad*."

"You ain't wrong," Andretta said slowly.

They sat in silence until Lucindy's stomach began to growl, so loud that everyone smiled. "You hush!" she said, and hit it lightly with her hand.

The sun had reached high noon, and though the porch shaded their bodies, it shone hot on their feet and legs. A house fly buzzed around first one and then the other, to be brushed absently aside. Now and then a leaf wandered down. Faced with changes as yet undefined, the thoughts of the women turned more and more inward. All three were grateful their mother had not died, but her living would be costly from now on. If one stayed, the other two would have to pay for it.

Elmo kept politely quiet, his eyes fixed on the road. Like actors on a stage, they waited for the old man to call out and let the ending begin.

RICK DeMARINIS

Gent

(FROM CUTBANK)

A YEAR AFTER MY FATHER SHOT HIMSELF my mother married a two-faced hardware salesman named Roger Trewly. In public, Roger Trewly smiled as if someone holding a gun on him had said, "Look natural, Roger." At home, though, he was usually cross and sullen and would rarely answer civilly if spoken to. He was a crack salesman and was once awarded a plaque engraved with the words *Ace of Hand-Held Tools*. There is a photograph that records the event. He is standing with the owner of the store, Mr. Fenwick, in front of a display of braces and bits, hammers, ripsaws, and planes. Both men are smiling, but the difference in their smiles has stuck in my mind through the years. Mr. Fenwick is smiling like a man who has just been found naked in the girls' gym and isn't at all humiliated by it. There's a ferocious gleam in his eyes challenging anyone to file a complaint. He looks like a well-to-do madman, capable of anything, absolutely sure of everything. Roger Trewly is smiling as though he's just spilled boiling coffee in his lap at the church social. His face shines with desperate sweat and his begging eyes are fixed on Mr. Fenwick. If you cover the lower half of Roger Trewly's face with your thumb, you will see that his small, pale eyes have no smile in them at all. They have a puzzled, frightened cast, wide with adrenalin. They are the eyes of a man who has understood nothing of the world in his thirty-five years. That anxious, kowtowing smile tries to hide this terrifying vertigo, but I don't think Roger Trewly fooled very many people. Mr. Fenwick, steely-eyed and successful, looks as though nothing had ever fooled him. When my father, who was a war hero, shot himself through the heart with his deer rifle, everyone was shocked. But when Roger Trewly jumped off the Mill Avenue bridge into the heavy rapids of the Far Cry River, no one in town was surprised, least of all my mother. "I saw it," she said. "I saw it coming."

Mother was only thirty-two years old the spring that Roger Trewly drowned himself, but four years of living with a terror-struck two-faced man had taken the bloom off her spirit. She didn't have gray hair yet, she didn't have wrinkled skin, she had not become bent or shaky or forgetful, but she acted like an older woman with not a whole lot left to live for. If you weren't a child, and could see things for what they were, you would have called her beautiful in spite of the lines and hollows of weariness that masked her true face. She was a petite, almost tiny woman with high, youthful breasts and her hair was the color of polished mahogany. She kept it long and she brushed it until it crackled with a suggestion of dark fire. She had large, widely spaced eyes, the gray-specked green of imperfect emeralds, and a smile that made you want to jump up and do chores. My father, who was a large, powerful man, called her "doll" or "midge." He loved to pick her up in his strong arms and whirl her through the house whistling or singing, like a happy giant whose dreams had come true at last.

"Ma, you're so pretty!" my sister, LaDonna, said one bright summer afternoon in 1952. This was a little over a year after Roger Trewly killed himself. Mother was dressed up for the first time since the funeral. "Look, Jack!" LaDonna said, pulling me into Mother's bedroom. "She looks like a princess!"

It was true. She was beautiful in her dark blue dress and white high-heeled shoes and little pillbox hat. Her face had recovered its sharp-edged prettiness. She looked young and exotic. Her perfume struck me like a shocking announcement. We both put our arms around her and hugged her tight. "Princess! Princess!" we yelled, imprisoning her in our linked arms. I'd turned twelve years old that spring and shouldn't have been carrying on like that, but I was as overwhelmed by her as

LaDonna was. She had come out of herself at last, like a butterfly out of its winter cocoon, and we clung to her as if we knew
there was a real danger of her flying away from us. But she
pried off our greedy arms and said, "Don't! You'll wrinkle me!
I'm only going out on a date!"

She went out into the living room where the man was waiting.
I hadn't realized that a stranger had entered the house. His
name was Gent Mundy, the owner of Mundy's Old Times
Creamery. LaDonna and I stood in front of Mother like a double shield between her and this man, but we were only a nui-
sance and she sent us outside to play. And when Gent Mundy
asked her to marry him several weeks later, we accepted the
news like the condemned victims of a rigged jury.

Gent lived in a large, slate-gray house next to his creamery on
the main east-west street of Far Cry. We were all invited there
to have dinner with him. After cookies and coffee in the living
room, he gave us a tour.

"This would be your room, Jackie," he said to me. "My" room
was on the second floor. It had a large dormer window that
looked out on the parking lot of the creamery where all the milk
trucks were kept when they were not making deliveries. The
room was about twice as big as the one I had at home, and the
walls had been freshly painted light blue. There was a "new"
smell in the room, and I realized then that all the furniture still
had price tags on it.

Next he showed us the room he and Mother would have. It
was half again as big as my room, and the bed in it had a bright
pink canopy. Mother sat on the bed and bounced lightly up and
down twice. "This *is* something," she said, the thin light of greed
sharpening her eyes. Gent sat next to her and the bed wheezed.
The depression he made in the bed forced her to sag against
him. She looked like a child next to his bulk.

"I think she's warming up to the idea, kids," he said, winking
nervously. He was bald, and the top of his head was turning
pink in mottled patches. It looked like a map of Mars, the rosy,
unknown continents floating in a white, fleshy sea. Gent Mundy
was a tall man. He had a heavy torso, but his legs were painfully
thin, almost spindly. His chest sloped out into a full, belt-strain-

ing stomach. His large head made his shoulders seem abnormally narrow. He had alert, pale blue eyes and a wide, friendly mouth that was fixed in a permanent half-smile, a smile warned off suddenly, as though by a cautionary second thought. He was an odd-looking man, but he was friendly and alive and open to everything that was going on around him. He wasn't powerful and wild like my father, but he wasn't two-faced and careful like Roger Trewly, either.

He was especially attentive to Mother. If she sighed, he would put his arm around her small waist as if to boost her morale. If she touched her nose before sneezing, he would quickly have his handkerchief ready. If she looked bored or disinterested, he would smoothly change to a livelier subject of conversation. If she began to rant at length about some ordinary injustice, he'd listen carefully to every word, and then, to prove he shared her concern, he'd repeat verbatim certain things she had said.

Some deep and fragile longing made him fall colossally in love with her. I almost winced to see it, even though I didn't understand what I was seeing or why it moved me to wince.

He made something of her name, Jade, and of her size. "Tiny perfect jewel," he once called her. "Jade, Jade, how I'd like to set you in gold and wear you on my finger!" When he said things like this, his eyes would get vague with tears.

LaDonna's prospective room was next to mine. Instead of fresh paint on the walls, it had new wallpaper — fields of miniature daisies against a light green background. "I had this done especially for you, honey," he told her, his voice low and secretive, as if it were a private matter between just the two of them.

Gent was forty-eight years old and had never been married. "I think I have a lot to offer you," he said, after the tour. We returned to the living room and sat down uneasily in the large, overstuffed chairs. Gent made some fresh coffee and poured each of us a cup. I picked up a *National Geographic* and thumbed through it. LaDonna picked up the silver cream pitcher. She brought it close to her face to study it. Mother held her steaming cup of coffee several inches from her lips, blowing thoughtfully. Careful lines appeared on her forehead. A tall clock ticked patiently in the polished hallway. A black woman with low-slung breasts and dusty feet was talking to a white man in a sun hel-

met. I turned the page to an article about funeral customs in
Sumatra. Gent was sweating now, and he mopped his head with
his napkin. "Well, no," he said, as if agreeing to some unspoken
criticism. "I'm no Casanova, I grant you that. I'm no Tyrone
Power, that's for sure! But I am moderately well off. I can
provide handsomely for all three of you. The milk business . . ."
and here he seemed to be stumped for the precise words. A
dreamy look came over his face and he smiled at the perplexity
of the thing in his mind. ". . . is, is a *good* business." His face
reddened, and his forehead was lacquered again with sweat.

Mother put the cup to her lips and drew a little hissing sound
from it that made all three of us lean toward her. We were poor.
Mother had a little pension, but it barely put food on the table
and paid the rent. My father was out of work when he shot
himself, and Roger Trewly, even though he was the Ace of
Hand-Held Tools, never made enough to keep up with the bills.

Mother set the cup down and said something. Her back was
straight and some untameable pride made the small muscles
around her mouth rigid.

"What was that, Jade?" Gent said, leaning closer to her. "What
was that your wonderful mother said, kids?"

LaDonna stood up. "It was yes," she said sternly. "Our wonderful mother said yes, she will be happy to marry you, Mr.
Mundy."

LaDonna was like that. She saw things for what they were and
she spoke her mind easily, and often with a sharp tongue.
Though she was only eleven years old at the time, she had her
future planned. She was going to be a scientist. She had no
doubts about this. Her hero was Albert Einstein. A picture of
the long-hair genius hung on her bedroom wall. She claimed to
understand the general drift of his writings, if not all the math
involved. She said that Einstein knew everything he would ever
know when he was sixteen, he just hadn't found the words to
put it in. She had an aggressive curiosity about nearly everything, and an ice-cold, relentless intelligence to back it up. I
always thought she was something special, one of the world's
truly unique people, but her detached brilliance sometimes worried me.

When she was seven she made a jigsaw puzzle out of a frog, a salamander, and a cat-killed flicker. She spread out their innards on the back-yard picnic table, trying to match them, organ for organ. The big and small differences fascinated her. Mother threw a fit when she saw the slimy, sun-pungent mess and called her Little Miss Frankenstein. But LaDonna was also affectionate and full of ordinary eleven-year-old ideas.

So when LaDonna said yes for Mother, it was with such crisp authority that Gent clapped his hands together and said, "Oh, Jade, you don't know how happy you've made me! You'll never regret this, I promise!"

LaDonna and I liked Gent, though he was overly neat and too concerned with cleanliness. One day, while visiting our house, he began to fidget. We were all sitting at the kitchen table waiting for Mother to take a box cake out of the oven. Finally Gent pushed away from the table and found himself an apron. "I'll clean up a little while we're waiting," he said. He began to sponge-clean the sink and the counter next to it. Then he went after the greasy stovetop with Ajax and a hard-bristle brush. When he finished that, he knelt down and searched the floor for dust balls. There were no dust balls. Dust that found its way into the kitchen got mixed almost instantly with the haze of grease that covered everything. Mother wasn't a very good cook and preferred to fry most of our food. When she cooked for us, grease hung in the air like fog. Gent ran a finger along the base of the counter. He stood up then, a gummy gray wad stuck to his uplifted finger, his half-smile bravely in place.

"Christ on a crutch, Gent," Mother said. "You don't have to do that." She stood up and tried to yank loose his apron ties. But Gent danced nimbly out of reach.

"No, no, Jade," he said. "Honestly, I don't mind at all. In fact, I like to tidy up. I've been a bachelor for nearly half a century!" He scraped and scrubbed until the whole kitchen gleamed. Mother watched him from her place at the table. She lit a cigarette and blew smoke noisily through her teeth. After Gent finished mopping the kitchen floor, he found the vacuum cleaner and went to work on the living-room carpet.

"No, no!" he yelled over the sucking roar, as if someone were trying to change his mind. "Let me do it! I don't mind a bit!"

He was wearing a suit. The apron had pink and white checks, with a ruffled trim. He had thrown his green, hand-painted tie over his left shoulder as if to keep it out of the way of the machine.

Mother got up and went outside. I watched her through the kitchen window. She crossed the back yard slowly and sat down at the picnic table. She lit another cigarette and stared into the hedge at the end of our property. A neighborhood cat jumped up on the table next to her, its vertical tail quivering, but Mother swept it away with a quick flash of her arm.

The night before Gent and Mother were to be married, Gent gave me a present. It was a dark blue suit with powerful gray stripes running through it. He also gave me a stiff, blue-white shirt and a shiny red tie with a picture of a trout painted on it. The trout had a red-and-white lure in its mouth. Big drops of water flew off its head like sweat.

"Christ God!" Mother said when she saw me in my new outfit. "Look at you, Jackie! It's the president of the First National Bank himself!" She was honestly taken by my appearance. She pressed both hands flat against her stomach and laughed nervously. I went into her bedroom and looked at myself in the full-length mirror. I raised an eyebrow and frowned and curled my lips, one side of my mouth up, the other side down. I didn't look bad. I felt I looked handsome in that ugly gangster way. "Say your prayers, sucker," I snarled, imitating Edward G. Robinson.

Gent fixed us dinner that day. Mother had allowed the kitchen to get grimy again, but Gent cleaned it before he started cooking. He was a good cook. He made a standing rib roast, scalloped potatoes, and three kinds of vegetables blanketed in a rich yellow sauce. I wore my blue suit to the table. LaDonna had received a new dress for the occasion. Gent was very generous to us. I had found a ten-dollar bill in the inside coat pocket of the suit, and LaDonna had found a five pinned to her skirts. I ate dinner like a steel robot, but still managed to get salad dressing on my tie and yellow sauce on my coat sleeve.

The wedding took place in a minister's back office. It was stuffy and hot in there, and my blue suit made me feel sick, so

I slipped out the door just as the minister was getting up a head of steam on the subject of the good marriage and how easily it can jump the tracks and wreck itself in the rocky ravine of neglect. Good grooming, for instance, said the minister. Married folks tend to let themselves go as they gradually become familiar with one another. I saw Gent wink at Mother when the minister said this, for Gent was nothing if not neat. And then, said the minister, there are the cat-footed evils of spite, inattention, and the always misguided sense of independence. Amen, Doc, said Gent, under his breath.

I felt better out in the street. It was a cool day in early autumn. I walked to the closest drugstore and bought a pack of cigarettes. The clerk didn't blink an eye. I guess I looked smoking-age in my blue suit, shirt and tie. I also bought a cigarette lighter that had the shape of a leaping fish. It looked pretty much like the trout that was jumping on my tie. The idea of my tie and cigarette lighter matching each other appealed to me.

I walked back to the church learning how to inhale. The smoke made me dizzy in an agreeable way. I knocked the ash off my cigarette several times so that I could use my fish-shaped lighter to light up again. Lighting up needed a style, and I studied myself in store windows trying to perfect one. When I reached the church, I sat down on the front steps and lit up again. Some kids ran by pointing at me and yelling, "I'm gonna te-ell, I'm gonna te-ell," but I blew some smoke at them and laughed suavely at their childishness.

After the wedding we went for a drive in the country in Gent's Buick Roadmaster, a black four-door sedan the size of a hearse. Gent parked next to an abandoned railroad depot. Mother and Gent walked down the old weedy railbed, and LaDonna and I explored the decaying brick depot. I actually found a set of ancient water-stained tickets that would have taken someone all the way to Chicago.

The windows of the depot were broken out and the floor was littered with a dank mulch of shattered glass and slimy leaves. I lit up a cigarette. LaDonna watched me with slowly widening eyes. I acted as though smoking were a trifle boring, as though smoking for us veterans were something to be endured fatalistically, like old wounds that would never quite heal.

I gave LaDonna a drag. Her brave curiosity wouldn't let her refuse. She drew a lungful of smoke. I could see that she wanted to choke it out, but she wouldn't let herself. "Give me one," she said, the words grating on her parched vocal cords. I gave her one and lit it for her. She inhaled again and blew the smoke furiously out her nose, her teeth grinding together in a tough smile.

"L.S.M.F.T.," I said, imitating the radio commercial.

"What?"

"Lucky Strike means fine tobacco," I said.

She looked at the white cylinder in her hand. "Tastes like burning rubber," she said.

We walked out onto the crumbling platform where people from another generation caught trains for Chicago. We could see Mother and Gent hugging down the railbed in the shade of an old rusted-out water tower. They kissed. Gent in his dark brown suit looked like a top-heavy bear. He was so much taller than Mother that he had to lean down and hunch his back as he gathered her in his arms. The kiss was long and awkward and Mother dropped her purse into the weeds. She tried to lean away from him to retrieve it, but Gent held her fast in his desperate arms, his legs spread for power. It looked like a bear had caught up with a Sunday picnicker. I took out my fish lighter and watched them through the orange flame.

My suit and tie made me look older, and smoking made me feel older. Feeling older widened my interests. I took a bunch of Gent's magazines up to my room once. I got them out of his office, which was a large paneled room next to the kitchen. Some of the magazines had full-color pictures of women wearing skimpy bathing suits. Others were of a more general interest. I read an article about the home life of Stone Age people. There were some drawings to go along with the article. The drawings showed short stubby women with furry tits tending a fire. They had faces only a zookeeper could love. In the hazy distance, a group of short men without foreheads were carrying a huge woolly carcass of some kind. The caption under this drawing said: "The Backbone of Domestic Harmony is the Successful Hunt."

I set the magazine aside and looked at the pictures of the

women in bathing suits. These were modern women — long-legged, smooth, with faces that were angelic and yet available. They seemed to radiate heat. The Stone Age men in the other magazine would have murdered entire forests full of woolly animals for a smile from one of those faces.

I'd been lying on top of my bed in my pajamas, but now I felt too restless and warm to go to sleep. I got up and put on my suit. I watched myself smoke cigarettes for a while in the mirror above my dresser. I looked good, I was developing style. I wished my neck weren't so skinny. I cinched my red tie, drawing the loose shirt collar tighter around my throat.

It was late, but I went into their room anyway. I guess I wanted some adult company. I snapped on the overhead light. There was a great rolling commotion in the canopied bed. I sat down in the chair next to Mother's vanity and lit a cigarette.

"Say, listen to this," I said, flipping open the magazine I had brought with me. "This story is about a day in the life of a linoleum cutter. It tells about this Stanley Wallach. He cuts linoleum twelve hours a day in Perth, Australia, and hopes to save enough money in twenty years to buy his own island. He's going to call it New Perth and crown himself king. King Stanley the First."

"Jackie," Mother said, sitting up in bed. "You shouldn't come barging into a bedroom like that. You're old enough to know better."

I felt suave in my suit. I put out my cigarette just so I could light another one. I wanted them to see my style. Gent was sitting on the edge of the bed, his back to me, his large pale head in his hands. He was in his shorts. I blew a recently perfected smoke ring toward them, winking.

"When did you start smoking?" Mother asked.

But I only crossed my legs and laughed in a sophisticated way, sort of tossing my head back and winking again, this time at the ceiling. I felt clever. I felt that I more or less had an adult's grasp of things.

"And there's this family," I continued, "who talk backasswards to each other, if you can swallow it. No one but themselves can get what they're saying. It's like a foreign country right in the middle of the neighborhood."

"Jack, old boy," said Gent, getting heavily to his feet. The lump in his long shorts swung as he stepped around the big bed. His bulky stomach rolled above his thin white legs. "Jack, you really ought to tap on a door before storming in like that."

I thought for a few seconds, then said, "Sklof, taht tuoba yrros."

"What?" Gent said.

"That's how they must do it," I said. "Talking backasswards."

Mother took a deep breath. It looked like she was about to smile. "Jackie . . ." she said.

I blew a fat doughnut straight up into the ceiling. "Okay, okay." I chuckled. "I can take a hint." I winked at them. Smoking had also given me a stylish chuckle, a husky little bark that trailed off into a world-weary wheeze. I stood up and yawned. I stubbed out my cigarette in their ashtray. "Guess I'll hit the old sackeroo," I said. "See you people in the morning."

I strolled slowly out of their room, as if the reluctance were theirs, not mine.

Money and a nice big house made all the difference to Mother. She now looked young and happy again. She had a lively bounce to her walk and she wore makeup every day. She bought herself a new dress on the first of every month and her collection of shoes outgrew her closet. She looked beautiful in the morning in her red silk duster and blue mules and she looked beautiful in the afternoon in her expensive dresses.

Gent was proud to have such a good-looking young woman for his wife and he made no secret of it. Her small size thrilled him, just as it had my father. But where my father would pick her up and dance her through the house, Gent seemed almost afraid to touch her, as if she were made of rare porcelain.

He would take us for Sunday rides in the Roadmaster just to show her off to the town. Mother would sit in the front seat next to Gent with her skirts hiked up for comfort, and LaDonna and I would sit in the back, reading the comic section. The Roadmaster had a radio, and Mother would search the dial for music as we idled in second gear through the streets of Far Cry.

The town on the north side of the river was usually smoky because of the teepee-shaped chip burners the lumber mills used to get rid of waste. On the south side, the air had a sulfurous sting to it because of the paper mill. On Sundays, though, the air on both sides of the river was not so bad. We'd drive down the tree-lined streets of the north side, and then, if we felt like it, we'd cross the Mill Avenue bridge and cruise the wider, treeless streets of the south side. Sometimes Gent would pull over and park and we'd listen to the radio for a while. People on the sidewalks, looking into the car, would smile and nod as if to approve our way of killing Sunday.

Mother had a baby by Gent Mundy. It was a big baby and the delivery was an ordeal. It gave her milk leg and she had to stay in bed for nearly a month after she got home from the hospital. The head of the baby was so large that for a time the doctor thought it would not be able to pass through the birth canal. And when it did pass, it tore her badly. Gent felt terrible about this. I saw him once kneeling at her bedside, crying loudly, his face in his hands. But Mother healed quickly and soon the big, happy-dispositioned baby became the central attraction at our house.

They named him Spencer Ted. Spencer Ted looked like Gent, and Gent couldn't get over it. "The Mundy heir," he'd say, amazed. If I was in earshot, he'd get flustered and add, "No offense to you, Jack." But it didn't matter to me since no boy of thirteen cares much about inheriting a creamery. "My precious strapping fellow," Gent would coo to the big, round-headed baby, and if either LaDonna or I was nearby, he'd insist, "But, say, I love you kids too, just as if you were my own!"

All this didn't matter to LaDonna or me. We liked Gent because he was easygoing and generous. He gave us practically anything we wanted. LaDonna hinted for a microscope of her own, and Gent went right down to the Sears outlet and ordered an expensive binocular microscope complete with lab kit. I barely complained one day about having to ride my old, rusty Iver-Johnson bike, and the next afternoon after school I found a beautiful new Schwinn on the front porch, complete with basket, headlight, foxtails, and horn.

It didn't matter to me or LaDonna that Gent loved Spencer Ted best because we loved the new baby too. He was happy as a cabbage and cute in an odd sort of way. All babies are more or less cute, but Spencer Ted's cuteness wasn't baby-cuteness. It was the cuteness of joke postcards, where unlikely combinations are relied on to produce a humorous effect. Like a fish wearing a saddle and a cowboy in the saddle twirling a rope, or a poodle smoking a pipe and reading the newspaper. With Spencer Ted, it was a fringe of red hair around his ears, which made him look like an old scholar, and a round, tomato-red nose, which made him look like a seasoned drinker. He had deep-set, coal-black eyes that missed nothing, and radiantly pink ears that bloomed under his fringe of hair like roses.

Spencer Ted seemed as pleased with the brand-new world as Gent was with his brand-new heir. Often LaDonna and I would take Spencer Ted out for a walk in his stroller, and when we did this, LaDonna liked to pretend that we were his parents. It was a game that tickled her, and she would say things such as "We must find a suitable nurse for our darling little man, dear." She would speak in a stagey voice and people near us would wink and chuckle, for we were only children ourselves.

Sometimes we would sit down on a park bench and LaDonna would hold Spencer Ted in her lap. Being held in a lap was a signal for him and he would begin turning his big round head impatiently, looking for a full breast. This made LaDonna nervous and she would give him his pacifier which only gentled him for a few seconds. He would spit the pacifier out, arch his back angrily, and then grind his soft, drunkard's face into LaDonna's milkless ribs.

"Mamma spank!" LaDonna once said, embarrassed by Spencer Ted's aggressive search for satisfaction, and Spencer Ted, arrested by her sharp, scolding voice, studied her like an old scholar studying an obscure text, his black eyes wide with alarm. LaDonna immediately regretted her tone. "Oh no, Spencey," she said. "Mamma would never spank *you*."

We always went to Grassy Lake on the Fourth of July. Grassy Lake was a recreational area for the people of Far Cry. There was a beach and several boat-launching ramps. In the late fall, old men would fish off the ramps with cane poles, but in the summer there were only bathers and boats at the lake.

Spencer Ted was almost one year old by the Fourth of July,

and we took him up to the lake thinking that he'd be thrilled with the fast boats, the long expanse of deep blue water, and the evening fireworks. But he was cranky and balked at everything we tried to interest him in. He sat under the beach umbrella with Gent, fussy and critical, while LaDonna and I made sand castles and Mother swam.

I didn't know Mother could swim, but she swam like a young girl out to the diving platform which was about fifty yards from shore. LaDonna and I watched her, amazed. When she reached the platform, she pulled herself easily out of the water and stood on the planks, shimmering with wet light. She took off her bathing cap, releasing her long shining hair. Then she found a sunny spot and lay down on her back.

The arch of her ribs, her nicely muscled legs, the graceful reach of her relaxed arms, and the mass of dark glossy hair pillowing her head and shoulders made all of us gaze out across the water like the stranded victims of a shipwreck afflicted with thirst-caused visions. It was like a spell. Finally Gent said, in dreamy baby talk, "Thaz you booly-full mamma, Spencey," and Spencer Ted, recognizing at last the impassable gulf between him and Mother, released a ragged forlorn sob.

LaDonna and I turned our attention back to our sand castles. They weren't very elaborate and we didn't mind wrecking them as soon as we got them built. We erected a city full of sloppy skyscrapers. "Let's A-bomb it," LaDonna said.

I was the B-29, arms out, rumbling through the hot sky, radio chatter of the crewmen alive in my head, sighting in on the muddy skyline of our city. Then, as I approached it, I picked up speed, bomb-bay doors open, crew tense, and I released the bomb, Fat Boy. I had to be Fat Boy then, and I fell on the city, back first, squashing it flat, and LaDonna made the A-bomb noise, the rolling boom and bleak sigh of the high sweeping wind.

We did this several times, and then I dove into the lake to wash off the mud. I swam out toward the diving platform, thinking to join Mother, but when I looked up I saw that there was a man standing behind her. He was big and heavily muscled. He had black hair, bright as freshly laid tar. He lifted his arms and flexed. The biceps jumped impossibly tall with cords of angry veins, violet under the oiled skin. Then he put his hands on his hips and drew in his stomach until his ribcage arched over the unnatural hollow like an amphitheater. His thighs from his kneecaps to hips were thick with bands of visible muscle. He moved from one pose to another, finally relaxing, hands on hips at a cocky angle, a swashbuckler's smile on his tanned face. Mother glittered like booty at his feet. But she acted as though she didn't see him, or even know he was there.

I swam back to shore and joined Gent and Spencer Ted under the umbrella. LaDonna was building another city. This one was futuristic, with tall spires and cylinders and oddly concave walls. I got a half-dollar from Gent and bought a package of fire-crackers — "ladyfingers" — and a package of "whistlers." I thought we could blow this city up with ordinary explosives, one building at a time. Gent and Spencer Ted took a nap. Gent was lying flat on his back with a towel over his face and Spencer Ted was tucked in the crook of his arm. I was afraid the "whistlers" might wake them, but they didn't.

After the city was wrecked, I watched Mother swim. She stroked the water like a professional channel swimmer, but she wasn't swimming back to us. She was swimming parallel to shore, away from the platform. The muscleman with the black hair was in the water too. He didn't swim as gracefully as Mother. The water churned around him and his black hair whipped from side to side. Even so, he swam much faster than Mother and was soon even with her. They treaded water for a while, about one yard apart. I thought I could hear them talk-ing. Then they swam back to the platform, side by side. He tried to match his stroke to hers, but it wasn't easy for him. While she looked smooth and natural, he looked drugged.

He climbed out of the water first, then helped Mother. He pretended that she was too heavy for him and that she was pulling him off balance. He somersaulted over her into the water with a gigantic splash. Mother climbed up onto the plat-form, laughing. He joined her and then did a handstand. He began to walk around the perimeter of the platform on his hands while Mother shook out her hair. Mother leaned sharply to one side and then to the other, combing her hair with her fingers, while the muscleman walked on his hands. It looked like some kind of crazy dance.

Gent and Spencer Ted were awake now and looking out across the water at Mother. Spencer Ted's bald head looked like a smaller version of Gent's. Spencer Ted lifted his fat white arm and pointed toward the diving platform. He moaned crankily and blew a fat spit bubble.

It was nearly evening. Soon the fireworks would begin.

ANDRE DUBUS

A Father's Story

(FROM BLACK WARRIOR REVIEW)

MY NAME IS LUKE RIPLEY, and here is what I call my life: I own a stable of thirty horses, and I have young people who teach riding, and we board some horses too. This is in northeastern Massachusetts. I have a barn with an indoor ring, and outside I've got two fenced-in rings and a pasture that ends at a woods with trails. I call it my life because it looks like it is, and people I know call it that, but it's a life I can get away from when I hunt and fish, and some nights after dinner when I sit in the dark in the front room and listen to opera. The room faces the lawn and the road, a two-lane country road. When cars come around the curve northwest of the house, they light up the lawn for an instant, the leaves of the maple out by the road and the hemlock closer to the window. Then I'm alone again, or I'd appear to be if someone crept up to the house and looked through a window: a big-gutted gray-haired guy, drinking tea and smoking ciga-rettes, staring out at the dark woods across the road, listening to a grieving soprano.

My real life is the one nobody talks about anymore, except Father Paul LeBoeuf, another old buck. He has a decade on me: he's sixty-four, a big man, bald on top with gray at the sides; when he had hair, it was black. His face is ruddy, and he jokes about being a whiskey priest, though he's not. He gets outdoors as much as he can, goes for a long walk every morning, and hunts and fishes with me. But I can't get him on a horse any-more. Ten years ago I could badger him into a trail ride; I had to give him a Western saddle, and he'd hold the pommel and bounce through the woods with me, and be sore for days. He's looking at seventy with eyes that are younger than many I've seen in people in their twenties. I do not remember ever feeling the way they seem to; but I was lucky, because even as a child I knew that life would try me, and I must be strong to endure, though in those days I expected to be tortured and killed for my faith, like the saints I learned about in school.

Father Paul's family came down from Canada, and he grew up speaking more French than English, so he is different from the Irish priests who abound up here. I do not like to make general statements, or even to hold general beliefs, about people's blood, but the Irish do seem happiest when they're dealing with misfortune or guilt, either their own or somebody else's, and if you think you're not a victim of either one, you can count on certain Irish priests to try to change your mind. On Wednesday nights Father Paul comes to dinner. Often he comes on other nights too and once, in the old days when we couldn't eat meat on Fridays, we bagged our first ducks of the season on a Friday, and as we drove home from the marsh, he said: For the purposes of Holy Mother Church, I believe a duck is more a creature of water than land, and is not rightly meat. Sometimes he teases me about never putting anything in his Sunday collection, which he would not know about if I hadn't told him years ago. I would like to believe I told him so we could have philosophical talk at dinner, but probably the truth is I suspected he knew, and I did not want him to think I so loved money that I would not even give his church a coin on Sunday. Certainly the ushers who pass the baskets know me as a miser.

I don't feel right about giving money for buildings, places. This starts with the pope, and I cannot respect one of them till he sells his house and everything in it, and that church too, and uses the money to feed the poor. I have rarely, and maybe never, come across saintliness, but I feel certain it cannot exist in such a place. But I admit, also, that I know very little, and maybe the popes live on a different plane and are tried in ways I don't know about. Father Paul says his own church, St. John's, is hardly the Vatican. I like his church: it is made of wood, and has a simple altar and crucifix, and no padding on the kneelers. He does not have to lock its doors at night. Still it is a place. He could say Mass in my barn. I know this is stubborn, but I can find no mention by Christ of maintaining buildings, much less erecting them of stone or brick, and decorating them with pieces of metal and mineral and elements that people still fight over like barbarians. We had a Maltese woman taking riding lessons, she came over on the boat when she was ten, and once she told me how the nuns in Malta used to tell the little girls that if they wore jewelry, rings and bracelets and necklaces, in purgatory snakes would coil around their fingers and wrists and throats. I do not believe in frightening children or telling them lies, but if those nuns saved a few girls from devotion to things, maybe they were right. That Maltese woman laughed about it, but I noticed she wore only a watch, and that with a leather strap.

The money I give to the church goes in people's stomachs, and on their backs, down in New York City. I have no delusions about the worth of what I do, but I feel it's better to feed somebody than not. There's a priest in Times Square giving shelter to runaway kids, and some Franciscans who run a bread line; actually it's a morning line for coffee and a roll, and Father Paul calls it the continental breakfast for winos and bag ladies. He is curious about how much I am sending, and I know why: he guesses I send a lot, he has said probably more than tithing, and he is right; he wants to know how much because he believes I'm generous and good, and he is wrong about that; he has never had much money and does not know how easy it is to write a check when you have everything you will ever need, and the figures are mere numbers, and represent no sacrifice at all. Being a real Catholic is too hard; if I were one, I would do with my house and barn what I want the pope to do with his. So I do not want to impress Father Paul, and when he asks me how much, I say I can't let my left hand know what my right is doing.

He came on Wednesday nights when Gloria and I were married, and the kids were young; Gloria was a very good cook (I assume she still is, but it is difficult to think of her in the present), and I liked sitting at the table with a friend who was also a priest. I was proud of my handsome and healthy children. This was long ago, and they were all very young and cheerful and often funny, and the three boys took care of their baby sister, and did not bully or tease her. Of course they did sometimes,

with that excited cruelty children are prone to, but not enough
so that it was part of her days. On the Wednesday after Gloria
left with the kids and a U-Haul trailer, I was sitting on the front
steps, it was summer, and I was watching cars go by on the road,
when Father Paul drove around the curve and into the driveway. I was ashamed to see him because he is a priest and my
family was gone, but I was relieved too. I went to the car to greet
him. He got out smiling, with a bottle of wine, and shook my
hand, then pulled me to him, gave me a quick hug, and said:
"It's Wednesday, isn't it? Let's open some cans."

With arms about each other we walked to the house, and it
was good to know he was doing his work but coming as a friend
too, and I thought what good work he had. I have no calling. It
is for me to keep horses.

In that other life, anyway. In my real one I go to bed early
and sleep well and wake at four forty-five, for an hour of silence. I never want to get out of bed then, and every morning I
know I can sleep for another four hours, and still not fail at any
of my duties. But I get up, so have come to believe my life can
be seen in miniature in that struggle in the dark of morning.
While making the bed and boiling water for coffee, I talk to
God: I offer Him my day, every act of my body and spirit, my
thoughts and moods, as a prayer of thanksgiving, and for Gloria
and my children and my friends and two women I made love
with after Gloria left. This morning offertory is a habit from my
boyhood in a Catholic school; or then it was a habit, but as I
kept it and grew older it became a ritual. Then I say the Lord's
Prayer, trying not to recite it, and one morning it occurred to
me that a prayer, whether recited or said with concentration, is
always an act of faith.

I sit in the kitchen at the rear of the house and drink coffee
and smoke and watch the sky growing light before sunrise, the
trees of the woods near the barn taking shape, becoming single
pines and elms and oaks and maples. Sometimes a rabbit comes
out of the treeline, or is already sitting there, invisible till the
light finds him. The birds are awake in the trees and feeding on
the ground and the little ones, the purple finches and titmice
and chickadees, are at the feeder I rigged outside the kitchen
window; it is too small for pigeons to get a purchase. I sit and

give myself to coffee and tobacco, that get me brisk again, and I watch and listen. In the first year or so after I lost my family, I played the radio in the mornings. But I overcame that, and now I rarely play it at all. Once in the mail I received a questionnaire asking me to write down everything I watched on television during the week they had chosen. At the end of those seven days I wrote in *The Wizard of Oz* and returned it. That was in winter and was actually a busy week for my television, which normally sits out the cold months without once warming up. Had they sent the questionnaire during baseball season, they would have found me at my set. People at the stables talk about shows and performers I have never heard of, but I cannot get interested; when I am in the mood to watch television, I go to a movie or read a detective novel. There are always good detective novels to be found, and I like remembering them next morning with my coffee.

I also think of baseball and hunting and fishing, and of my children. It is not painful to think about them anymore, because even if we had lived together, they would be gone now, grown into their own lives, except Jennifer. I think of death too, not sadly, or with fear, though something like excitement does run through me, something more quickening than the coffee and tobacco. I suppose it is an intense interest, and an outright distrust: I never feel certain that I'll be here watching birds eating at tomorrow's daylight. Sometimes I try to think of other things, like the rabbit that is warm and breathing but not there till twilight. I feel on the brink of something about the life of the senses, but either am not equipped to go further, or am not interested enough to concentrate. I have called all of this thinking, but it is not, because it is unintentional; what I'm really doing is feeling the day, in silence, and that is what Father Paul is doing too on his five- to ten-mile walks.

When the hour ends I take an apple or carrot, and I go to the stable and tack up a horse. We take good care of these horses, and no one rides them but students, instructors, and me, and nobody rides the horses we board unless an owner asks me to. The barn is dark and I turn on lights and take some deep breaths, smelling the hay and horses and their manure, both fresh and dried, a combined odor that you either like or you don't. I walk down the wide space of dirt between stalls, greeting the horses, joking with them about their quirks, and choose one for no reason at all other than the way it looks at me that morning. I get my old English saddle that has smoothed and darkened through the years, and go into the stall, talking to this beautiful creature who'll swerve out of a canter if a piece of paper blows in front of him, and if the barn catches fire and you manage to get him out he will, if he can get away from you, run back into the fire, to his stall. Like the smells that surround them, you either like them or you don't. I love them, so am spared having to try to explain why. I feed one the carrot or apple and tack up and lead him outside where I mount, and we go down the driveway to the road and cross it and turn northwest and walk then trot then canter to St. John's.

A few cars are on the road, their drivers looking serious about going to work. It is always strange for me to see a woman dressed for work so early in the morning. You know how long it takes them, with the makeup and hair and clothes, and I think of them waking in the dark of winter or early light of other seasons, and dressing as they might for an evening's entertainment. Probably this strikes me because I grew up seeing my father put on those suits he never wore on weekends or his two weeks off, and so am accustomed to the men, but when I see these women I think something went wrong, to send all those dressed-up people out on the road when the dew hasn't dried yet. Maybe it's because I so dislike getting up early, but am also doing what I choose to do, while they have no choice. At heart I am lazy, yet I find such peace and delight in it that I believe it is a natural state, and in what looks like my laziest periods I am closest to my center. The ride to St. John's is fifteen minutes. The horses and I do it in all weather; the road is well plowed in winter, and there are only a few days a year when ice makes me drive the pickup. People always look at someone on horseback, and for a moment their faces change and many drivers and I wave to each other. Then at St. John's, Father Paul and five or six regulars and I celebrate the Mass.

Do not think of me as a spiritual man whose every thought during those twenty-five minutes is at one with the words of the Mass. Each morning I try, each morning I fail, and know that always I will be a creature who, looking at Father Paul and the altar, and uttering prayers, will be distracted by scrambled eggs, horses, the weather, and memories and daydreams that have nothing to do with the sacrament I am about to receive. I can receive, though: the Eucharist, and also, at Mass and at other times, moments and even minutes of contemplation. But I cannot achieve contemplation, as some can; and so, having to face and forgive my own failures, I have learned from them both the necessity and the wonder of ritual. For ritual allows those who cannot will themselves out of the secular to perform the spiritual as dancing allows the tongue-tied man a ceremony of love. And, while my mind dwells on breakfast, or Major or Duchess tethered under the church eave, there is, as I take the Host from Father Paul and place it on my tongue and return to the pew, a feeling that I am thankful I have not lost in the forty-eight years since my first Communion. At its center is excitement; spreading out from it is the peace of certainty. Or the certainty of peace. One night Father Paul and I talked about faith. It was long ago, and all I remember is him saying: Belief is believing in God; faith is believing that God believes in you. That is the excitement, and the peace; then the Mass is over, and I go into the sacristy and we have a cigarette and chat, the mystery ends, we are two men talking like any two men on a morning in America, about baseball, plane crashes, presidents, governors, murders, the sun, the clouds. Then I go to the horse and ride back to the life people see, the one in which I move and talk, and most days I enjoy it.

It is late summer now, the time between fishing and hunting, but a good time for baseball. It has been two weeks since Jennifer left, to drive home to Gloria's after her summer visit. She is the only one who still visits; the boys are married and have children, and sometimes fly up for a holiday, or I fly down or west to visit one of them. Jennifer is twenty, and I worry about her the way fathers worry about daughters but not sons. I want to know what she's up to, and at the same time I don't. She looks athletic, and she is: she swims and runs and of course rides. All my children do. When she comes for six weeks in summer, the house is loud with girls, friends of hers since childhood, and new ones. I am glad she kept the girl friends. They have been young company for me and, being with them, I have been able to gauge her growth between summers. On their riding days, I'd take them back to the house when their lessons were over and they had walked the horses and put them back in the stalls, and we'd have lemonade or Coke, and cookies if I had some, and talk until their parents came to drive them home. One year their breasts grew, so I wasn't startled when I saw Jennifer in July. Then they were driving cars to the stable, and beginning to look like young women, and I was passing out beer and ashtrays and they were talking about college.

When Jennifer was here in summer, they were at the house most days. I would say generally that as they got older they became quieter, and though I enjoyed both, I sometimes missed the giggles and shouts. The quiet voices, just low enough for me not to hear from wherever I was, rising and falling in proportion to my distance from them, frightened me. Not that I believed they were planning or recounting anything really wicked, but there was a female seriousness about them, and it was secretive, and of course I thought: love, sex. But it was more than that: it was womanhood they were entering, the deep forest of it, and no matter how many women and men too are saying these days that there is little difference between us, the truth is that men find their way into that forest only on clearly marked trails while women move about in it like birds. So hearing Jennifer and her friends talking so quietly, yet intensely, I wanted very much to have a wife.

But not as much as in the old days, when Gloria had left but her presence was still in the house as strongly as if she had only gone to visit her folks for a week. There were no clothes or cosmetics, but potted plants endured my neglectful care as long as they could, and slowly died; I did not kill them on purpose, to exorcise the house of her, but I could not remember to water them. For weeks, because I did not use it much, the house was as neat as she had kept it, though dust layered the order she had made. The kitchen went first: I got the dishes in and out of the dishwasher and wiped the top of the stove, but did not return cooking spoons and potholders to their hooks on the wall, and soon the burners and oven were caked with spillings, the refrigerator had more space and was spotted with juices.

The living room and my bedroom went next; I did not go into the children's rooms except on bad nights when I went from room to room and looked and touched and smelled, so they did not lose their order until a year later when the kids came for six weeks. It was three months before I ate the last of the food Gloria had cooked and frozen: I remember it was a beef stew, and very good. By then I had four cookbooks, and was boasting a bit, and talking about recipes with the women at the stables, and looking forward to cooking for Father Paul. But I never looked forward to cooking at night only for myself, though I made myself do it; on some nights I gave in to my daily temptation, and took a newspaper or detective novel to a restaurant. By the end of the second year, though, I had stopped turning on the radio as soon as I woke in the morning, and was able to be silent and alone in the evening too, and then I enjoyed my dinners.

It is not hard to live through a day, if you can live through a moment. What creates despair is the imagination, that pretends there is a future, and insists on predicting millions of moments, thousands of days, and so drains you that you cannot live the moment at hand. That is what Father Paul told me in those first two years, on some of the bad nights when I believed I could not bear what I had to: the most painful loss was my children, then the loss of Gloria whom I still loved despite or maybe because of our long periods of sadness that rendered us helpless, so neither of us could break out of it to give a hand to the other. Twelve years later I believe ritual would have healed us more quickly than the repetitious talks we had, perhaps even kept us healed. Marriages have lost that, and I wish I had known then what I know now, and we had performed certain acts together every day, no matter how we felt, and perhaps then we could have subordinated feeling to action, for surely that is the essence of love. I know this from my distractions during Mass, and during everything else I do, so that my actions and feelings are seldom one. It does happen every day, but in proportion to everything else in a day, it is rare, like joy. The third most painful loss, which became second and sometimes first as months passed, was the knowledge that I could never marry again, and so dared not even keep company with a woman.

On some of the bad nights I was bitter about this with Father
Paul, and I so pitied myself that I cried, or nearly did, speaking
with damp eyes and breaking voice. I believe that celibacy is for
him the same trial it is for me, not of the flesh, but the spirit:
the heart longing to love. But the difference is he chose it, and
did not wake one day to a life with thirty horses. In my anger I
said I had done my service to love and chastity, and I told him
of the actual physical and spiritual pain of practicing rhythm:
nights of striking the mattress with a fist, two young animals
lying side by side in heat, leaving the bed to pace, to smoke, to
curse, and too passionate to question, for we were so angered
and oppressed by our passion that we could see no further than
our loins. So now I understand how people can be enslaved for
generations before they throw down their tools or use them as
weapons, the form of their slavery — the cotton fields, the
shacks and puny cupboards and untended illnesses — absorb-
ing their emotions and thoughts until finally they have little or
none at all to direct with clarity and energy at the owners and
legislators. And I told him of the trick of passion and its slaking:
how during what we had to believe were safe periods, though
all four children were conceived at those times, we were able
with some coherence to question the tradition and reason and
justice of the law against birth control, but not with enough
conviction to soberly act against it, as though regular satisfaction
in bed tempered our revolutionary as well as our erotic desires.
Only when abstinence drove us hotly away from each other did
we receive an urge so strong it lasted all the way to the drugstore
and back; but always, after release, we threw away the remaining condoms; and after going through this a few times, we knew
what would happen, and from then on we submitted to the
calendar she so precisely marked on the bedroom wall. I told
him that living two lives each month, one as celibates, one as
lovers, made us tense and short-tempered, so we snapped at
each other like dogs.

To have endured that, to have reached a time when we
burned slowly and could gain from bed the comfort of lying
down at night with one who loves you and whom you love, could
for weeks on end go to bed tired, and peacefully sleep after a
kiss, a touch of the hands, and then to be thrown out of the

marriage like a bundle from a moving freight car, was unjust, was intolerable, and I could not or would not muster the strength to endure it. But I did, a moment at a time, a day, a night, except twice, each time with a different woman and more than a year apart, and this was so long ago that I clearly see their faces in my memory, can hear the pitch of their voices, and the way they pronounced words, one with a Massachusetts accent, one midwestern, but I feel as though I only heard about them from someone else. Each rode at the stables and was with me for part of an evening; one was badly married, one divorced, so none of us was free. They did not understand this Catholic view, but they were understanding about my having it, and I remained friends with both of them until the married one left her husband and went to Boston, and the divorced one moved to Maine. After both those evenings, those good women, I went to Mass early while Father Paul was still in the confessional, and received his absolution. I did not tell him who I was, but of course he knew, though I never saw it in his eyes. Now my longing for a wife comes only once in a while, like a cold: on some late afternoons when I am alone in the barn then I lock up and walk to the house, daydreaming, then suddenly look at it and see it empty, as though for the first time, and all at once I'm weary and feel I do not have the energy to broil meat, and I think of driving to a restaurant, then shake my head and go on to the house, the refrigerator, the oven; and some mornings when I wake in the dark and listen to the silence and run my hand over the cold sheet beside me; and some days in summer when Jennifer is here.

Gloria left first me then the church, and that was the end of religion for the children, though on visits they went to Sunday Mass with me, and still do, out of a respect for my life that they manage to keep free of patronage. Jennifer is an agnostic, though I doubt she would call herself that, any more than she would call herself any other name that implied she had made a decision, a choice, about existence, death, and God. In truth she tends to pantheism, a good sign I think; but not wanting to be a father who tells his children what they ought to believe, I do not say to her that Catholicism includes pantheism, like onions in the stew. Besides, I have no missionary instincts and do not believe everyone should or even could live with the Catholic faith. It is Jennifer's womanhood that renders me awkward. And womanhood now is frank, not like when Gloria was twenty and there were symbols: high heels and cosmetics and dresses, a cigarette, a cocktail. I am glad that women are free now of false modesty and all its attention paid the flesh; but still it is difficult to see so much of your daughter, to face the deep and unabashed sensuality of women, with no tricks of the eyes and mouth to hide the pleasure she feels at having a strong young body. I am certain, with the way things are now, that she has very happily not been a virgin for years. That does not bother me. What bothers me is my certainty about it, just from watching her walk across a room or light a cigarette or pour milk on cereal.

She told me all of it, waking me that night when I had gone to sleep listening to the wind in the trees against the house, a wind so strong that I had to shut all but the lee windows, and still the house cooled; told it to me in such detail and so clearly that now, when she has driven the car to Florida, I remember it all as though I had been a passenger in the front seat, or even at the wheel. It started with a movie, then beer and driving to the sea to look at the waves in the night and the wind, Jennifer and Betsy and Liz. They drank a beer on the beach and wanted to go in naked but were afraid they would drown in the high surf. They bought another six-pack at a grocery store in New Hampshire, and drove home. I can see it now, feel it: the three girls and the beer and the ride on country roads where pines curved in the wind and the big deciduous trees swayed and shook as if they might leap from the earth. They would have some windows partly open so they could feel the wind; Jennifer would be playing a cassette, the music stirring them, as it does the young, to memories of another time, other people and places in what is for them the past.

She took Betsy home, then Liz, and sang with her cassette as she left the town west of us and started home, a twenty-minute drive on the road that passes my house. They had each had four beers, but now there were twelve empty bottles in the bag on the floor at the passenger seat, and I keep focusing on their sound against each other when the car shifted speeds or changed directions. For I want to understand that one moment out of all her heart's time on earth, and whether her history had any bearing on it, or whether her heart was then isolated from all it had known, and the sound of those bottles urged it. She was just leaving the town, accelerating past a nightclub on the right, gaining speed to climb a long gradual hill, then she went up it, singing, patting the beat on the steering wheel, the wind loud through her few inches of open window, blowing her hair as it did the high branches alongside the road, and she looked up at them and watched the top of the hill for someone drunk or heedless coming over it in part of her lane. She crested to an open black road, and there he was: a bulk, a blur, a thing running across her headlights, and she swerved left and her foot went for the brake and was stomping air above its pedal when she hit him, saw his legs and body in the air, flying out of her light, into the dark. Her brakes were screaming into the wind, bottles clinking in the fallen bag, and with the music and wind inside the car was his sound already a memory but as real as an echo, that car-shuddering thump as though she had struck a tree. Her foot was back on the accelerator. Then she shifted gears and pushed it. She ejected the cassette and closed the window. She did not start to cry until she knocked on my bedroom door, then called: "Dad?"

Her voice, her tears, broke through my dream and the wind I heard in my sleep, and I stepped into jeans and hurried to the door, thinking harm, rape, death. All were in her face, and I hugged her and pressed her cheek to my chest and smoothed her blown hair, then led her weeping to the kitchen and sat her at the table where still she could not speak, nor look at me; when she raised her face it fell forward again, as of its own weight, into her palms. I offered tea and she shook her head, so I offered beer twice then she shook her head, so I offered whiskey and she nodded. I had some rye that Father Paul and I had not finished last hunting season, and I poured some over ice and set it in front of her and was putting away the ice but stopped and got another glass and poured one for myself too, and brought the ice and bottle to the table where she was trying to get one of her long menthols out of the pack, but her fingers jerked like severed snakes, and I took the pack and lit one for her and took one for myself. I watched her shudder with her first swallow of rye, and push hair back from her face, it is auburn and gleamed in the overhead light, and I remembered how beautiful she looked riding a sorrel; she was smoking fast, then the sobs in her throat stopped, and she looked at me and said it, the words coming out with smoke: "I hit somebody. With the *car.*"

Then she was crying and I was on my feet, moving back and forth, looking down at her asking Who? Where? Where? She was pointing at the wall over the stove, jabbing her fingers and cigarette at it, her other hand at her eyes, and twice in horror I actually looked at the wall. She finished the whiskey in a swallow and I stopped pacing and asking and poured another, and either the drink or the exhaustion of tears quieted her, even the dry sobs, and she told me; not as I tell it now, for that was later as again and again we relived it in the kitchen or living room, and if in daylight fled it on horseback out on the trails through the woods, and if at night walked quietly around in the moonlit pasture, walked around and around it, sweating through our clothes. She told it in bursts, like she was a child again, running to me, injured from play. I put on boots and a shirt and left her with the bottle and her streaked face and a cigarette twitching between her fingers, pushed the door open against the wind, and eased it shut. The wind squinted and watered my eyes as I leaned into it and went to the pickup.

When I passed St. John's I looked at it, and Father Paul's little white rectory in the rear, and wanted to stop, wished I could as I could if he were simply a friend who sold hardware or something. I had forgotten my watch but I always know the time within minutes, even when a sound or dream or my bladder wakes me in the night. It was nearly two; we had been in the kitchen about twenty minutes; she had hit him around one-fifteen. Or her. The road was empty and I drove between blowing trees; caught for an instant in my lights, they seemed to be in panic. I smoked and let hope play her tricks on me; it was neither man nor woman but an animal, a goat or calf or deer on the road; it was a man who had jumped away in time, the collision of metal and body glancing not direct, and he had limped home to nurse bruises and cuts. Then I threw the cigarette and hope both out the window and prayed that he was alive, while beneath that prayer, a reserve deeper in my heart, another one stirred: that if he were dead, they would not get Jennifer.

From our direction, east and a bit south, the road to that hill and the nightclub beyond it and finally the town is, for its last four or five miles, straight through farming country. When I reached that stretch I slowed the truck and opened my window for the fierce air; on both sides were scattered farmhouses and barns and sometimes a silo, looking not like shelters but like unsheltered things the wind would flatten. Corn bent toward the road from a field on my right, and always something blew in front of me: paper, leaves, dried weeds, branches. I slowed approaching the hill, and went up it in second, staring through my open window at the ditch on the left side of the road, its weeds alive, whipping, a mad dance with the trees above them. I went over the hill and down and, opposite the club, turned right onto a side street of houses, and parked there, in the leaping shadows of trees. I walked back across the road to the club's parking lot, the wind behind me, lifting me as I strode, and I could not hear my boots on pavement. I walked up the hill, on the shoulder, watching the branches above me, hearing their leaves and the creaking trunks and the wind. Then I was at the top, looking down the road and at the farms and fields; the night was clear, and I could see a long way; clouds scudded past the half-moon and stars, blown out to sea.

I started down, watching the tall grass under the trees to my right, glancing into the dark of the ditch, listening for cars behind me; but as soon as I cleared one tree, its sound was gone, its flapping leaves and rattling branches far behind me, as though the greatest distance I had at my back was a matter of feet, while ahead of me I could see a barn two miles off. Then I saw her skid marks: short, and going left and downhill, into the other lane. I stood at the ditch, its weeds blowing; across it were trees and their moving shadows, like the clouds. I stepped onto its slope, and it took me sliding on my feet then rump to the bottom where I sat still, my body gathered to itself, lest a part of me should touch him. But there was only tall grass, and I stood, my shoulders reaching the sides of the ditch, and I walked uphill, wishing for the flashlight in the pickup, walking slowly, and down in the ditch I could hear my feet in the grass and on the earth, and kicking cans and bottles. At the top of the hill I turned and went down, watching the ground above the ditch on my right, praying my prayer from the truck again, the first one, the one I would admit, that he was not dead, was in fact home, and began to hope again, memory telling me of lost pheasants and grouse I had shot, but they were small and the colors of their home, while a man was either there or not; and from that memory I left where I was and while walking the ditch under the wind was in the deceit of imagination with Jennifer in the kitchen, telling her she had hit no one, or at least had not badly hurt anyone, when I realized he could be in the hospital now and I would have to think of a way to check there, something to say on the phone. I see now that, once hope returned, I should have been certain what she prepared me for: ahead of me, in high grass and the shadows of trees, I saw his shirt. Or that is all my mind would allow itself: a shirt, and I stood looking at it for the moments it took my mind to admit the arm and head and the dark length covered by pants. He lay face down, the arm I could see near his side, his head turned from me, on its cheek.

"Fella?" I said. I had meant to call, but it came out quiet and high, lost inches from my face in the wind. Then I said, "Oh God," and felt Him in the wind and the sky moving past the stars and moon and the fields around me, but only watching me as He might have watched Cain or Job, I did not know which, and I said it again, and wanted to sink to the earth and weep till I slept there in the weeds. I climbed, scrambling up the side of the ditch, pulling at clutched grass, gained the top on hands and knees, and went to him like that, panting, moving through the grass as high and higher than my face, crawling under that sky, making sounds too like some animal, there being no words to let him know I was here with him now. He was long; that is the word that came to me, not tall. I knelt beside him, my hands on my legs. His right arm was by his side, his left arm straight out from the shoulder, but turned, so his palm was open to the tree above us. His left cheek was clean shaven, his eye closed, and there was no blood. I leaned forward to look at his open mouth and saw the blood on it, going down into the grass. I straightened and looked ahead at the wind blowing past me through grass and trees to a distant light, and I stared at the light, imagining someone awake out there, wanting someone to be, a gathering of old friends, or someone alone listening to music or painting a picture, then I figured it was a night light at a farmyard whose house I couldn't see. *Going,* I thought. *Still going.* I leaned over again and looked at dripping blood.

So I had to touch his wrist, a thick one with a watch and expansion band that I pushed up his arm, thinking *he's left-handed,* my three fingers pressing his wrist and all I felt was my tough fingertips on that smooth underside flesh and small bones, then relief, then certainty. But against my will, or only because of it, I still don't know, I touched his neck, ran my fingers down it as if petting, then pressed and my hand sprang back as from fire. I lowered it again, held it there until it felt that faint beating that I could not believe. There was too much wind. Nothing could make a sound in it. A pulse could not be felt in it, nor could mere fingers in that wind feel the absolute silence of a dead man's artery. I was making sounds again; I grabbed his left arm and his waist, and pulled him toward me, and that side of him rose, turned, and I lowered him to his back, his face tilted up toward the tree that was groaning, the tree and I the only sounds in the wind. Turning my face from his, looking down the length of him at his sneakers, I placed my ear on his heart, and heard not that but something else, and I clamped a hand over my exposed ear, heard something liquid and alive, like when you pump a well and after a few strokes you hear air and water moving in the pipe, and I knew I must raise his legs and cover him and run to a phone, while still I listened to his chest, thinking *raise with what? cover with what?* and amid the liquid sound I heard the heart then lost it, and pressed my ear against bone, but his chest was quiet, and I did not know when the liquid had stopped, and do not know now when I heard air, a faint rush of it, and whether under my ear or at his mouth or whether I heard it at all. I straightened and looked at the light, dim and yellow. Then I touched his throat, looking him full in the face. He was blond and young. He could have been sleeping in the shade of a tree, but for the smear of blood from his mouth to his hair, and the night sky, and the weeds blowing against his head, and the leaves shaking in the dark above us.

I stood. Then I kneeled again and prayed for his soul to join in peace and joy all the dead and living; and doing so, confronted my first sin against him, not stopping for Father Paul, who could have given him the last rites, and immediately then my second one, or, I saw then, my first, not calling an ambulance to meet me there, and I stood and turned into the wind, slid down the ditch and crawled out of it, and went up the hill and down it, across the road to the street of houses whose people I had left behind forever, so that I moved with stealth in the shadows to my truck.

When I came around the bend near my house, I saw the kitchen light at the rear. She sat as I had left her, the ashtray filled, and I looked at the bottle, felt her eyes on me, felt what she was seeing too: the dirt from my crawling. She had not drunk much of the rye. I poured some in my glass, with the water from melted ice, and sat down and swallowed some and looked at her and swallowed some more, and said: "He's dead."

She rubbed her eyes with the heels of her hands, rubbed the cheeks under them, but she was dry now.

"He was probably dead when he hit the ground. I mean, that's probably what killed — "

"Where was he?"

"Across the ditch, under a tree."

"Was he — did you see his face?"

"No. Not really. I just felt. For life, pulse. I'm going out to the car."

"What for? Oh."

I finished the rye, and pushed back the chair, then she was standing too.

"I'll go with you."

"There's no need."

"I'll go."

I took a flashlight from a drawer and pushed open the door and held it while she went out. We turned our faces from the wind. It was like on the hill, when I was walking, and the wind closed the distance behind me: after three or four steps I felt there was no house back there. She took my hand, as I was reaching for hers. In the garage we let go, and squeezed between the pickup and her little car, to the front of it, where we had more room, and we stepped back from the grill and I shone the light on the fender, the smashed headlight turned into it, the concave chrome staring to the right, at the garage wall.

"We ought to get the bottles," I said.

She moved between the garage and the car, on the passenger side, and had room to open the door and lift the bag. I reached out, and she gave me the bag and backed up and shut the door and came around the car. We sidled to the doorway, and she put her arm around my waist and I hugged her shoulders.

"I thought you'd call the police," she said.

We crossed the yard, faces bowed from the wind, her hair blowing away from her neck, and in the kitchen I put the bag of bottles in the garbage basket. She was working at the table: capping the rye and putting it away, filling the ice tray, washing the glasses, emptying the ashtray, sponging the table.

"Try to sleep now," I said.

She nodded at the sponge circling under her hand, gathering ashes. Then she dropped it in the sink and, looking me full in the face, as I had never seen her look, as perhaps she never had, being for so long a daughter on visits (or so it seemed to me and still does: that until then our eyes had never seriously met), she crossed to me from the sink, and kissed my lips, then held me so tightly I lost balance, and would have stumbled forward had she not held me so hard.

I sat in the living room, the house darkened, and watched the maple and the hemlock. When I believed she was asleep I put on *La Bohème*, and kept it at the same volume as the wind so it would not wake her. Then I listened to *Madame Butterfly*, and in the third act had to rise quickly to lower the sound: the wind was gone. I looked at the still maple near the window, and thought of the wind leaving farms and towns and the coast, going out over the sea to die on the waves. I smoked and gazed out the window. The sky was darker, and at daybreak the rain came. I listened to *Tosca*, and at six-fifteen went to the kitchen where Jennifer's purse lay on the table, a leather shoulder purse crammed with the things of an adult woman, things she had begun accumulating only a few years back, and I nearly wept, thinking of what sandy foundations they were: driver's license, credit card, disposable lighter, cigarettes, checkbook, ballpoint pen, cash, cosmetics, comb, brush, Kleenex, these the rite of passage from childhood, and I took one of them — her keys — and went out, remembering a jacket and hat when the rain struck me, but I kept going to the car, and squeezed and lowered myself into it, pulled the seat belt over my shoulder and fastened it and backed out, turning in the drive, going forward into the road, toward St. John's and Father Paul.

Cars were on the road, the workers, and I did not worry about any of them noticing the fender and light. Only a horse distracted them from what they drove to. In front of St. John's is a parking lot; at its far side, past the church and at the edge of the lawn, is an old pine, taller than the steeple now. I shifted to third, left the road, and aiming the right headlight at the tree, accelerated past the white blur of church, into the black trunk growing bigger till it was all I could see, then I rocked in that resonant thump she had heard, had felt, and when I turned off the ignition it was still in my ears, my blood, and I saw the boy flying in the wind. I lowered my forehead to the wheel. Father Paul opened the door, his face white in the rain.

"I'm all right."

"What happened?"

"I don't know. I fainted."

I got out and went around to the front of the car, looked at the smashed light, the crumpled and torn fender.

"Come to the house and lie down."

"I'm all right."

"When was your last physical?"

"I'm due for one. Let's get out of this rain."

"You'd better lie down."

"No. I want to receive."

That was the time to say I wanted to confess, but I have not and will not. Though I could now, for Jennifer is in Florida, and weeks have passed, and perhaps now Father Paul would not feel that he must tell me to go to the police. And, for that very reason, to confess now would be unfair. It is a world of secrets, and now I have one from my best, in truth my only, friend. I have one from Jennifer too, but that is the nature of fatherhood.

Most of that day it rained, so it was only in early evening, when the sky cleared, with a setting sun, that two little boys, leaving their confinement for some play before dinner, found him. Jennifer and I got that on the local news, which we listened to every hour, meeting at the radio, standing with cigarettes, until the one at eight o'clock; when she stopped crying, we went out and walked on the wet grass, around the pasture, the last of sunlight still in the air and trees. His name was Patrick Mitchell, he was nineteen years old, was employed by CETA, lived at home with his parents and brother and sister. The paper next day said he had been at a friend's house and was walking home, and I thought of that light I had seen, then knew it was not for him; he lived on one of the streets behind the club. The paper did not say then, or in the next few days, anything to make Jennifer think he was alive while she was with me in the kitchen. Nor do I know if we — if I — could have saved him.

In keeping her secret from her friends, Jennifer had to perform so often, as I did with Father Paul and at the stables, that I believe the acting, which took more of her than our daylight trail rides and our night walks in the pasture, was her healing. Her friends teased me about wrecking her car. When I carried her luggage out to the car on that last morning, we spoke only of the weather for her trip — the day was clear, with a dry cool breeze — and hugged and kissed, and I stood watching as she started the car and turned it around. But then she shifted to neutral and put on the parking brake and unclasped the belt, looking at me all the while, then she was coming to me, as she had that night in the kitchen, and I opened my arms.

I have said I talk with God in the mornings, as I start my day, and sometimes as I sit with coffee, looking at the birds, and the woods. Of course He has never spoken to me, but that is not something I require. Nor does He need to. I know Him, as I know the part of myself that knows Him, that felt Him watching from the wind and the night as I kneeled over the dying boy. Lately I have taken to arguing with Him, as I can't with Father

Paul who, when he hears my monthly confession, has not and
will not hear anything of failure to do all that one can to save
an anonymous life, of injustice to a family in their grief, of
deepening their pain at the chance and mystery of death by
giving them nothing — no one — to hate. With Father Paul, I
feel lonely about this, but not with God. When I received the
Eucharist while Jennifer's car sat twice-damaged, so redeemed,
in the rain, I felt neither loneliness nor shame, but as though
He were watching me, even from my tongue, intestines, blood,
as I have watched my sons at times in their young lives when I
was able to judge but without anger, and so keep silent while
they, in the agony of their youth, decided how they must act; or
found reasons, after their actions, for what they had done.
Their reasons were never as good or as bad as their actions, but
they needed to find them, to believe they were living by them,
instead of the awful solitude of the heart.

I do not feel the peace I once did: not with God, nor the
earth, or anyone on it. I have begun to prefer this state, to
remember with fondness the other one as a period of peace
I neither earned nor deserved. Now in the mornings while I
watch purple finches driving larger titmice from the feeder, I
say to Him: I would do it again. For when she knocked on my
door then called me, she woke what had flowed dormant in my
blood since her birth, so that what rose from the bed was not a
stable owner or a Catholic or any other Luke Ripley I had lived
with for a long time, but the father of a girl.

And He says: I am a Father too.

Yes, I say, as You are a Son Whom this morning I will receive;
unless You kill me on the way to church, then I trust You will
receive me. And as a Son You made Your plea.

Yes, He says, but I would not lift the cup.

True, and I don't want You to lift it from me either. And if
one of my sons had come to me that night, I would have phoned
the police and told them to meet us with an ambulance at the
top of the hill.

Why? Do you love them less?

I tell Him no, it is not that I love them less, but that I could
bear the pain of watching and knowing my sons' pain, could
bear it with pride as they took the whip and nails. But You never

had a daughter, and if You had, You could not have borne her passion.

So, He says, you love her more than you love Me.

I love her more than I love truth.

Then you love in weakness, He says.

As You love me, I say, and I go with an apple or carrot out to the barn.

MAVIS GALLANT

Lena

(FROM THE NEW YORKER)

IN HER PRIME, by which I mean in her beauty, my first wife, Magdalena, had no use for other women. She did not depend upon women for anything that mattered, such as charm and enjoyment and getting her bills paid; and as for exchanging Paris gossip and intimate chitchat, since she never confided anything personal and never complained, a man's ear was good enough. Magdalena saw women as accessories, to be treated kindly — maids, seamstresses, manicurists — or as comic minor figures, the wives and official fiancées of her admirers. It was not in her nature to care what anyone said, and she never could see the shape of a threat even when it rolled over her, but I suspect that she was called some of the senseless things she was called, such as "Central European whore" and "Jewish adventuress," by women.

Now that she is nearly eighty and bedridden, she receives visits from women — the residue of an early wave of Hungarian emigration. They have small pink noses, wear knitted caps pulled down to their eyebrows, and can see on dark street corners the terrible ghost of Béla Kun. They have forgotten that Magdalena once seemed, perhaps, disreputable. She is a devout Catholic, and she says cultivated, moral-sounding things, sweet to the ears of half a dozen widows of generals and bereft sisters of bachelor diplomats. They crowd her bedside table with bottles of cough mixture, lemons, embroidered table napkins, jars of honey, and covered bowls of stewed plums, the juice from which always spills. They call Magdalena "Lena."

She occupies a bed in the only place that would have her — a hospital on the northern rim of Paris, the color of jails, daubed with graffiti. The glass-and-marble lobby commemorates the flashy prosperity of the nineteen sixties. It contains, as well as a vandalized coffee machine and a plaque bearing the name of a forgotten minister of health, a monumental example of the art of twenty years ago: a white foot with each toenail painted a different color. In order to admire this marvel, and to bring Magdalena the small comforts I think she requires, I need to travel a tiring distance by the underground suburban train. On these expeditions I carry a furled umbrella: the flat, shadeless light of this line is said to attract violent crime. In my wallet I have a card attesting to my right to sit down, because of an accident suffered in wartime. I never dare show the card. I prefer to stand. Anything to do with the Second World War, particularly its elderly survivors, arouses derision and ribaldry and even hostility in the young.

Magdalena is on the fourth floor (no elevator) of a wing reserved for elderly patients too frail to be diverted to nursing homes — assuming that a room for her in any such place could be found. The old people have had it drummed into them that they are lucky to have a bed, that the waiting list for their mattress and pillow lengthens by the hour. They must not seem too capricious, or dissatisfied, or quarrelsome, or give the nurses extra trouble. If they persist in doing so, their belongings are packed and their relatives sent for. A law obliges close relatives to take them in. Law isn't love, and Magdalena has seen enough distress and confusion to make her feel thoughtful.

"Families are worse than total war," she says. I am not sure what her own war amounted to. As far as I can tell, she endured all its rigors in Cannes, taking a daily walk to a black-market restaurant, her legs greatly admired by famous collaborators and German officers along the way. Her memory, when she wants to be bothered with it, is like a brief, blurry, self-centered dream.

"But what were you *doing* during those years?" I have asked her. (My mother chalked Gaullist slogans on walls in Paris. The father of my second wife died deported. I joined the Free French in London.)

"I was holding my breath," she answers, smiling.

She shares a room with a woman who suffers from a burning rash across her shoulders. Medicine that relieves the burning seems to affect her mind, and she will wander the corridors, wondering where she is, weeping. The hospital then threatens to send her home, and her children, in a panic, beg that the treatment be stopped. After a few days the rash returns, and the woman keeps Magdalena awake describing the pain she feels — it is like being flogged with blazing nettles, she says. Magdalena pilfers tranquillizers and gets her to take them, but once she hit the woman with a pillow. The hospital became nasty, and I had to step in. Fortunately, the supervisor of the aged-and-chronic department had seen me on television, taking part in a literary game ("Which saint might Jean-Paul Sartre have wanted most to meet?"), and that helped our case.

Actually, Magdalena cannot be evicted — not just like that. She has no family, and nowhere to go. Her continued existence is seen by the hospital as a bit of a swindle. They accepted her in the first place only because she was expected to die quite soon, releasing the bed.

"Your broken nose is a mistake," she said to me the other day. My face was damaged in the same wartime accident that is supposed to give me priority seating rights in public transport. "It lends you an air of desperate nerve, as if a Malraux hero had wandered into a modern novel and been tossed out on his face."

Now, this was hard on a man who had got up earlier than usual and bought a selection of magazines for Magdalena before descending to the suburban line, with its flat, worrying light. A man who had just turned sixty-five. Whose new bridge made him lisp. She talks the way she talked in the old days, in her apartment with the big windows and the sweeping view across the Seine. She used to wear white, and sit on a white sofa. There were patches of red in the room — her long fingernails and her lipstick, and the Legion of Honor on some admirer's lapel. She had two small, funny dogs whose eyes glowed red in the dusk.

"I heard you speaking just the other day," she went on. "You were most interesting about the way Gide always made the rounds of the bookstores to see how his work was selling. Actually, I think I told you that story."

"It couldn't have been just the other day," I said. "It sounds like a radio program I had in the nineteen fifties."

"It couldn't have been you, come to think of it," she said. "The man lisped. I said to myself, 'It *might* be Édouard.' "

Her foreign way of speaking enchanted me when I was young. Now it sharpens my temper. Fifty years in France and she still cannot pronounce my name, Édouard, without putting the stress on the wrong syllable and rolling the *r*. "When you come to an *r*," I have told her, "keep your tongue behind your lower front teeth."

"It won't stay," she says. "It curls up. I am sorry." As if she cared. She will accept any amount of petulance shown by me, because she thinks she owes me tolerance: she sees me as youthful, boyish, to be teased and humored. She believes we have a long, unhampered life before us, and she expects to occupy it as my wife and widow-to-be. To that end, she has managed to outlive my second wife, and she may well survive me, even though I am fourteen years younger than she is and still on my feet.

Magdalena's Catholic legend is that she was converted after hearing Jacques Maritain explain neo-Thomism at a tea party. Since then, she has never stopped heaping metaphysical rules about virtue on top of atavistic arguments concerning right and wrong. The result is a moral rock pile, ready to slide. Only God himself could stand up to the avalanche, but in her private arrangements he is behind her, egging her on. I had to wait until a law was passed that allowed divorce on the ground of separation before I was free to marry again. I waited a long time. In the meantime, Magdalena was writing letters to the pope, cheering his stand on marriage and urging him to hold firm. She can choose among three or four different languages, her choice depending on where her dreams may have taken her during the night. She used to travel by train to Budapest and Prague wearing white linen. She had sleek, fair hair, and wore a diamond hair clip behind one ear. Now no one goes to those places, and the slim linen suits are crumpled in trunks. Her mind is clear, but she says absurd things. "I never saw her," she said about Juliette, my second wife. "Was she anything like me?"

"You did see her. We had lunch, the three of us."

"Show me her picture. It might bring back the occasion."

"No."

They met, once, on the first Sunday of September 1954 — a hot day of quivering horizons and wasps hitting the windshield. I had a new Renault — a model with a reputation for rolling over and lying with its wheels in the air. I drove, I think, grimly. Magdalena was beside me, in a nimbus of some scent — jasmine, or gardenia — that made me think of the opulent, profiteering side of wars. Juliette sat behind, a road map on her knee, her finger on the western outskirts of Fontainebleau. Her dark hair was pulled back tight and tied at the nape of her neck with a dark-blue grosgrain ribbon. It is safe to say that she smelled of soap and lemons.

We were taking Magdalena out to lunch. It was Juliette's idea. Somewhere between raspberries-and-cream and coffee, I was supposed to ask for a divorce — worse, to coax from Magdalena the promise of collusion in obtaining one. So far, she had resisted any mention of the subject and for ten years had refused to see me. Juliette and I had been living together since the end of the war. She was thirty now, and tired of waiting. We were turning into one of those uneasy, shadowy couples, perpetually waiting for a third person to die or divorce. I was afraid of losing her. That summer, she had traveled without me to America (so much farther from Europe then than it is today), and she had come back with a different coloration to her manner, a glaze of independence, as though she had been exposed to a new kind of sun.

I remember how she stared at Magdalena with gentle astonishment, as if Magdalena were a glossy illustration that could not look back. Magdalena had on a pale dress of some soft, floating stuff, and a pillbox hat tied on with a white veil, and long white gloves. I saw her through Juliette's eyes, and I thought what Juliette must be thinking: Where does Magdalena think we're taking her? To a wedding? Handing her into the front seat, I had shut the door on her skirt. I wondered if she had turned into one of the limp, pliant women whose clothes forever catch.

It was Juliette's custom to furnish social emptiness with some rattling anecdote about her own activities. Guests were often grateful. Without having to cast far, they could bring up a narrative of their own, and the result was close to real conversation. Juliette spoke of her recent trip. She said she was wearing an American dress made of a material called cotton seersucker. It washed like a duster and needed next to no ironing.

For answer, she received a side view of Magdalena's hat and a blue eye shadowed with paler blue. Magdalena was not looking but listening, savoring at close quarters the inflections of the French Protestant gentry. She knew she was privileged. As a rule, they speak only to one another. Clamped to gearshift and wheel, I was absolved of the need to comment. My broken profile had foxed Magdalena at first. She had even taken me for an impostor. But then the remembered face of a younger man slid over the fraud and possessed him.

Juliette had combed through the *Guide Michelin* and selected a restaurant with a wide terrace and white umbrellas, set among trees. At some of the tables there were American officers, in uniform, with their families — this is to show how long ago it was. Juliette adjusted our umbrella so that every inch of Magdalena was in the shade. She took it for granted that my wife belonged to a generation sworn to paleness. From where I was sitting, I could see the interior of the restaurant. It looked cool and dim, I thought, and might have been better suited to the soft-footed conversation to come.

I adjusted my reading glasses, which Magdalena had never seen, and stared at a long handwritten menu. Magdalena made no move to examine hers. She had all her life let men decide. Finally, Juliette wondered if our guest might not like to start with asparagus. I was afraid the asparagus would be canned. Well, then, said Juliette, what about melon. On a hot day, something cool followed by cold salmon. She broke off. I started to remove my glasses, but Juliette reminded me about wine.

Magdalena was engaged in a ritual that Juliette may not have seen before and that I had forgotten: pulling off her tight, long gloves finger by finger and turning her rings right side up. Squeezed against a great sparkler of some kind was a wedding ring. Rallying, Juliette gave a little twitch to the collar of the washable seersucker and went on about America. In Philadelphia, a celebrated Pentecostal preacher had persuaded the Holy

Spirit to settle upon a member of the congregation, a woman whose hearing had been damaged when she was brained by a flying shoe at a stock-car race. The deaf woman rose and said she could hear sparrows chirping in High German, on which the congregation prayed jubilant thanks.

Juliette did not stoop to explain that she was no Pentecostalist. She mentioned the Holy Spirit as an old acquaintance of her own class and background, a cultivated European with an open mind.

We were no longer young lovers, and I had heard this story several times. I said that the Holy Spirit might find something more useful to attend to than a ruptured eardrum. We were barely ten years out of a disastrous war. All over the world, there were people sick, afraid, despairing. Only a few days before, the president of Brazil had shot himself to death.

Juliette replied that there were needs beyond our understanding. "God knows what he wants," she said. I am sure she believed it.

"God wanted Auschwitz?" I said.

I felt a touch on my arm, and I looked down and saw a middle-aged hand and a wedding ring.

With her trained inclination to move back from rising waters, Juliette made the excuse of a telephone call. I knew that her brief departure was meant to be an intermission. When she came back, we would speak about other things. Magdalena and I sat quietly, she with her hand still on my arm, as if she had finally completed a gesture begun a long time before. Juliette, returning, her eyes splashed with cold water, her dark hair freshly combed, saw that I was missing a good chance to bring up the divorce. She sat down, smiled, picked up her melon spoon. She was working hard these days, she said. She was translating an American novel that should never have been written. (Juliette revealed nothing more about this novel.) From there, she slid along to the subject of drastic separations — not so much mine from Magdalena as divorcement in general. Surely, she said, a clean parting was a way of keeping life pleasant and neat? This time, it was Magdalena's hearing that seemed impaired, and the Holy Spirit was nowhere. The two women must have been thinking the same thing at that moment, though

for entirely different reasons: that I had forfeited any chance
of divine aid by questioning God's intentions.

It was shortly before her removal to the hospital that Magdalena
learned about Juliette's death. One of her doddering friends
may have seen the notice in a newspaper. She at once resumed
her place as my only spouse and widow-to-be. In fact, she had
never relinquished it, but now the way back to me shone clear.
The divorce, that wall of pagan darkness, had been torn down
and dispersed with the concubine's ashes. She saw me delivered
from an adulterous and heretical alliance. It takes a convert to
think "heretical" with a straight face. She could have seen Juliette burned at the stake without losing any sleep. It is another
fact about converts that they make casual executioners.

    She imagined that I would come to her at once, but I went
nowhere. Juliette had asked to be cremated, thinking of the
purification of the flame, but the rite was accomplished by clank-
ing, hidden, high-powered machinery that kept starting and
stopping, on cycle. At its loudest, it covered the voice of the
clergyman, who affirmed that Juliette was eyeing us with great
good will from above, and it prevailed over Juliette's favorite
recordings of Mozart and Bach. Her ashes were placed in a
numbered niche that I never saw, for at some point in the funeral service I lost consciousness and had to be carried out. This
nightmare was dreamed in the crematorium chapel of Père La-
chaise cemetery. I have not been back. It is far from where I
live, and I think Juliette is not there, or anywhere. From the
moment when her heart stopped, there has been nothing but
silence.

Last winter, I had bronchitis and seldom went out. I managed
to send Magdalena a clock, a radio, an azalea, and enough
stamps and stationery to furnish a nineteenth-century literary
correspondence. Nevertheless, the letters that reached my
sickbed from hers were scrawled in the margins of newspapers,
torn off crookedly. Sometimes she said her roommate had lent
her the money for a stamp. The message was always the same:
I must not allow my wife to die in a public institution. Her pink-
nosed women friends wrote me, too, signing their alien names,
announcing their titles — there was a princess.

It was no good replying that everybody dies in hospital now. The very idea made them sick, of a sickness beyond any wasting last-ditch illusion. Then came from Magdalena: "On Saturday at nine o'clock, I shall be dressed and packed, and waiting for you to come and take me away."

Away from the hospital bed? It took weeks of wangling and soft-soaping and even some mild bribery to obtain it. Public funds, to which she is not entitled, and a voluntary contribution from me keep her in it. She has not once asked where the money comes from. When she was young, she decided never to worry, and she has kept the habit.

I let several Saturdays go by, until the folly had quit her mind. Late in April I turned up carrying a bottle of Krug I had kept on ice until the last minute and some glasses in a paper bag. The woman who shares her room gave a great groan when she saw me, and showed the whites of her eyes. I took this to mean that Magdalena had died. The other bed was clean and empty. The clock and the radio on the table had the look of objects left behind. I felt shock, guilt, remorse, and relief, and I wondered what to do with the wine. I turned, and there in the doorway stood Magdalena, in dressing gown and slippers, with short white hair. She shuffled past me and lay on the bed with her mouth open, struggling for breath.

"Shouldn't I ring for a nurse?" I said, unwrapping the bottle.

"No one will come. Open the champagne."

"I'd better fetch a nurse." Instead, I made room on the table for the glasses. I'd brought three, because of the roommate.

Magdalena gasped, "Today is my birthday." She sat up, apparently recovered, and got her spectacles out from under the pillow. Leaning toward me, she said, "What's that red speck on your lapel? It looks like the Legion of Honor."

"I imagine that's what it is."

"Why?" she said. "Was there a reason?"

"They probably had a lot to give away. Somebody did say something about 'cultural enrichment of the media.' "

"I am glad about the enrichment," she said. "I am also very happy for you. Will you wear it all the time, change it from suit to suit?"

"It's new," I said. "There was a ceremony this morning." I sat down on the shaky chair kept for visitors, and with a steadiness that silenced us both I poured the wine. "What about your neighbor?" I said, the bottle poised.

"Let her sleep. This is a good birthday surprise."

I felt as if warm ashes were banked round my heart, like a residue of good intentions. I remembered that when Magdalena came back to Paris after the war, she found her apartment looted, laid waste. One of the first letters to arrive in the mail was from me, to say that I was in love with a much younger woman. "If it means anything at all to you," I said, the coals glowing brighter, "if it can help you to understand me in any way — well, no one ever fascinated me as much as you." This after only one glass.

"But perhaps you never loved me," she said.

"Probably not," I said. "Although I must have."

"You mean, in a way?" she said.

"I suppose so."

The room became so quiet that I could hear the afternoon movie on television in the next room. I recognized the voice of the actor who dubs Robert Redford.

Magdalena said, "Even a few months ago this would have been my death sentence. Now I am simply thankful I have so little time left to wander between 'perhaps' and 'probably not' and 'in a way.' A crazy old woman, wringing my hands."

I remembered Juliette's face when she learned that her menopause was irreversible. I remembered her shock, her fright, her gradual understanding, her storm of grief. She had hoped for children, then finally a child, a son she would have called Thomas. "Your death sentence," I said. "Your death sentence. What about Juliette's life sentence? She never had children. By the time I was able to marry her, it was too late."

"She could have had fifteen children without being married," said Magdalena.

I wanted to roar at her, but my voice went high and thin. "Women like Juliette, people like Juliette, don't do that sort of thing. It was a wonder she consented to live with me for all those years. What about her son, her Thomas? I couldn't even have claimed him — not legally, as long as I was married to you. Imagine him, think of him, applying for a passport, finding out he had no father. Nothing on his birth certificate. Only a mother."

"You could have adopted Thomas," said Magdalena. "That way, he'd have been called by your name."

"I couldn't — not without your consent. *You* were my wife. Besides, why should I have to adopt my own son?" I think this was a shout; that is how it comes back to me. "And the inheritance laws, as they were in those days. Have you ever thought about that? I couldn't even make a will in his favor."

Cheek on hand, blue eyes shadowed, my poor, mad, true, and only wife said, "Ah, Édouard, you shouldn't have worried. You know I'd have left him all that I had."

It wasn't the last time I saw Magdalena, but after that day she sent no more urgent messages, made no more awkward demands. Twice since then she has died and come round. Each time, just when the doctor said, "I think that's it," she has squeezed the nurse's hand. She loves rituals, and she probably wants the last sacraments, but hospitals hate that. Word that there is a priest in the place gets about, and it frightens the other patients. There are afternoons when she can't speak and lies with her eyes shut, the lids quivering. I hold her hand, and feel the wedding ring. Like the staunch little widows, I call her "Lena," and she turns her head and opens her eyes.

I glance away then, anywhere — at the clock, out the window. I have put up with everything, but I intend to refuse her last imposition, the encounter with her blue, enduring look of pure love.

MARY HOOD

Inexorable Progress

(FROM THE GEORGIA REVIEW)

THERE'S NOT MUCH DIFFERENCE between a bare tree and a dead tree in winter. Only when the others begin to leaf out the next spring, and one is left behind in the general green onrush, can the eye tell. By then it is too late for remedy. That's how it was with Angelina: a tree stripped to the natural bone, soul-naked in the emptying wind. She was good at pretending; she hung color and approximations of seasonal splendor on every limb, and swayed like a bower in the autumn gales around her, but her heart was hollow, and her nests empty. You could tell a little something by her eyes, with their devious candor (like a drunk's), but her troubles, whatever they were, didn't start with the bottle, and after a while, the bottle wasn't what stopped them.

Glory Be to the Father she sang the Sunday before Labor Day. She wore her neckline low, her hem and heels and spirits as high as fashion and propriety would allow.

And to the Son and to the Holy Ghost
When she warbled in the sanctuary, her freckled bosom rippled in vibrato. She left no fingerprints on the salver as she dropped in her tithe.

As It Was in the Beginning
She kept herself retouched, forever presenting the same bright portrait to the saints.

Is Now and Ever Shall Be
Her cordial eyes, fixed in bravado, were shining windows, bolted against bad weather.

World without End, Amen
Behind them, fear, that restless housecat, paced.
Amen.
She hated many things, but Sundays most of all.

The congregation settled in for the sermon now that it was paid
for. To her daughter beside her Angelina whispered, "Listen,
Bon" — as though she were still a fidgety child, impervious as
stone, around whose innocence the words and water of life
would pour unproved; as though Bonnie were still six, to be
cajoled into rectitude (or at least silence) with carefully doled
bribes of Lifesavers tasting of the scented depths of her purse.
   Part of what Angelina hated about Sundays was sitting alone
in church while her husband went fishing or hunting. The way
he saw it, he always made it up to her afterward, but from black-
powder season to doe days she might as well have been a widow.
Of course, Bonnie was growing up there beside her, but it wasn't
the same. To make sure nobody thought she was getting re-
signed to it, or ever would, Angelina always reserved a space
beside her in the pew, so the world would know at a glance that
Chick was expected back.
   Sometimes she thought more than was reasonable about who
was missing. Sometimes she dreamed about her stillborn son;
every month just before her period she dreamed about him.
Perhaps he was just born and they laid him wailing, wriggling,
on her belly. Or perhaps he was a little older, running to her
with a pine-cone pipe, calling, "See what I found? Come see!"
She always recognized him, who he would have been. Once she
dreamed they were camping in hunting season and he came
fretting up, arms out in a "Love me, love me, mama," pose, and
she gave him a bloody fox foot to teethe on, to hush him. She
never told Chick about the dreams, nor what it was she had
been suffering in her sleep when she cried "Help!" and woke
them both.
   Here lately she had been dreaming about her mother; always
the same thing: just before they sealed the coffin (her mother
had died in April), she saw her mama's eyelids flicker; no one
believed her (suddenly everybody was a stranger; dark-suited,
efficient, looming, they closed ranks against her, and she cried

Stop! but they did not stop), and the inexorable progress toward the dark, the sealing, the lowering, the losing sight of, the closing went on until she woke herself dry-mouthed, heart pounding, telling herself it was only a dream. Its persistence shamed her, haunted her; she could not tell anyone how she felt, that she had got off too light, that she deserved worse than heartbreak. She had felt that way from the beginning; indeed, had tried to comfort the comforters at the funeral. The feeling of guilt, of some punishment deserved, haunted her through the summer until one night she dreamed she had a pain in her left breast, and the sensation of pain woke her like a noise, like a light. She lay panting in fright, unable to disbelieve, or perhaps unwilling. Waking fully, she investigated and found a lump: a dream come true. It somehow satisfied her; it was her secret. She would not see a doctor; she knew how it went. Her mother had died of such a lump. Sometimes Angelina imagined herself wasted like that; when she raised her own hand before her eyes she saw her mother's skeleton instead.

Angelina lost her appetite. She began cleaning out closets. During a rainy spell she got out the carton of snapshots and began putting them in an album for Bonnie, labeling who and what and when. She smoked heavily (Bonnie always after her to quit, saying, "Mama, I want you around") and the fruitcake brandy (a bottle had lasted five years) vanished in one afternoon. When Elsie Bland and her boy Jude came in the afternoon to pick windfall apples on shares, Angelina crouched close against the kitchen cabinet, out of sight, while they knocked and knocked. After a while they went away. When Bonnie got home from school, she found her mama rubber-legged, penitent, incapacitated. Bonnie cleaned up, mopped, ran the laundry through, and had the place aired out and sweet-smelling when Chick got home. They called it the flu that time; there were other times . . .

Lost in reverie, Angelina did not realize the service was over; Bonnie was touching her arm and saying, "Mama? Mama!" and it made her start. She stood perhaps too quickly, for she had to stop a moment, resting her hand on the rubbed pew-end till the stained glass on her periphery swung and settled. Then she walked down (it seemed uphill) the burgundy carpet in which her sharp heels picked little dimples, and out into the dazzling sunlight, her left hand holding up the bulletin to fend off the noon. Reverend Martin made his small remarks at the door, gentle pleasantries served with a handshake to each departing member. He was speaking to Angelina, but she couldn't make out the words. All around her thrummed an expectant, dimming silence like the instant between lightning and thunder. She turned away, troubled, from the lips soundlessly moving, and shut her eyes against the intolerable glare off the whited church front. Very suddenly the porch tilted up and she pitched down the steps, unconscious before she relinquished the Reverend's hand, which is why (the doctor said later) there were no bones broken.

She told the doctor some of what she had been going through; not the dreams, not the brandy. He gave her something for her nerves and arranged for a biopsy on the lump. Overnight in the hospital, and she would know for sure (but she *was* sure!). Chick gave up a bow-and-arrow weekend to be with her; he was what she saw when she opened her eyes after the surgery; he was the one who exulted, "Benign." But she didn't believe him. Hadn't they lied to her mother? Finally, finally they persuaded her.

Relieved, yet oddly disappointed, she went home determined to make the most of her spared life. At Sunday-night services she laid her cigarettes on the altar rail and asked for prayer to help her kick the habit. Dust gathered on the unopened conscience bottle of brandy. She built up to four miles of brisk walking every morning and was able to sleep without medication. She took up crafts, and began hooking a rug for Bonnie's room. ("Do something for yourself," Bonnie said, when her mama finished that and began a matching pillow, but Angelina said, "Doing for others, that's the reason we're here.")

The doctors advised her to cut out caffeine too, and she was able to break a fourteen-cup-a-day habit. ("Jesus can fix anything," she told her neighbor as they jogged in the fine fall weather.) For her forty-third birthday Chick bought her a hair-fine chain with a gold charm: PERFECT it announced. She fastened it on and wore it along with the little silver cross her mother left her. She was on a streak of pure happiness.

But, of course, there is no such thing unalloyed. Cakes fall. Cars break down. A roofing staple manages to penetrate the week-old steel radial. The eggs on the top shelf of the refrigerator freeze. Dogs, even the most kindly treated, chase cats, wander, bark well off cue. Bills get lost in the mails. Angelina's streak ended with vapor lock. She had been shopping for groceries for the week; they and milk and frozen foods were in the trunk when the car cut out. She had an appointment in an hour, so she took a shortcut in repairs; rather than wait for the car to cool, she ran in the bait shop and bought a bag of ice and held it to the hot engine, and the engine block cracked. Still, she expected sympathy, not a scolding, and could hardly believe it when Chick roared up behind the wrecker and jumped out and began yelling, "How can you be so goddamn stupid!" before God and the gathering crowd. And while he was on the subject, why didn't she wash the car once in a while? A little soap in a bucket of water wouldn't kill her . . .

She pointed out (while the wrecker hooked up) that she might have more motivation if the car were in her name. (Nothing was; not the house, not the lot at Hammermill, nor the pontoon, nothing. "I bet if I polished the Revereware I'd find his Social Security number engraved on the bottom," she fumed later.) She rode in the wrecker, wouldn't ride with Chick.

"A thousand bucks for a new engine," he told her as she climbed into the wrecker. "You want it fixed, *you* earn it." As though what she did, what she was, wasn't worth anything to him! To say it like that before the wide world! If he meant it, about her paying for the repairs, he only meant it when he said it, not a moment later, but it pleased Angelina to prolong the quarrel. Nothing he thought to do could stop it now. It must run its course, like a disease.

Tuesday was election day. Angelina had been on her way to the courthouse to be sworn in as poll chief for Deerfield when the car tore up and she and Chick had boiled over. Grace Arnold had had to be the one to run up to Hammermill for the materials. She offered Angelina a ride election day, too, and came by before 6:30 that morning with her car loaded with supplies (extension cord, flag, posterboard, hampers of lunch and magazines, folding chairs). Angelina was waiting at the foot of the drive with a look of righteous malice on her face; she got in bragging what she had done (looking a little scared, too): she had locked Chick's truck in the garage, along with the ladder, and had thrown both sets of keys up on the roof, as high as indignation would allow.

How he solved the problem Grace never knew, but he came in to vote around noon. They had the precinct set up in the Fish and Game Clubhouse, the old school on the pine hill, high enough so you could see the traffic passing by on the road; the magnolia blocked the north view, but you could see the cars a half-mile off looking south, and Grace, with her bright eye, spotted the blue truck and said, "Isn't that Chick?" Instantly, Angelina fled. They could hear her in back, dropping incorrect change through the Coke machine, over and over. Grace signed Chick up and he voted; it didn't take very long. When the curtains swept open and he emerged, cheerful with done duty, he glanced all around, encountering nowhere his wife. He didn't inquire.

"All right, then," he said, pocketing his hands and staring out the window toward the reservoir where a yellow boat sped along. It looked as if Chick might be going to announce something, but he didn't, just mentioned the weather, and went on out jingling his keys loudly enough so that if you were listening and interested in the back of the building, you could hear them. He cast another proud look at the sky as he got into his truck, as though it were all his doing, as though he had invented blue.

"He said, 'Have a nice day,' " Grace told Angelina when she came back to her chair.

"A *good* day," Angelina corrected. "He didn't mean me." She gave a little laugh, a single bark of desperation.

At the end of the day they closed the door, took down the notices of penalties and warnings, counted and recapped, signed the quadruplicate forms, sorted the papers into the proper envelopes, posted the results, and loaded the stuff (chairs, cushions, crochet, magazines, thermoses, flag, and extension) into Grace's car and headed for the courthouse at Hammermill. The key to the Fish and Game Clubhouse stayed between times in the cash register at Bully's store, so they stopped by there and Angelina ran in with it. When she came back out, she had a shock: it felt like terror; it felt like triumph. There was Chick, his truck parked alongside Grace's car on the far side of the gas pumps. Without a pause or hitch Angelina got back into Grace's Monte Carlo as though she hadn't *seen*, but Grace knew better.

"Aw, honey, can't you budge just a little?" Grace cried. "Please! I'll take care of this." She patted the official boxes with the state seals on the side. Angelina hesitated. Almost too long. They heard Chick's truck crank, final offer.

At the last possible instant, Angelina jumped out and ran across, leaning a little forward on her wedgies as though battling headwinds. Chick offered her a hand up, but she ignored it. When they drove out, Angelina was stiff-backed, eyes shut. Chick hung a vehement right onto the road home, tipping her over against his shoulder. "Thanky ma'am," Chick said. He had that energized look he always wore when he had a secret; Angelina suspected some grand gesture, perhaps he had bought her another car . . .

But when they got home (and they rode, after his "thanky," without speaking, in an uneasy truce) it wasn't a new car at all. They had cooked supper and done the laundry, that was the surprise. They helped out. Bonnie stood with the sheets in her arms and Chick went over to help her fold them. Were they waiting for praise? Angelina took a look at the table with its little bouquet of persimmon leaves and oak and sourwood. Candles, too, and Sunday dishes. Everything in its proper place. They didn't need her, that's what they were saying! They could get along without her! (She mentioned that.)

Bonnie's stricken face in the candlelight was more than Angelina could bear.

"Don't 'Mama, please' me! I've had enough of your whining about how things ought to be! It's not going to be 'Mommy and Daddy' on their wedding cake, and Santa and the Easter Bunny like a roof over you, and happily ever after all your life! The roof leaks. It blows off in chunks. It rots. It stinks! You have to save yourself, don't you 'Mama, Mama' me, don't you 'Now, Angelina, honey' me!" She jerked her shoulder from Chick's grasp and sent herself to bed without supper. To punish herself or them? She lay wondering as the codeine in her migraine medication took effect.

Later she woke in terror and loneliness. The house was so silent all around her. She put out her hand and Chick was there; he hadn't left her; he hadn't given up on her. He wanted her. A real treaty, mouth to mouth, was signed. In the morning she made a last-minute call to the Avon lady (order was going in that day) for that chain and charm necklace Bonnie had admired, a peace offering. And she gave in about music camp. She told Bonnie that afternoon, said they'd just have to learn to get along without Bonnie this once, even if it was Thanksgiving, since it meant so much to the girl. She helped her fill out the forms (a church-run retreat): Who is the most influential person in your life? Bonnie paused at that blank and considered. Angelina had absolutely no doubt.

"Jesus Christ," she told her. "Write it in."

Bonnie, who had been about to write "parents," blushed, ashamed she had not even thought of it.

"Write it in," Angelina said again. Bonnie wrote.

After Christmas Angelina canvassed door to door, handing out pamphlets ("ERA — The Trojan Horse"), saying till she was numb, "I'm Mrs. Chester Cole, I'd like to speak with you a few moments on a subject vital to the survival of the American home and leave you some literature to study." Mixed results.

"You Jehovah's Witness?" The woman peered out through the rusty screen, reaching for the pamphlet, holding it to the sun, studying the illustrated cover. "Are you for or against?"

And Angelina said, "I hope you'll read and then pass it on to your friends; write your congressmen and legislators — "

"Them Jehovah's Witness stay and stay. I tell her, lady, please, my carrots is scorching, but she just sits like she never smelled smoke."

"If you or your friends have any questions — "

"Mormon fellers the same. Nice-looking boys prayed and prayed on me. Left me a whole book to read. Say they're coming back."

"I thank you for your time," Angelina said.

At another house she tried to interest the woman in joining the bus rally to the capitol.

"Shoot, I got me a job, ma'am. You let someone else have my seat." She handed the pamphlet back. "I'm only home today because of the flu. Head's aching so bad I can't read."

"And thank you for your time," Angelina said.

When she stopped by Grace's for more brochures, Grace reminded her about printing costs.

"So you think I'm throwing them out of an airplane over the reservoir?" Angelina pried off her boots and rested her legs on the coffee table. "Although I might as well . . ." She rubbed her ankles. "Just look. Mama's feet did the same, swelled so they nearly burst. Be so much easier to *phone*."

Grace kept on counting out pamphlets. She had something new, a Xeroxed page from the *Congressional Record*. "A copy for each field worker," she said, handing Angelina hers.

"You ever get the idea what's the use?" Angelina wondered.

"Tomorrow we're going to run off another thousand 'Things You Can Do' fact sheets — "

"Nobody listens," Angelina said. "You ever notice?"

" — getting some of those bumper stickers and litter bags (did I show you those? around here somewhere) and maybe get some of those — "

"I guess you never did notice," Angelina decided. "I bet I could tell you I was going home and pipe a bottle of Valium and sleep till the daisies sprung and you'd say — "

" — like stop signs, real cute; they're red and say STOP; we could pass them out at the bank on Saturday."

Angelina zipped her boots back on and stood up. "May I quote you? And you'd say . . ."

"Why, anything you can use," Grace said, flattered, smiling, puzzling it out. (Something like that, if you remember it later, is the only hint you get, the kind of joke the whole world makes one down day or another.)

But Angelina didn't have her mind made up; she was still trying. She made lists of things to get done, lists for the day, the week, the month; goals for the coming year. She drove over to the house and went through her mother's clothes, one closet at a time, and made all those decisions without crying for help, or receiving any. She had the trunk and the back seat of her Maverick (Chick got the engine rebuilt before Christmas) crammed with sacks and boxes for Goodwill and was on her way there, Ash Wednesday, when she had more car trouble. This wasn't like the old trouble; this time the car stalled and she couldn't get it to restart. She coasted down to the stop sign at the corner and set the brake, resting her head on the wheel and considering her luck. She rolled her window down and wished she had a cigarette. It was unsettling to be sitting there, stalled, with the faint scent of her mother's household all around her. Was it a sign she wasn't supposed to get rid of all the stuff? She decided to walk home. It wasn't half a mile.

As she got out, a voice said, "I thought it was you. I've been watching you. What were you doing, praying?"

Angelina whirled around and there stood Ginnie Daniels, in pristine Adidas, with a dry sweatband holding back her hair. She pressed her hand on the stitch in her side.

"That Roy. I told him I couldn't keep up. Maybe I lied when I said I was doing three miles a day, but he promised to go slow, then he said never mind. Said he'd go on without me. And he did!"

"I'd offer you a lift," Angelina said, "but my car's conked out."

"Maybe it's flooded," Ginnie said. "Maybe you flooded it." She walked over and reached in and gave the hood latch a yank. "Let's see."

They stood there listening to the oil drip back into the pan.

"You know something about cars?" Angelina hoped.

"Me?" Ginnie blew a pink bubble. "Nah." She spelled F-O-X-Y in the dust on the air cleaner, careful of her nails. She noticed the gold charm at Angelina's throat and pointed at it. "Going to get me one of those. Maybe the one that says '10.' "

Reminded, Angelina raised her hand to her throat and touched the little cross. "Do you believe in prayer?" she asked, with that incandescent look people had about gotten used to.

Ginnie blinked and formed another bubble, enlarging it slowly to cosmic proportions. It burst. "Couldn't hurt."

Angelina laid her hands on certain blue objects under the hood. Then she got in and turned the key. The car cranked instantly.

Ginnie slammed the hood. "Praise the Lord anyway," she drawled, settling herself on the seat, propping her feet on the dash. "You can drop me off at the light in town."

"I can remember when you were born," Angelina said as Ginnie lit a cigarette. "I went to your mama's shower."

"Yeah?"

"It goes so fast."

"The faster the better . . . I'm getting me a T-roof Z for graduation," Ginnie said. She made a gesture of running through gears. "We're already planning what to do. Not going to spray SENIORS on the bridges or LEGALIZE POT on the water tower . . . Kid stuff . . . They'll remember us a while . . . Raise us a little hell . . . Going down to Daytona, Lauderdale maybe . . ."

Angelina frowned, remembering. "Our class went to Panama City."

"Bet you had a ball," Ginnie said indulgently.

"One of the boys hit a cow in the rain. Wiped out his brand-new T-bird. The girl with him went right through the windshield. It blinded her. Broke Danny's neck, they said instantly."

"Yeah?" Ginnie shook her head. "Wow." She pointed up ahead. "This is my corner." When they stopped, Ginnie got out and stretched. "Beats jogging. Thanks a bunch for the lift." She hipped the door shut.

"Something always happens," Angelina realized.

"Ma'am?" Ginnie peered back in at her.

"Death," Angelina said.

When she got home from the trip to Goodwill, JoJo was missing. The dog didn't come in for supper, and in the night when Angelina got up and walked around the yard, calling, there was no sign of him. He had never stayed out all night before.

"If only I had locked him in the garage when I left!" Angelina, pacing, making coffee, calling, and the lights on managed to rouse the household. Bonnie stood in the glare of the kitchen and pled for her mama not to get upset.

"Why do you think it's you? Why do you have to be the one?" Bonnie asked.

"Because I'm guilty," Angelina said simply. "Who else is to blame?"

Chick stood in the door, backlit, haloed by moths, and called to Angelina out wandering in the yard to come to bed, to be sensible. But she had to take the lantern and search along the roadside for his body if he had been hit by a car . . . She didn't find him.

From the first they ruled out stealth; he wasn't the sort of dog you'd kidnap for ransom. He was a stray mutt puppy who required so much medical attention when he took up with them that it kept Angelina's mind off the stillbirth of their son. She sometimes bragged that JoJo's vet bills ran as much as a pediatrician's, and early on, when Chick, holding up the silly little green sweater she had crocheted for the dog, teased, "Without JoJo, Bonnie would be an only child," Angelina's sudden tears had washed the remark completely away. Now she couldn't shake the feeling that her prayer to get the Maverick going (but hadn't she said *Thy* will?) had cost her the dog.

"Christ's sake, it's nobody's fault!" Chick said. He pretended not to worry, but she heard him in the woods whistling the come-here-boy note that JoJo had always run to. They searched for a week, night and day, patrolling the near roads and calling, calling. When Chick said, "Face it," and Bonnie said, "He was getting old," Angelina said, "Was? Was!" and went on looking, after Bonnie went to school, after Chick drove away to work. She walked early. Later, she and her jogging partner made the rounds: no clues, no telltale ravens, nothing.

The Friday before Palm Sunday was frosty. Angelina was jogging alone and she smelled something. She tried to kid herself, but she cut the run short and with growing dread, she followed the old wagon road to the hilltop. There was a springhouse, fallen in for years, smothered in vinca and lilies in season. The pool was dark and leaf-clotted. That's where he lay; that's where JoJo had died. It might have been his heart; it might have been poison. What difference now?

He lay with his head a little way over the lip of the pool. After considering, she decided to take only his collar; his collar and tags only would she salvage for burial. When she touched him, it surprised her; he was warm. A little steam rose from his body, the work of worms. She caught the leather of the collar in her hands and began to unfasten it. The unforeseen: as she tried to slip the collar off, the dog's head detached itself and fell ripely into her hands. Angelina caught it. She tried to put it back. Tried beyond reason to put it back. She cried out and stood and stomped and shook herself free of the maggots which had climbed past her elbows. She scooped the collar out of the water and ran, ran without looking back.

Chick took care of it that night. When he asked if she wanted the collar buried in the little grove of dogwoods, Angelina didn't care.

Sometime during the week of Easter Angelina made up her mind. On Wednesday after Easter she took Chick's good dark suit to the cleaners and on the way home she stopped in the Van Shop to buy a replacement Windbreaker for Bonnie, who had left hers on the school bus again — the third one the girl had lost. Chick had said, "Let her do without," the only way to teach her. "But here I am again," Angelina told the clerk.

"Same with my kids," the clerk agreed. "What would they do without us?"

Angelina considered that a moment, her pen poised above the check. "I don't know," she admitted. She signed her name gravely, as to a warrant, as though lives and honor were at stake. The sound the check made as she tore it from the book, that papery final complaint, made her sad. Tears stung her eyes.

"Going to be pretty today. Even prettier tomorrow. Not a cloud in the — oops, spoke too soon," the clerk said, pointing. Shoulder to shoulder they examined the sky through the amber sun film.

"That cloud's looking for me," Angelina laughed. "I washed my car." She laughed, as though she recognized it of old. The heavy door with its COME ON IN decal and cowbell swung shut behind her. The clerk called, "See you," and Angelina raised her hand.

She drove home and got there in time to answer the phone: Grace reminding her about the Tupperware party. "Two-thirty," Grace said. "A little early so we can talk. Been missing you lately."

"Two-thirty," Angelina lied.

She wrote a note and with the TODAY IS THE FIRST DAY magnet

pinned it to Thursday: "Blue suit ready at noon." She wrote it in red to catch Chick's eye. He would be needing that suit.

She wasn't hungry; hadn't eaten all day. She felt lightheaded and breezy, the way she had felt when she was about to be married, when she knew the tremendous doom and peace of being sure, of knowing her fate, of being espoused, and trusting her choice. She sat in Chick's chair, with its shape martyred to his. She could faintly smell his hairdressing. She reached toward the little table and turned on the reading lamp. The Bible fell open to the place she had marked with a rose from her mother's funeral blanket. She read; then — in the center of a clean page of paper — she made a note, folded it, sealed it into an envelope. She wasn't going to mail it; she didn't need a stamp. She left it on the table.

After that, she filled the bird feeder which the squirrels had raided again. She walked down to the mailbox and read the weekly news on her way back up the drive. There was a pine cone on the steps; she picked it up and dropped it in the kindling bin. There were handprints on the refrigerator; she buffed them away and put up the rag. It was time to be on her way. Angelina glanced around the house; everything was tidy. She picked up her pocketbook and went out. In a moment she unlocked and went back in, to check if she had unplugged the coffee maker (she had), and after that she got away.

She drove slowly down the road, her window open, breathing in the sweet scent of crab apples. She kept to the old familiar routes, heading out west as far as Tubby's Lake, then circling back toward town. She drove past Grace's street, but didn't turn in. Every landmark she passed seemed to lurch up at her, dragging her back. She drove on, determined. Everything caught her eye.

VidALiA ONiON a new sign announced, paint still wet. It was propped against the front wheel of a car backed up to the railroad tracks on the dead side of the depot. A man and his children were busy, were happy, arranging cabbages on the fenders. There were trays of tomatoes and (she craned to be sure) the year's first peaches. A baby sat in the driver's seat tooting the horn. As Angelina went by, the baby leaned from the window and waved a tattered little Rebel flag.

At the next corner Angelina stopped (YIELD TO PEDESTRIANS was painted man-tall in the road both ways) to let Mrs. Nesby in her fresh print dress cross the street on her way to the library to return a Janice Holt Giles. She blew Angelina a God-bless-you kiss. A quarter of a mile farther north the Highway Department was surveying. The yellow Travelall was parked with its doors open, and a flagman was stopping traffic in both directions.

"Left . . . left . . . left . . . right — WHOA! Whoa!"

Tap-tap-tap. They were using an ax for a hammer to drive the pins in.

It was warm enough for the chain pullers and target men to go shirtless. Their visibility vests were stark against their winter-pale skin. Each man (there were six, Angelina noticed: six strong men, like pallbearers) had hold of the tape or chain or stick or rod. The ledger man stared through the transit and shouted, "Left . . . left . . . left . . . good — WHOA!" and then again the tap-tap-tap.

The flagman noticed Angelina checking her watch. "Won't be long now," he estimated. The crew was already snaking its way down the street toward the next mark. Then the flagman swung his STOP sign out of service to SLOW and waved her past. "Sorry for the delay," he called.

Angelina drove north till she came to the scar where the new road was being graded. She turned down the diminishing old farm track toward the reservoir and rode till the young weeds and brambles scratched and clawed her to a stop. She could feel the earth rumbling from the prime movers a mile away chewing up the red hills into four lanes. She set the brake and rolled up the window against the dust. She left her pocketbook and keys. She took only the little pistol.

She had not been here before. She looked around her for a place. There were bird's-foot violets in the dry clay. She had always loved them, yet none she ever transplanted survived to bloom the next year. She bent to pick one, then changed her mind. A C-130 on a training flight made a slow turn and headed out over the lake toward the mountains. She watched it till it was only a noise on the horizon, then she sought out the tender green shade beneath a broken willow. She aimed the gun approximately at her heart and pulled the trigger.

The noise as much as the charge toppled her. She thought, I should have been lying down! Too late. She had planned to cease instantly, and this delay caused her chagrin; she failed, as she had all her life, by degrees. She stared up into the ferny, fretted crown of the willow. Oh soon, oh soon oh soon, she panted, laboring to deliver herself of this final burden, life. She lay watching the sky go white as a shell over her. All the color bled from the day. A jay spotted her, flew over to investigate, hopped lower in the branches, and cried THIEF! THIEF! as he flew away west to shrill the news. Soon that sound was lost in the surf-roar of her inner ear, and Angelina lost contact . . .

No one had the least notion. They called around when she failed to show up at the Tupperware party, and Grace finally called Chick at work. But he didn't begin worrying until Bonnie called too; she was due at the orthodontist's and Angelina had not come by school to pick her up as she had promised. Chick guessed then it was car trouble. No one guessed it would turn out like it did.

The reservoir manager noticed her car on toward sundown, went to check on it, and found her, so she didn't have to lie out there all night.

She was in surgery till nearly midnight, and in the waiting room the little crowd of shocked well-wishers gradually thinned to Angelina's husband, her father, her daughter, and a few silent comforters. Bonnie, from the first, felt indicted, never mind who pulled the trigger. She was her mother's child all right, and the tenderest victim. She kept to herself, and spent hours in the restroom; Chick could hear her congested crying but didn't know how to help her. He couldn't even help himself. When the surgeon came out and told them Angelina would live, Bonnie had her mama's note, tear-stained now and folded, folded, folded into triviality, as though it were some everyday something that could be forgotten, left behind in an ashtray, lost in a pocket, unimportant. (All the note said was "Job 7" — that's all she wrote, addressed To Whom It May Concern, not To Chick and Bonnie, not even Sorry, not even Love, as though in forgetting everything she lived for she forgot them first. Bonnie had looked the quote up in the little white calf-bound King James Angelina gave her for Christmas. She read and reread that whole early chapter from "Is there not an appointed time?" to the last exulting despair of "For now I shall sleep in the dust; and thou shalt seek me in the morning but I shall not be.") Bonnie, in a wizened whisper in the general echoing ignorance, asked the surgeon, asked anyone, "Why?" She turned on them all, on herself in the dark glass of the midnight windows and shouted it this time, "Why didn't she want to read to the end of the book?"

Which is, of course, the question. Her father, her grandfather, Reverend Martin, Dr. Spence, the neighbors — all met her harrowing wild gaze for a moment only, then looked away.

In the morning they let Chick go in to see her for five minutes. Angelina was awake, but she lay with her eyes shut against him, her chin aimed at God. She knew as well as if she were floating in a corner of the ceiling looking down at him exactly what Chick was doing, heard him lift the one chair and turn it around and straddle it and sit, knew he was resting his chin on his fists, watching her. Four of his minutes, then thirty seconds more, elapsed. Finally she had to open her eyes and let him in.

"Oh, babe," he said when she looked his way. "You very nearly broke my heart."

She beat at the bed with her pale hands, clawing at the IVs in her wrists that tethered her to life. The nurse came, then another, and they restrained her. Chick turned at the door for a last look.

Septic with regret, he didn't have time to arrange his face before Bonnie saw him. Terrified, she cried, "She didn't die, did she? She'll have another chance?"

He thought of Angelina lying there small and sharp-eyed and at bay somehow, vulnerable but valiant, like a little beast who would gnaw off its own foot to escape the trap.

"Another chance," he said.

DONALD JUSTICE

The Artificial Moonlight

(FROM ANTAEUS)

Coconut Grove, 1958

THE LANGS, Hal and his wife Julie, were giving a party.

From the screen porch of their apartment you could see, strung out across the bay, the colored lights of the neighborhood sailing club — the Langs did not belong — and, farther out, the bulky shadows of the members' boats riding at anchor. Almost always, with nightfall, there would be a breeze. It came from the bay and across the bayshore road past the shaggy royal palms bordering the driveway, cooling the porch like a large and efficient fan.

But tonight was one of those rare end-of-summer nights without any saving breeze. It was past midnight, and still the apartment felt oppressive and close. The heat was spoiling the party. It was a going-away party for an old friend of the Langs', Jack Felton, whom they saw now only when he came home from graduate school to visit his parents, and in a day or two, with summer over, he would be taking off for Europe on a Fulbright. But it was not only the heat. Some vague melancholy of departure and change seemed to have settled over everyone and everything.

In the back room a record player was turning, unattended. Sounds of the jazz of a dozen years ago, early Sarah Vaughan, drifted out to the porch. The casual guests, the friends of friends, had all departed. The few who remained looked settled in, as though they might stay forever, listless and bored, some on the sagging wicker chair and settee, and some on the floor cushions brought out from the stuffy back rooms. They looked as though they might never move again, not even to flip the stack of records when the music ended.

If anyone did, it would probably be Julie herself. Of the Langs, Julie was the dependable one. Five afternoons a week she worked as a legal stenographer, while her husband kept up appearances by giving occasional painting lessons to the daughters of tourists. Yet except for a shortage of money from time to time they lived with as much freedom from care and nearly as much leisure as the well-to-do. Approaching their thirties, they seemed as perpetually youthful as movie stars.

The odd hours they kept could be hard on Julie, and occasionally she retired early. She would be so wound up that she could not sleep and would have to read for a long time before her eyes closed. It was an intense sort of reading, beyond simple pleasure. One wall of their bedroom was filled with books, and sometimes when they made love without turning the lights off she caught herself innocently letting her eyes rove across the titles on the spines of the larger books. Once or twice Hal had complained of this publicly, to her embarrassment, but she seemed unable to change.

Alone in their bedroom, reading or not, she liked the sound of conversation floating back late at night from the porch. It was soothing, like the quiet, washing sound of an ocean. It was hot back there, and there was a little fan she could reach out for and turn on, but she did not often use it. She liked the warm weather; she could not imagine living anywhere but Miami.

Still, there were nights when Julie felt left out of things. Their friends all drank, and, except on the most ceremonial occasions, Julie did not. Of course the feeling went beyond that. She would suspect them of planning something incalculably exciting from which she was to be excluded. Unreasonable, but there was nothing she could do about the feeling. Julie gazed with half-closed eyes across the porch at her husband, where he sat perched on an arm of the old wicker settee, bending down to speak to a tall blond woman in slacks. She wondered if she would ever be able to trace this feeling of hers back to its source. How far back would she have to go? She was an orphan, adopted by a couple old enough to be her grandparents, long ago dead. Could it be as simple as that? She thought, sometimes, that she might have Spanish blood. That would account for her dark coloring, for her thick black eyebrows, her almost blue-black hair, which only a few days before she had cut short, despite Hal's protests.

In the back room now the record stopped and another dropped down from the stack — Duke Ellington, slow and bluesy. Shutting her eyes, Julie took a sip of the plain orange juice in her glass and, leaning back, crossed her legs. One tiny sandaled foot, the nails that afternoon painted a deep blood-red for the party, commenced to swing nervously back and forth, back and forth, to some inner rhythm of her own.

However serious his life elsewhere might have become, Jack had kept his old reputation locally for stirring things up. He wondered if the others were waiting for him to take some initiative now. After all, the party was for him.

But he was not the same person they remembered, not really. Whenever he came back home now it was as if the curtain had risen on a new act, with the same actors, but the playwright had without notice shifted the course of the action. It was impossible to point to a time when everything had been as it should be, but that time must have existed once. They all felt it. And lately, to Jack, every change — the divorce of one couple, the moving away of another — came as an unwelcome change.

As for himself, Jack knew that he seemed quieter than he used to seem. In fact, he was. He had no wish to pretend otherwise, but in a very small way, just as he could imagine his friends doing, he missed his old self. He sat now very quietly, stretched out on his floor cushion, leaning back against the wall, his long legs folded in a lazy tangle before him. He looked half-asleep. But behind his glasses his eyes were still open. It might have seemed that he was listening to the music, except that it had stopped.

He had intended to listen. He had stacked the records himself, some of his favorites. Then, just as the unforgotten sounds had begun to bear him back toward his own adolescence, it had struck him suddenly why the girl sitting beside him, to whom he had been talking desultorily for the last twenty minutes or so, was wearing so loose and unbecoming a blouse — tardily, for she was, if not very far along, nevertheless visibly pregnant. To Jack, who had known her all his life, the realization came like a blow. When those very records were being cut, this girl, Susan, who was almost certainly the youngest person in the room, had been listening obediently to the nuns of her grammar school, wearing the blue-and-white uniform Jack still remembered. The summer before, when he had last seen her, Susan had not even been married. And already her husband, Robert or Bob, the sallow, sleepy-looking fellow in the corner who never had much to say, had got her pregnant.

For the time being Jack could concentrate on nothing but this, this fact that to him seemed so irremediably, if obscurely, wrong.

Hal was bending down, whispering into the blond woman's ear. Not that there was anything important to be said, but there was a pleasure in merely leaning toward her in that way, some momentary illusion of intimacy. What he had to say was only that soon they would be out of vodka.

And then he sighed. There was a sort of perfume coming, apparently, from a spot just behind her ear. Green was her married name, Karen Green, and Hal had known her longer than he had known his wife. As far back as high school he had had a hopeless crush on her, but never before had he noticed how peculiarly large and yet shapely her left ear was, from which the hair was drawn back, and how many little whorls it contained, impossible to count. Was she wearing her hair some new way?

Hal leaned closer and whispered, "Of course we could always go out to Fox's for more. More vodka."

It was half a question. It was the tone he always adopted with Karen, the tone of casual flirtation, just as though they were in school together still.

A rustling stirred in the palms outside, the first sign of something like a breeze. For a moment the wind rose, the rolled tarpaulins high up on the screen seemed to catch their breath.

All at once, borne to them on the faint edge of wind, they

heard a dance band playing, not very far away, a rumba band
— snarling trumpet, bongo drums, maracas. Had it been playing all this time? Everyone listened. Jack straightened up and
peered about the room, somewhat crossly, like a person roused
from an interesting dream.

"The Legion dance," someone called out.

The large, good-looking man, who from his cushion beside
Julie Lang's chair had also been watching Hal and the blond
woman, climbed to his feet. This was Sid Green, Karen's husband. Standing, he loomed larger than anyone else in the
group.

Normally unassertive, Sid heard his own voice calling across
the porch, "Hey, Hal, you by any chance a member?" To himself
his voice sounded unexpectedly loud, as if it contained some
challenge he did not wish to issue more directly.

"For Christ's sake, Sid, the *Foreign* Legion maybe, not the
American."

"If somebody was a member, we could go to the dance," Sid
said. "I mean if anybody wanted to."

"Crash it?" the pregnant girl asked.

"Oh, maybe not," Sid said, looking around, and even his flash
of enthusiasm was fading.

"I don't know," Hal said, with a glance at Sid's wife beside
him.

"Oh, let's do go!" Julie cried out suddenly from across the
porch. "For God's sake, let's do something! Just wait a minute
till I change my shoes." And kicking her sandals off, fluffing
her short crop of hair out as she went, she hurried back through
the dark apartment toward the bedroom.

But when she returned it was apparent that something was
wrong. Hal and Karen were missing, and Jack as well. Julie
peered into the corner where the other women were sitting —
Susan and a girl named Annabelle, who appeared to be sound
asleep.

"Aren't you coming?" Julie asked nervously.

"Not me," Susan said, placing one hand on her stomach. "Not
in my condition." Her silent husband beamed, as if Susan had
said something witty or perhaps flattering to him.

Julie felt more uncomfortable than ever. She had never been

a mother, and she was a good deal older than Susan, seven or eight years at least, but she did not think that Susan and her husband would intentionally try to embarrass her. Everyone knew that she had never wanted children, that she preferred her freedom.

Julie turned to Sid; their eyes met. He was quiet, too quiet to be amusing in the way that Hal and even Jack could sometimes be, but really quite good-looking in his athletic fashion, dark and mysterious, withheld. They knew very little about Sid. Was it true that his family had money? If only, Julie thought, he would volunteer himself more, like Hal. But at least Sid could be managed.

"Come on, you," she said, taking him by the hand and pulling. "Let's catch up with the others."

Meekly, Sid allowed himself to be led out the door.

On the dock it was very quiet. Only stray phrases of the Cuban trumpet carried out that far.

As they had walked out onto the dock, which was floated on an arrangement of great, slowly rusting oil drums, it had bobbed and swayed with every step. By now it had settled down. The three of them — Hal and Karen and Jack — sat dangling their legs over the end, looking out at the anchored boats which the water rocked as gently as cradles. Above the water, very bright, as if left over from some festivity, were strung the lights of the sailing club. All of the lights together cast a strange glow on the dark waters of the bay, a thin swath of artificial moonlight which reached out perhaps halfway toward the long, indistinct blur of the nearest island.

Jack wanted to touch the water, see how cold it was. Carefully he set the drink he had brought with him down upon the planking and removed his loafers.

Not that he meant to swim. But as he thrust one leg down, and his toes touched water, which was not as cold as expected, he found himself thinking of a woman they all knew, a woman named Roberta, who had once lived in the apartment above the Langs, and how she sometimes used to swim out to the island, which was no more than a dark, low line on the horizon. There was nothing to do out there; it was a mere piney arm of sand.

She would wait just long enough to catch her breath and then swim back. That was all. It would not have been, if you were a swimmer, very dangerous. There were plenty of boats along the way to catch hold of if you tired.

Perhaps they were all thinking of Roberta just then, for when Hal asked, out of the blue, if they knew that Roberta was in San Francisco, Karen said, "Funny, I was just thinking of that time she drove her car into the bay."

"Well, not quite all the way in," Hal said. "It stalled, you know."

Hal was the authority on the stories they told about people they used to know. There was a good-sized collection of them, recounted so often the identities of the participants tended to blur, and the facts themselves were subject to endless small revisions and adjustments.

"I thought it was a palm tree that stopped her," Jack commented, rather sourly. He had never been one of Roberta's admirers. At the time, she had seemed a silly romantic girl, mad for attention. He tried to recall her face but could not. Had it been pretty? He seemed to remember it as pale, rather moon-shaped, but perhaps that was someone else's, someone more elusive still.

"You're right," Hal agreed. "There was a palm tree somewhere, but where?" He began to reconstruct. "The car must have caromed off the palm and gone on into the bay. Yes, partway in. I seem to picture it hanging over the edge, sort of."

"I always thought she did it on purpose," Karen said.

"No, it was an accident." On that point Hal was definite.

Gradually a deeper melancholy settled over them. All around, the small dinghies tied up at the dock nosed familiarly against the wood. One was painted a vivid orange and white, the colors of the sailing club. A car passed behind them along the bayshore road, swiftly, heading for Miami proper.

Karen looked out across the bay. "Well, she should have done it on purpose. That would have made sense. It would have been — oh, I don't know . . ."

Off and on all evening Jack had been wondering what, if anything, was on between Hal and Karen. Karen was very beautiful,

more beautiful than she had been ten years ago, just out of high
school, when everyone, himself and Hal too, as he remembered,
was buzzing around her. Experience had only ripened her; she
made him think of some night-blooming flower the neighbors
call you out to see. Probably just then — at that very minute,
Jack would have liked to believe — she was at the absolute peak
of her beauty. The next summer, surely by the summer after,
she would have crossed the invisible line they were all approaching. On the other side of that line strangers would no longer
find her quite so remarkable to look at, only old friends like Hal
and himself, who would remember her face as it had been lit
momentarily by the driftwood fire of some otherwise forgotten
beach picnic, or more likely as it was now, shaped by the glow
of the lights strung out from the dock over the water.

He recalled a story of Hal's, a story he did not much like to
think of, of how Hal and a girl Jack didn't know had rowed out
to the island one night and stayed till dawn. Thinking about the
story now, with the island itself so near, Jack began to feel curiously giddy, as if the dock were starting to bob again.

"What about the island?" he asked.

"What about it?" Karen said.

"What about going out to the island?"

"I couldn't swim that far," she said. "Not nearly."

"Not swim. We borrow one of these dinghy things. Ask Hal.
He's done it before."

Hal grinned. "Right. The night watchman, he sleeps back in
that little shack. Besides, he doesn't really give a damn."

In a moment they were climbing down into the orange-and-
white dinghy, a trickier operation than it looked. Whenever one
of them put a foot down, exploring, the boat seemed to totter
almost to the point of capsizing. Jack could not hold back a snort
of laughter.

"Shh," Hal said.

"I thought he didn't give a damn," Karen said, tittering.

"Shh," Jack said. "Shh."

Once they were all seated, Hal took up the oars. They were
just casting off, Jack had just managed to slip the rope free,
when they heard footsteps coming up the walk. The rope
dropped with a thick splash.

"Hey, we see you down there," a voice called, and Karen recognized it as her husband's. Just behind him stood Julie, their shadows bent out over the water.

"Shh," Karen hissed. Already the current was bearing them out, and there was a wide dark patch between boat and dock.

"Come on back."

"Can't. Current's got us."

But Hal was able to plant one oar firmly in the water and with that the boat began to turn in a slow circle.

"How was the dance?" Hal called politely.

For reply Julie stamped her foot on the dock. "Come on back," she called.

"Tell me, Julie, I sincerely want to know how it was."

"Oh, Hal, stop it."

"Actually they were very nice about it," Sid said, "but we felt kind of out of place."

"I feel kind of out of place right here," said Jack, dizzy with the motion of the boat.

"Oh, you're all drunk," Julie said. "Every one of you is hopelessly drunk and besotted."

It ended with Sid and Julie untying another dinghy and climbing into it. Quietly then the two boats glided out with the mild current through the lighted water.

Under the lights Jack felt like an escaping prisoner caught in the beam of a spotlight, and he closed his eyes, distinctly giddy now. When he looked again, they were already emerging from the shadows of the anchored boats into the clear space beyond, where it was dark. The other boat was no longer in sight. Hal feathered the oars, and they drifted with the flow, letting Sid and Julie catch up. It was very still. They could hear Sid grunting over the oars before they saw his dinghy coming up, gaining fast. In the dark his bent-over shape looked like part of the ghostly, gliding boat. Their eyes had become used to the dark by now, and they were near enough to make out ahead the narrow strip of sand edged with stunted pines that marked the shore of the island. A moment later the outline of a landing pier with several large nets spread out to dry on skeletal frames came into sight. Hal pointed the boat that way and resumed rowing.

The pier was rickety but apparently safe. When Hal leaped out, the others followed.

Karen lived with the vaguely troubling impression that some-one, some man, had all her life been leaning toward her, about to touch her. It was like a dream. Instinctively she wished to draw back but could not. Moments ago, on the island, lying on the little beach, with Hal leaning toward her, whispering some-thing about exploring the island a little farther down, around the point, she had consented without a thought, without strict attention to the words. Tomorrow, thinking back over it, excus-ing herself, she might suppose that she had thought Hal meant for the others to come too, but now, with that little moment still round and clear in her mind, she could admit that she had come away under no such illusion. She could not understand why she had come. Karen was not in any way angry with her husband, and she had never felt the least tremor of desire for Hal, who was simply an old friend.

Her earliest recollection of Hal was of a brash, rebellious boy in high school, a loud talker, but solitary, whom she had seen once standing alone after classes at the end of a long corridor puffing away at — strange! — a cigar, much too advanced for his years. Perhaps that was why she had been tempted to come with him now, that fragment of memory. Hal had looked up from the end of the corridor and seen her watching him puff away at the forbidden cigar, though neither had spoken at the time, nor, for that matter, had either brought the incident up since. Karen was not certain that Hal would remember it. Even if he did not, Karen believed that out of that moment, in some not-to-be-explained way, this moment had come, and that it was in some way inevitable that the two of them should be standing together now, around the point from the beach where the oth-ers were lying, though not yet so far off as to keep an occasional murmur of voices from drifting their way.

Hal was no longer leaning toward her. He had taken her hand to lead her across one stretch of slippery rocks, but he had not otherwise touched her. He was talking softly and at incredible length about a book he was reading, a novel about some boys marooned on an island. Of all things! Karen thought, slightly indignant. Of all things! She had failed at the outset to catch the novelist's name, and the conversation by now was too far advanced to ask. Hal seemed to have reached the point of criticizing the style of the writer. *Seemed* — she could not really say. Her attention was failing, fading. She was overcome by a feeling of surrender, a sense of division that was almost physical, in which she stood watching herself disappear over the water, which was dark, of a deep gemlike hue, and astonishingly calm.

In the distance she could hear Sid's laughter. She had the most vivid sensation of his anxiety and of Julie's as well. She wished she might do something to alleviate it, but it was as if Hal's voice going on and on endlessly about the novel she would never read were fixing her, or a part of her, to a certain point, pinning her there, draining her of all power, while the rest of her drifted out, out . . . If only Sid would raise his voice and call her! She remembered the after-supper games of hide-and-seek as a child with her large family of sisters and a brother. One game in particular was among her most persistent memories, one that recurred even in her dreams. She was crouching behind a prickly bush — for years afterward she could go to that same bush and point it out; she knew exactly where it stood on the lawn of her parents' house. She was the last one of all the sisters not yet found by her brother, who was "It," and she could hear her brother's footsteps coming through the dusk and then his soft voice calling, almost whispering, "Karen? Karen? Karen?" And she ran to him and threw her arms around him, whereupon her brother, who was quite a few years older and much larger than she — he was only playing the game as a favor to his sisters — lifted her from the ground and swung her around and around until they both fell to the grass, overcome with laughter and relief.

How tired she was! She wanted Hal to stop talking. She was ready. She wanted him to touch her; she wanted whatever was going to happen to begin. Love! And yet she could not bring herself to say to him that it would be all right, that whatever he did or did not do scarcely mattered any longer.

Jack woke from a sound sleep feeling cold. He was alone.

He sat up and listened, a little apprehensively, for some

sound to indicate where the others might be. Except for the water that was licking up along the sand almost to his feet and out again, the silence was complete. Where had they gone? He took it for granted that they were off exploring the island, two by two probably, but by what pairs and for what purpose he hardly considered. His curiosity, brimming not long before, had gone flat.

Somewhere he had misplaced his glasses. Groping in the sand near where he had been sleeping, failing to find them, he blinked out across the water into the sky. The first faint streaks and patches of light were beginning to show. For a long time he sat, reluctant to get up and start looking for the others. He did not like the idea of stumbling across them in the dark, especially half-blind as he was. For the time being he did not care if he never saw any of them again. His stomach felt a little queasy, but he was not sure if it was from drinking. It might have been from emotion. In any case, he had been through worse.

Only after he had made his way back along the path to the landing pier and seen that the boats were missing did he realize what had happened. They had left him behind; they had abandoned him on the island.

At first he was simply angry. He peered as well as he could toward land. The sailing-club lights were still burning over the water. That he could see, but no farther. It was beginning to get light, and soon, he knew, the night watchman would wake up and turn the lights off. Already the lights were beginning to look superfluous. What a stupid joke this was, he thought. He imagined the story they would make out of it — the night they marooned Jack on the island! For a moment he considered the chance of swimming back, like Roberta. If he could make seventy or eighty yards on his own, there would be plenty of boats to hang on to. But the water looked cold, and his stomach was too unsettled.

Cold after the warmth of the night, he wrapped his arms around his shoulders. He felt as alone as he could ever remember having felt, and in an unfamiliar place, a place he could not even, without his glasses, see clearly, all fuzzy and vague — the last absurd touch. Any minute his teeth would start chattering. Standing there like that, realizing how foolish and pointless it was, for he must have been very nearly sober by then, he began to call their names out as loud as he could, one after the other — a kind of roll call — whether out of annoyance or affection he did not pause to consider. *Hal, Sid, Karen, Julie!* He had no idea how far his voice carried over the water, and in any case there was no answer.

At last he sat down on the little rickety pier and began to wait for someone to come and rescue him. And gradually, sitting there, beginning to shiver with the morning cool, Jack reflected, absurdly enough, that he was to be the hero of whatever story came to be told of the night. A curious form of flattery, but flattery of a sort. He had been singled out. At once he felt better about the evening. The party — it had not been a dead loss, after all. He almost found himself forgiving them for having abandoned him; eventually perhaps he would forgive them, forgive them everything, whatever they had done or not done. Without him, whatever had happened — and he did not want to know yet what that was, afraid that his new and still fragile sense of the uniqueness of the evening might evaporate once he knew — would not have happened. In some way, he was responsible. In any case, he would have forgiven them a great deal — laughter, humiliation, even perhaps betrayal — as they would forgive him practically anything. He saw all that now. Well, it was a sentimental time of night — the very end of it — and he had had a lot to drink, but he was willing to believe that the future would indeed be bleak and awful without such friends, willing to take their chance with you, ready even to abandon you on a chunk of sand at four A.M. for nothing but the sheer hell of it. And he was, for the moment, remarkably contented.

Brighton, 1980

The apartment building the Langs had lived in had been gone since the late sixties. There had been a boom. The fine old house — one of the oldest in the area, one to which Indians just before the turn of the century had come up across the bay in their canoes to trade — had lasted as long as any, but it had succumbed in the end to time and money. In any case, it would have been quickly dwarfed by the new high-rises looming around it. On its site stood one of the poshest of the latest generation of high-rises, expensive and grand, with glass and impractical little tilted balconies painted in three bold colors. Admittedly, it had been and was still a grand site, with a marvelous sweeping view of the bay, the little masted boats thick on the water, like blown leaves.

But it was the people who concerned Jack. And he knew none of the new people. In his own place, when he went there now, he felt uncomfortable and alien.

One day — twenty years and more had passed — sitting in a flat in Brighton, England, looking idly out over the gray, disturbed sea in a direction he thought must be toward home, Jack began making a sort of mental catalogue of all his friends from that period. He had not thought it out in advance. The idea just came to him, and he began. He was trying to remember everyone who was together at a certain time in the old life, at a precise moment even, and the night of his going-away party came back to him.

The list began with Susan's son, the one she had been pregnant with at the time, and Jack was pleased with himself for having thought to include her child-to-be in his recollection. She never had another. The son, he had heard, was a fine, intelligent boy, off at college somewhere, no trouble to anybody. Jack had not seen him since the boy started grammar school. The boy's name slipped his memory, but he did remember, if not very clearly, curls and a sort of general shying away from the presence of grownups.

The sallow husband — Robert or Bob — had been some trouble or had some trouble. Drinking? Whatever in the past had caused his silence, he was to sink deeper and deeper into it over the years. Eventually he had found his way back north to Philadelphia, into his father's business, a chain of liquor stores. Just the thing, Jack thought ruefully, just the thing.

Susan herself was another story, though not much of one. She owned a small stucco house in the Grove, almost hidden by shrubs and palms and jacarandas. Her time seemed to go into nothing at all, unless it was a little gardening, but it surely went. She had no time for anything, certainly not for friends, and never or very rarely ventured out. She kept a few cats, quite a few. Their number grew.

The great surprise was Sid, the only one to have become famous. Not exactly famous, Jack acknowledged, but well-known. No one had sensed the power and ambition hidden so quietly in Sid back then, certainly not Karen. From small starts, from short sailing trips down into the Keys, later out to the Bahamas, Sid had taken the great dare of a long solo sail across the Atlantic, kept a journal, and published an account of the voyage. Modestly popular. Later, other adventures, other books. He was married now to a minor movie actress, past her prime but still quite beautiful — a brunette, not at all like Karen in appearance — and they lived most of the year, predictably somehow, in southern France. (It was true — his family had had some money.) Jack had recently had occasion to call on them on the continent and found that he enjoyed his visit immensely. Sid had become voluble, a great smiler — of all of them, the most thoroughly and happily changed.

Karen, on the other hand, had been through three more husbands. Two daughters, one of them married, with a daughter of her own. It seemed incredible to Jack that Karen, of all people, should have become a grandmother. It was like a magic trick, seen but not believed. Sometimes, of an evening, as they sat talking over a drink beside the current husband's pool, the bug light sending out its intermittent little zap, he had caught a sidelong glimpse of the former Karen, a Karen absolute and undiminished, still slender, seemingly remote, cool if not cold, not to be found out. Some secret she had, and it had kept her beautiful. Her present husband was often ill, and there was a bad look around her own eyes. She looked away from you much of the time. She had never done anything of any importance in her life, and everybody had always loved her for herself alone. What happiness!

Julie, as she had wished, never had had any children. Over the years she had gone a little to corpulence, but her foot, surprisingly tiny still, still swung back and forth to some nervous rhythm of her own. She, who had always abhorred and fled from the cold, ran a bookstore now in Boston. She had become an expert on books. The way Jack had of explaining this to himself — he had browsed in her shop once or twice when in the city — was simply that she had liked to read, always. Those nights Hal had been out catting around she had read. She had read and read and she had always loved books and, in the end, it had come to this. She seemed satisfied.

Nor was Hal — the great romantic, Hal — a totally lost cause, even though he had, in his maturity, held down a steady job, the same job now, for ten or eleven years, easily a record for him. He managed a gallery. He was perfect for it, a gallery in the Grove popular with everyone, wealthy tourists especially. It also provided him the contacts with women he seemed to need — wives, daughters, perhaps even a youthful grandmother or two. Women, young and old, some beautiful, some rich, pursuing Hal, who was not getting any younger. He let his colorful shirts hang out usually, over a slight belly, wore dark glasses much of the time, rode out his hangovers with good grace and considerable experience. He still painted, excellent miniatures, obsessively detailed, with the clear jeweled colors of Byzantine work. He sold everything he made and never set too high a price, though it was certain he could demand more if he chose. But no, he was as happy as he deserved, perhaps happier. Not married — it was easier that way. Some nights he liked being alone.

Several of his friends, Jack realized, were actually happy. The shape of their futures must always have been there, somehow, just as eye color is built into the chromosomes before birth. Impossible to read, all the same, except backward, as with some obscure Eastern language. Or perhaps the night of the party had been a sort of key, and it had been clear, or should have been clear then, that the Langs would never last, not as a couple, and if the Langs went, then the Greens constituted a doubtful case; and something in the way her husband had cast his silent, wary, unfathomable glances at the pregnant Susan might have hinted at some future division between them as well. Now no one was married to the right person. No one, as Jack would have it, would ever be married to the right person again. The time when everything was as it should be was always really some other time, but back then, that summer, it had seemed near.

From the window of the flat he could see only a little corner of the sea, and he wanted, for some reason, to be closer to the water. Dressing warmly, Jack walked down to the parade, braced himself against the baby gale and walked and walked, for forty minutes or so. He found himself down on the shingle, almost alone there. It was too nasty a day for there to be much company. A big boat hung on the horizon. Jack thought back to the beach of the little sandy bay island and he guessed that what had happened that night must be why he had ventured down to the sand now, to which he almost never descended. Here in this foreign place he felt again that he was on a little island, isolated, the last civilized speck, himself against a faceless and unpredictable world — unknowable, really. Jack felt like calling out the names again, the names of his friends, but of course he did not. He could not even remember how he had been rescued that other time, who it was that had come out in a dinghy for him, risking the wrath of the sleepy night watchman. Probably Sid. Julie had cooked a nice breakfast — he remembered that. No one would be coming to rescue him now, not that he needed rescuing or wanted rescuing, even in the sort of half-dreaming state he had fallen into. But the thought did occur to him, in passing.

STEPHEN KIRK

Morrison's Reaction

(FROM THE GREENSBORO REVIEW)

DURING THE COURSE of his thirty years of practice, Dr. Herman Morrison had developed a strong aversion to the brand of dentistry that he called "hack work." He could still enjoy the sense of accomplishment that followed a difficult session of inlay casting or bridge construction, since each case demanded a creative solution to its unique set of problems. Even the semiannual checkups that occupied his mornings were varied enough to spare him the boredom of routine.

But willful, gross neglect always stirred in Morrison feelings of depression and futility. He had witnessed too much suffering in patients who had inherited everything from mild malocclusion to poor enamel, who might have practiced perfect hygiene and still been doomed to pain. When the odor of decay from what could have been healthy teeth and gums was so overpowering that it negated the alcoholic reek of antiseptic mouthwash — so stifling that he was forced to dismiss professional etiquette and stuff his nostrils with cotton and breathe through his mouth — Morrison was inclined to forgive grudgingly.

Duane Vincent was unwilling or unable to provide a dental history, claiming to have no records with any doctor. New patients often choose a dentist at the recommendation of a friend or coworker. Who had sent him to Morrison? Vincent could not say. Had he picked Morrison's name from the telephone book? Was he a stranger to the area? Vincent's curtness discouraged further questions. Morrison made an effort at light conversation, but Vincent was equally evasive about his private life, his family and his interests, volunteering only that he was "in business, downtown."

Morrison's patience was showing its first signs of inconstancy as he neared sixty. His greatest desire was that the days leading to his retirement be uneventful, and he would have liked to pass Vincent on to one of his colleagues by pleading a full schedule. But despite the subtle suggestion that he look elsewhere for treatment, Vincent had followed up their preliminary meeting with another unannounced visit to the office, and then another. Morrison insisted upon a series of five sessions over a period of weeks, yet Vincent would concede only one follow-up for the installation of caps and the painting of visible fillings. Vincent's determination had finally won the single three-hour afternoon appointment he desired.

While Morrison was washing his hands, Margaret McLain settled Vincent in the chair and clipped a bib around his neck. Vincent was physically small, but he had the stern, intimidating presence of a successful man accustomed to having his way. Outwardly, he possessed the virtues of evident education and meticulous dress that Morrison highly valued. If he wished to draw a connection between Vincent's excellent appearance and the oral corruption that made him so puzzling, Morrison had to pursue the implications of a face still pitted and scarred by the memory of acne. He rolled Vincent's sleeve, swabbed his arm, and tore the sterile covering from the syringe that had been waiting on his tray. Vincent didn't stop him until he had penetrated the ampule and begun to draw the anesthesia.

"Is that a general?"

"Of course," Morrison answered. "It's sodium pentothal."

"I don't want it."

"It'd be easier for both of us. I administer generals almost every day. It doesn't even have to be a shot. I can give you ether or ethyl chloride gas."

"No," Vincent said, "I won't have it. I prefer to stay awake."

"I'll have to pump you full of Novocain if that's the case."

"That'll be fine."

Morrison was not inclined to retreat behind a steady stream of mindless, happy chatter like many doctors. He directed Mrs. McLain to get eight syringes and an equal number of two-milliliter ampules of Novocain from the cabinet, while he himself disposed of the sodium pentothal, wheeled the analgesic unit into place on Vincent's left side, and checked the nosepiece and the pressure gauge.

"This is nitrous oxide — laughing gas. It'll help you relax."

"I'm relaxed enough," Vincent answered. "My stomach couldn't take it. Gas makes me sick."

"Nonsense. Nitrous oxide is extremely mild. It rarely causes any illness. You'd be conscious at all times. You may be sorry if you refuse."

"I doubt it." Vincent waved his hand in dismissal. "It's pure poison."

Morrison never failed to be surprised when a patient who needed extensive work balked at the use of anesthesia, though he had seen it many times. He called it superstition.

He sterilized Vincent's mandibular gum and prepared a syringe. Rather than the more common deep block, Morrison chose twin plexus injections for their greater protection. Forcing Vincent's mouth open wide, he pinched the gum hard with the thumb and forefinger of his left hand — his technique for drawing attention away from the point of entry — and jabbed the needle through the tightened skin near the left lateral incisor. He pulled the plunger back to affirm that he had not entered a minor blood vessel, then depressed it slowly until the cartridge was emptied. After repeating the procedure near the right lateral incisor, Morrison exited the room to await the Novocain's effect.

In advanced cases like Vincent's, multiple enamel surfaces are decimated, often on the adjacent sides of neighboring teeth. Among his four mandibular incisors, for example, there were no fewer than five cavities. The condition of his premolars and molars was almost as bad. The cavity of the maxillary right first molar had penetrated the enamel and dentin to the soft pulp at the center of the tooth, which causes the nerve swelling of toothache. So much tissue was destroyed that it would have to be temporarily plugged, and then capped with gold or porcelain at the follow-up appointment. Eleven other premolars and molars required similar treatment. The maxillary left wisdom tooth would have to be extracted, as would the mandibular right, which was impacted. Vincent had also developed gingivitis, a painful inflammation of the gums associated with poor hygiene. Dense plaque covered most of his enamel surfaces not eroded by cavities.

Upon Morrison's return, Mrs. McLain folded a towel to cover Vincent's eyes and adjusted the tip of the suction unit behind his lower gum. Morrison attached a diamond drill to his high-speed handpiece. He would pull the two wisdom teeth only after completing all the cavity restorations, so reducing the chance of impurities entering his incisions. He packed the area of the mandibular left second molar with gauze before he inserted the drill and his hand mirror.

Vincent stiffened at the whir and the initial impact, but Morrison helped him get accustomed to the pressure with several gentle bursts. Mrs. McLain began to mix silver amalgam filling, timing her progress carefully, since each preparation had to be discarded if not used within three or four minutes. Morrison bored to a conservative depth and removed his handpiece to exchange the diamond for a smoother carbide bur before piercing the dentin and entering the sensitive pulp. He packed the amalgam mixture, polished it with a steel bur, scraped away the remaining plaque, and moved on to the first molar.

Each time Morrison removed his handpiece to change accessories, Vincent would gnaw his lower lip, peeling back the layers of skin.

"That's a nervous habit," Morrison finally told him. "You'd be surprised how many patients need a stitch or two. You can't taste your blood, remember. And it's a difficult place to heal as well. I'd advise you to stop now."

Vincent closed his mouth, lifted a corner of the towel, and directed a defiant stare at Morrison, who was left holding his instruments in the air for several uncomfortable moments.

The restorations were without further incident until Morrison reached the right first premolar, another of the major pulp cavities that would have to be capped. As he bore into the black region with a diamond drill, the weakened tooth split vertically to a point somewhere below the gum line with an audible crack that made Vincent wince, though he could not have experienced pain. Morrison used his explorer to verify that the nerve was undamaged. He decided to apply a coagulant and postpone action until he had completed all the maxillary restorations, when he would extract the premolar along with the wisdom teeth.

Morrison had planned another pair of plexus blocks for the upper jaw. He sterilized the gum and injected near the left lateral incisor, yet Vincent complained before he could prepare a second syringe.

"That's about enough. I'm not a lab animal."

"It takes two shots to numb the entire jaw," Morrison answered.

"I've never heard of that."

"I can give you single injections from now on if you insist, but they're not fully effective in this kind of work."

"But you're only drilling, not pulling teeth," Vincent said, his speech beginning to slur. "I shouldn't even need Novocain."

"You most certainly should if the cavities are as deep as these. It's standard practice."

"Standard practice. Do you know what I think of standard practice?" Vincent laughed, waving his hand and wrist in a gesture of finality. When he lowered the towel over his eyes and folded his arms triumphantly across his chest, Morrison continued to stand idly for a minute, both mystified and angry.

The dual injections were merely a precaution, it was true. Novocain never remains completely localized. And the drill's water spray was designed to provide comfort without anesthesia. Vincent's mouth was reasonably well protected.

But Morrison considered the fractured premolar a different matter. It would soon grow intolerably painful unless it received a second dosage in accompaniment with the first maxillary injection. Still, Vincent protested as soon as Morrison tried to swab his lower gum.

"What the hell are you doing?"

"Don't worry, this is for the broken tooth. You'll need this one."

"I'll tell you when I need it."

"I'm afraid that may be a little late."

"Then I guess it'll be my mistake, won't it?"

Morrison's hands twitched. He could find no reply.

When he had to drill the unanesthetized right side of the upper jaw, Morrison used only fine carbide burs, but at each pulp cavity he could not help touching nerve tissue. Vincent began to sweat, the muscles tightening along the length of his body.

With four teeth remaining, Mrs. McLain was finally unable to meet the demand for amalgam mixture. Morrison's irritation at the delay was transferred effortlessly to Vincent. His eyes were drawn to the acne scars he found so repugnant. Both of Vincent's lips were badly chewed and bleeding freely by now, and he looked from underneath the towel with insolence and a studied nonchalance, as if wordlessly complaining about the wait.

"Why didn't you come to me at the first toothache?" Morrison suddenly asked. "How could you stand it? The pain must have been horrible."

"Toothaches? They're not so bad. They're overrated."

"Overrated! That's not what my patients tell me every day. When was the last time you brushed your teeth? Do you even remember?" Vincent laughed in reply. "Really, you can tell me that, can't you? Why don't you take care of yourself? Is it hard?"

"I'm a busy man. I don't have the time."

"I consider it a form of self-mutilation."

"Don't feel obliged to judge me, Doctor. Just go about your business."

Morrison resumed his work with the fresh preparation of amalgam, inspired by a dangerous new energy that contained none of his customary prudence. The coarsest diamond drills should be used only in conjunction with anesthesia, yet Morrison simply guessed at the extent of each remaining cavity and bored to the maximum depth without troubling himself about all the tiresome gradations to carbide burs. Why should he agonize if he took a little healthy enamel along with the decay? He hadn't wanted the case in the first place. And Vincent seemed to have welcomed the disease into his own mouth. Why should he be bothered by the thought of causing pain when Vincent himself was unconcerned? How could he respect a patient who wouldn't concede his trust to thirty years of professional experience? The sound of the drill was no longer a series of cautious bursts, but a single menacing drone. Vincent clenched and unclenched his fists spasmodically and buried the back of his head in the cushion.

When it came time to prepare for extraction of the maxillary left wisdom tooth and his offer of Novocain was again rejected with exasperating coolness, Morrison caught himself trying to force the needle past Vincent's outstretched hand. Mrs. McLain was staring at him strangely. Morrison dropped the loaded syringe into the sink and left the room.

He could hear Mrs. McLain pleading with Vincent.

"You must have Novocain. You're being foolish. Extractions are considered surgery. Some patients insist on general anesthesia, or even on going to the hospital. You'll be very sorry. Why don't you let me give you the injection?"

Vincent's response was inaudible, yet it was obvious that his attitude was unchanged. Morrison made himself a cup of coffee. The X-ray area was crowded with lab equipment and plastic cutaway models of teeth, but the waiting room was neutral and empty. Morrison pushed through the outer door and paced the floor for several minutes before he was calm enough to take a seat.

He considered refusing Vincent further treatment. The fractured premolar would have to be removed, of course, but the wisdom teeth did not really demand immediate attention. Vincent should have had them extracted fifteen years ago, when their growth began to misalign his molars.

But Morrison had committed himself. A dentist must live by his word. It was honor and pride. It was dignity, honesty, courage, and professionalism.

There is something about a dentist's chair that drives people toward the extremes of cowardice or bravado. Just after his fiftieth birthday, Morrison had undergone root-canal surgery to drain an abscess. Though he knew his dentist to be the finest available, and thoroughly understood the operation, he still could not escape the sensation of great vulnerability which he had recognized but vaguely in so many of his patients. It is frightening to have to place the power of pain in the hands of another.

But Morrison had also operated on half a dozen patients — religious zealots and supposed self-hypnotists — who refused anesthesia. Granted, each eventually demanded to be drugged, yet a few stood the scalpel for fifteen minutes and more without complaint. At bottom, anesthesia and even pain itself are subjective. While a two-milliliter dosage of Novocain is considered fully effective for an hour, for example, one person may writhe after ten minutes while the next may deny any discomfort after two or three hours. Morrison had to acknowledge that the best judge of Vincent's suffering was probably Vincent himself.

He reentered his offices nearly as relaxed as he had been at the start of the day.

"Where the hell were you?" Vincent asked.

"I think I'm entitled to a cup of coffee."

"Good for you. And what about me? I'm paying you to get me out of here as quickly as possible. Don't forget that. I can't afford to waste my time. Take your break after you've finished."

The fractured premolar must have been excruciating by now. And while one new filling is foreign, twenty are intolerable. But if on the other hand Vincent were trying to bait or intimidate him, then Morrison certainly could not understand his objective.

"As you like," he answered. "I'm not about to argue again."

When he applied pressure to the area of the maxillary left wisdom tooth, Morrison was pleased to discover that the last of the three injections was still largely effective. After sterilizing the gum, he packed it with gauze, directed Mrs. McLain in positioning the suction tip, and took his scalpel.

He made an incision down either side of the gum to the point below the crown where the roots begin to form an inverted V, then inserted an exolever underneath the tooth and out the back of its socket. Morrison had guessed that Vincent's gingivitis was a symptom of a general weakness of the gums, yet a few preliminary thrusts, using the jawbone for leverage, proved that the roots were firm. Vincent sank lower in the chair and tried to swallow, but Morrison judged that he felt little pain.

A small horizontal incision on either side of the gum allowed him to clamp the crown tightly with forceps. He yanked violently and the tooth came cleanly and easily. After moving the suction tip to draw the blood flow, Morrison searched for root fragments, packed the torn tissue loosely enough to allow for swelling, and sutured.

The mandibular anesthesia had worn off long ago. He manip-

ulated the fractured premolar in hopes that Vincent would surrender quickly, but despite the unnerving cracking noises, and
though he rocked his head in obvious discomfort, there was no
request for Novocain.

The worst damage was confined to the crown, so that the
roots were part of the larger section. Morrison extracted the
smaller piece and made vertical incisions along the roots. Because the gum in that region was particularly poor, he worked
with forceps alone, and was careful to clamp only the most solid
portion of the crown to prevent the tooth from shattering. Vincent began to bit Morrison's fingers convulsively during every
instrument exchange. He now sweated profusely. His hand
strayed nervously to pick at his facial scars while his gum was
being prepared for the final extraction.

"Have you changed your mind?" Morrison asked. "You won't
enjoy this one, I promise you."

Vincent removed the towel from his eyes.

The mandibular right wisdom tooth was impacted, having
erupted horizontally into the second molar without breaking the
surface of the gum. Morrison would cut on the underside of the
tooth until he could bend it upward in its socket. When the edge
of its crown was forced above the height of the second molar,
he would use forceps to extract it at an angle from its growth.

He began with a vertical incision along the second molar to
the depth of the lower edge of the wisdom tooth — actually its
side, had it erupted properly — and then cut horizontally toward the roots. After a quarter of an inch, Morrison inserted a
chisel through the gum and pushed upward, but could not raise
the tooth above the second molar. Vincent bit Morrison's fingers
sharply when he substituted the chisel for his scalpel — perhaps
only a sign that his jaws were cramping from being held open
almost three hours.

Vincent was pallid and his pupils were dilated, suggesting the
onset of shock. Lifting his knees toward his chest so that his
shoes were flat on the seat cushion, he wrapped his arms around
his body and hugged himself. He leaned toward the cuspidor as
he began swallowing blood, only to have Morrison pull him back
— the flow was severe, and he had to extract and suture as
rapidly as possible.

Morrison cut a quarter of an inch deeper and exchanged scalpel for chisel, but Vincent bit him again, so hard this time that it must have been malicious. When Morrison forced the tooth upward, Vincent nearly fainted at the violence of the effort. Morrison had failed again. Vincent gagged and strained for the cuspidor, but Morrison jerked him back and plunged his scalpel into the incision.

Choking, Vincent grabbed Morrison's wrist and held him firmly. His face was drained of blood, yet it was not contorted by pain. It was merely peaceful. Morrison suddenly saw it, the misshapen, mocking smile of a new satisfaction. Enraged, he broke free and drove his scalpel not along the underside of the tooth but straight down toward the jawbone with a mangling, sawing motion.

Mrs. McLain struggled with his arm, and then tried to wrestle him away. "Doctor! Doctor!"

SUSAN MINOT

Thorofare

(FROM THE NEW YORKER)

"I'M NOT ABOUT TO TRUST THIS GUY," Delilah said after the undertaker excused himself from the reception room. She craned her neck and peered down the hall after him. We could hear cabinets whining open and snapping shut.

"He can't find her," she said. My sister didn't like being waited on.

"Be quiet," I said. "He'll hear you."

"I don't care," she whispered, and gave me a frustrated look. "What's taking him so long?"

"Maybe after a while they lose track. Most people probably aren't left here so long."

"That's for sure," said Delilah, and rolled her eyes.

For a year and a half after our mother died, Dad had avoided the subject of her ashes, and they remained at the funeral home. Now, a month after remarrying, he asked me and Delilah, who was home after graduating from college, to pick them up.

Delilah resumed her watch, her mouth slack with fascination. I turned my back to her and went to the bay window. It was May, and across the street kids in a playground were having a muddy recess, pushing each other over and screaming. Inside, it was quiet. A few chairs were lined up against the wall. My heart was doing peculiar, anxious things.

"Finally," whispered Delilah behind me. I turned around. She was swinging her boot nonchalantly.

The undertaker came out with a white box. "Here you are, Miss Vincent," he said to me. I thought him rather young for an undertaker. He had beige hair, sprayed in place.

Delilah eyed him. "Are you sure it's her?"

He smiled without showing his teeth and didn't answer.

I took the box. It was cardboard, a little taller than an ice-cream carton, and narrower.

"How do you know?" Delilah asked him.

"There is a card," he said with a sigh.

Delilah and I exchanged glances. For a moment we stood there dumbly, unsure of how to proceed.

"Is that it?" I asked.

"Yes," he said. "Everything else has been taken care of."

By whom I couldn't imagine at the time. It wasn't exactly our father's thing.

Outside, the sun was weak. We got into the car Dad had bought when I moved home to take care of Minnie, the youngest of the seven of us. I handed the box to Delilah, in the passenger seat. "It's heavy," I said, trying to act normal.

We looked at each other. Her face was pale. She put the box in her lap. "I can't believe this is her," she said.

"It's not."

"I know." She stared off. "But you know what I mean."

We drove through the small streets of Marshport. It was the middle of the day, and there was little traffic — repair trucks, and station wagons with housewives in them. We wound along the shore, going in and out of sight of the ocean — Boston's tiny skyline far away to the south — passing the stone walls, the hidden mansions.

"Should we look inside?" I asked. I had the drugged feeling of being separate from myself, as if someone else's hands were on the steering wheel.

Delilah lit a cigarette and threaded the match through a crack in the window. She took a deep drag. I put out two fingers and she handed it to me. "O.K.," she said.

She untucked the top; it was flimsy, with a zigzag edge. She picked out a card and held it up in front of me. It said "Rose Marie Vincent" in script.

"Jesus," I said.

Delilah looked at the road. "Slow down, Sana," she said. "You're as bad as Gus." Our oldest brother, Gus, had cracked up the same car twice.

"What's it in?" I asked, keeping my eyes on the road.

"A Baggie." She slid it out by its knot. "Weird," she said. "It's all white chunks."

I shuddered. "It's the bones," I said.

She peered closer, undaunted. "You know, they kind of look like shells."

"Oh God, Delou," I said, and held out the cigarette, and without looking over at me she took it back.

The morning Mum died, I stood in the dim light of the TV room. Dad was a wreck, mute, his face bloated. The boys were on the couch, Gus in the middle, with each hand on a younger brother's knee, Sherman and Chickie staring dumbly ahead. I had just returned from visiting college friends to find our driveway crowded with cars. Two hours before, on her way to the market, Mum's car had been hit by a train. The shock had been absolute. I steadied myself, holding on to the low mantelpiece. I told Dad, "She wanted to be cremated." It came out level, flat.

No further devastation could have shown on his face. "She did?"

Everything was different — another world suddenly. My brothers looked as if all the air had been socked out of them. Minnie had been taken out of first grade to stay with some friends for the day.

"Yes, she wanted her ashes sprinkled in the thorofare. I remember her saying so up there last summer."

Dad looked at me with horror. People were passing by the doorway, mixing in the hall, whispering and then drifting away when they saw our dark conference. I remained through it all like some strange pillar — hollow and weightless. Back in the kitchen, Mum's friends were making ham sandwiches on our carving board. Men had their business suits on. Caitlin, the oldest, was on her way home from New York. Delilah had gone to Florida after Christmas. She didn't even know yet.

Ellen Grady, one of our only Catholic friends, was in the TV room with us. "I'm not sure cremation's allowed in the Church," she said. I looked at her. My mother was dead. I turned to Dad. "I know it's what she wanted." We were Catholic, like Mum. Though his family was Protestant, Dad had no religion. He didn't know where to look; he didn't know about any of this.

It turned out that the body had to be present at the funeral

Mass. We hid the casket by covering it with daffodils. They wanted a dress to put her in. Caitlin, Delilah, and I went through her closets. Caitlin pulled one from the hanger.

"But I love that dress," Delilah said. It was lilac blue with little block prints. "And they're just going to burn it."

"It was her favorite, though," Caitlin said.

We all stared at it, nodding.

Delilah put the ashes away in the sideboard in the dining room. The whirring in the kitchen was Pat, Dad's new wife, making dinner. When we were little, Pat had been a friend of Mum's. When Pat got divorced and went to work in town, Mum tried to fix her up with someone a couple of times, but it didn't work out. The summer after Mum died, Pat started asking Dad out to lunch.

When Dad got home from work, he went straight to the hall table. "We got Mum's ashes," I told him while he leafed through the mail.

He turned to me with a blank face. "Thank you," he said.

Delilah came around the corner. "Don't you want to see them?"

He cleared his throat. "Certainly," he said.

She led him off toward the dining room. "See?" I heard her say. "They kind of look like shells."

I went into the living room, where no one ever was. Pat had taken down the curtains to be cleaned, and the yellow sunset came flooding through the French doors. A new painting — one Pat had brought — hung over the couch. The rug was gone, and there was a polished wooden floor I'd never seen before. During the past year, when the house had been under my care, things had deteriorated. Already, Pat had painters in for the upstairs bedrooms, and Mr. Parsons had come to look at the rot on the front porch.

I sat on the arm of a chair. I couldn't make out what Dad and Delilah were saying, but I heard her voice working itself into a high pitch. Then I heard Dad say, "No." Immediately, Delilah was tearing up the stairs. "But she's my mother, too!" she cried.

Out in the hall I ran into Minnie, wide-eyed, with Sherman and Chickie hovering behind her.

"What's her problem?" said Chickie. At fourteen, he was the

youngest of the boys, gangly and awkward, with dark, nervous eyes. His hand plucked at tufts of hair.

Upstairs a door slammed. Sherman stood there, hulking, silent as usual. Down the corridor I saw Dad heading for the kitchen.

"Delilah thinks we should scatter some of Mum's ashes here," I told them. "Dad's not wild about the idea."

"Why not?" said Minnie.

"You never know, hon," I said.

"I thought we were bringing them to Maine," said Sherman, deadpan.

"We are," I said, and put my hand on his shoulder. It was rock-hard; he flinched.

We were leaving the next morning. Every Memorial Day weekend, we opened the house on North Eden. This trip, we were taking Mum's ashes to throw in the thorofare, the channel that ran between the islands.

Caitlin appeared on the stairs. "Are we fighting already?" She had come up that afternoon from New York, where she worked in an ad agency, and had changed into her regular clothes.

"It's Dad and Delilah," I said.

"Oh," Caitlin said, as if that explained it.

We went into the TV room to watch the news. Everyone was home that night, except for Gus, who was up in Maine already, in college. He was meeting us the next day at the North Eden ferry. I sat next to Chickie on the couch, and we put our feet up beside the neat stacks of magazines on the table. Minnie lay on the floor, and Caitlin tried to make conversation with Sherman. How was school? Fine. How was lacrosse? All right. I told her he was high scorer. "That's great," she said, hitting a pillow. "Good for you." Sherman kept his eyes on the TV. Chickie was flipping through *Life*. When he turned the pages, I saw how his fingers trembled.

About twenty minutes later Dad bellowed up the stairs for Delilah. We kept quiet in the TV room and listened.

"What?" came her suffering voice. She was probably collapsed on her bed.

"Come down here," said Dad.

"Why?"

"Come down here," he repeated.

Footsteps crossed the ceiling above us, then came thumping down the stairs. "What do you want?" she said.

"Come with me," he said matter-of-factly.

We heard her stop. "*Where*, Dad?"

He was perfectly calm. "Come along."

She let out a huge sigh and continued heavily down the steps. "I'm coming, but where?"

The screen door opened and they went outside on the terrace.

Caitlin leaned over to Minnie. "See where they're going." Minnie hopped up, and her pigtailed head disappeared around the door.

We waited till Minnie returned. "They're by Dad's garden," she said eagerly.

Caitlin took her by the arms and looked into her face. "What are they doing?"

"O.K.," she said, and went out again. This time she spoke from the hall. "They've got the box with Mum's ashes." We all got up and went into the hall.

We clustered around the window. Dad and Delilah were standing at the edge of the lawn. Behind them the spring trees made a light-green screen, and beyond it the ocean was flat. Dad held the box as Delilah reached inside. She pulled back her fist and flung some white bits over the garden. Dad's chin was drawn in against his Adam's apple, his mouth peculiar and tight. When Delilah turned back toward the house, we saw her dark, glassy eyes and ducked away before she caught us watching.

For dinner that night we had rack of lamb. Pat had made a frozen lemon soufflé for dessert. Somehow she kept her neat size-six figure, though Dad had already put on a few pounds.

We drove up in two cars. Caitlin and Minnie went with Dad and Pat in the station wagon. Delilah and I took the boys, who slept in the back the whole way. We had the box with Mum's ashes in our car.

Gus and his girlfriend, Sarah, were already at the ferry landing, sitting on their knapsacks. He gave me a bear hug.

"How'd you get here?" said Chickie, looking worried.

"Hitched."

"What," said Sherman when he saw Gus. "Are you trying to grow a beard?"

Gus shrugged amiably.

"Dad'll love that," said Delilah.

Gus put his arm around Sarah. "Well, good for Dad," he said.

As we were buying our tickets, Caitlin said, "I should have brought Harry."

"I thought you broke up," I said.

"We did," she said. "Kind of. I don't know what's going on."

The ferry was still running on the winter schedule. Despite the cold, we stood at the upper railing the whole way over, our hair and collars flapping, and pointed out certain islands to Sarah — Barnacle, Waterman's, the Dumplings — and passed the gong. The bay was rough and gray and flashing with sun. Pat stayed in the car and read magazines while Dad, who could never sit still, walked back and forth between her and us.

The lilacs had just come out in Maine, and forget-me-nots were tangled in the grass behind the laundry room. The house used to be a warehouse, set at the edge of a wide dock, with bay windows only inches above the water at high tide. There were signs of winter wear — the piling supports under the living room were awry; flooding had left a watermark on the wainscoting in the downstairs hall.

The next day, it was bright out and blustery. In the morning, Caitlin and I took our tea and sat on the box under the empty window boxes, out of the wind.

Delilah came out, being careful not to spill her mug of coffee. "She's in there making lobster gumbo already," she told us.

"Where are the boys?" asked Caitlin. She tilted her face to the white sky and closed her eyes.

"Still sacked out." Delilah put a cigarette between her lips and tried to light matches against the wind.

Through the railing we could see Dad down on the float getting the boat ready. "He wants to go as soon as they're up," I said.

"Which will be forever," said Caitlin, her eyes still shut.

I took Delilah's cigarette and lit it for her, crouching beside the shingles, and gave it back. "Is Pat coming with us?" I asked.

Delilah dragged on her cigarette and looked at me like I was crazy. "No. Why should she?"

"I don't know. I just thought maybe . . ."

Caitlin said, "Yah. I was wondering, too."

"No way," Delilah said. "Just the family. Sarah's not coming, either."

I looked at Caitlin. "Do you think you're getting any sun?"

"Yes," she said defensively.

"No way," said Gus, coming around the corner. He arched his back and yawned, stretching. "No . . . waay . . ."

Caitlin opened her eyes. "It's about time you got up," she said.

Usually, loading everybody into the boat was a major operation. We scrambled and fought for seats, balancing books and towels and the iced-tea cooler, arguing about where to have the picnic, ordering the boys to cast off, making Minnie do up her life jacket. Today we went through it as if we were stepping on eggshells.

Dad waited at the controls. Minnie crawled into Gus's lap, nestling in his bulky jacket. Delilah, with the white box, stood next to Dad. Chickie was still on the dock, his hair blowing in his eyes, keeping an unsteady hold on the bow railing while Sherman untied the stern. It was all done without a sound. Sherman tossed the rope in over the gas tanks and stepped stiffly in, looking down.

Caitlin said, "Sherman, aren't you going to be cold?" We had bundled ourselves in sweaters and had hats on; Sherman wore nothing over his flannel shirt. He said nothing and sat down heavily on the seat in front of the Plexiglas windshield.

"Sherman," she said again, her voice especially gentle. "It's going to be cold out there."

He folded his thick arms across his chest and gave her a neutral look. "O.K., Caitlin," he said.

Even though there were few boats in the harbor, Dad waited till we were well out of the moorings before pushing the boat into full throttle. The gray water sped by, the surface waves crisscrossing. Passing the first point, we saw the Washburns'

house, with its windows boarded up. When we entered the
wider thorofare, the stronger wind hit us with a blast. To
the north was the rolling shore of North Eden, and south were
the uninhabited islands, in a line toward the east: Driftwood,
Black Island, Fling, Storm Head.

The boat began to slow down. Sherman made a face against
the wind; Caitlin started scratching at something on her dun-
garees. The bow fell slightly, and Delilah looked back over the
stern, where the wake was flattening out. Dad, holding his chin
high, continued to look forward, checking for lobster pots. Gus's
hands were cupped over his mouth, warming them, his eyes cast
to the side. Chickie glanced back and forth between Dad and
where we were heading, to see which spot he'd choose. Tentatively, Minnie hoisted herself from Gus's lap and tried to look
interested in something over the side of the boat.

We puttered along this way slowly for a while.

"This is good," Delilah said, but Dad went on surveying the
surrounding water. I turned Minnie around and leaned her
shoulders against me.

The waves smacked the sides when the engine went into idle.
After Dad cut the motor, we spun slightly and dipped in and
out of the swells, and it was suddenly quiet except for the wind.
Chickie gave Gus a hand up off the floor. We turned to Dad.

Delilah was opening the flap of the box; Dad took it from her,
extracting the bag himself.

"All right," he said. "Minnie first." He held the bag from
underneath.

As I eased Minnie toward him, she hesitated. "What'll I do?"
she said.

Dad lowered the bag near the side.

I said, "Just take a handful, Min."

Caitlin smoothed one of her pigtails. "Just take a little, honey,
and throw it over."

"How?" Minnie held her palm up flat. Her clear eyes were
watering over.

"It's O.K.," said Gus. "Just take as much as you can."

Minnie looked at Dad and kept blinking. He held the bag out.

Chickie moved her aside. "Here," he said. "I'll go and show
her." His lanky hand went into the bag and grappled awk-

wardly. It looked for a moment as if he and Dad were struggling
with each other. Pressing his free hand against the side of the
bag, Chickie pulled out a handful of ashes. When he threw
them, low, the heavier bits landed scuttling in a line, and the
wind carried the finer white dust a little way through the air.
He bent down to Minnie. "There," he said in his trembling
voice. "See?"

Dad lowered the bag and she put in her tiny hand, drew out
a tight fist, and threw an exuberant overhand, releasing it late,
so it shot into the water just inches from the boat. She gave us a
pleading, embarrassed look.

"That was fine," I said, and touched her sleeve. "You want to
do it again?" She shook her head, chewing on her bottom lip.

"Sherman," Dad said. We were going by age now.

Sherman always had the strongest throw. When we skipped
rocks off the beach, his stone would go skittering farther than
anyone else's. He took his handful, keeping himself at a distance
from the bag, as if it were contaminated. He tossed the ashes
loosely and didn't bother to see where they landed.

Gus frowned in his direction and moved up. He fitted both
hands into the bag, pulled them out, and then let them go like
a golf swing, flinging the ashes in a great arc. With the wind,
they speckled down like rain.

"Wow," said Delilah facetiously.

She went next, keeping her back straight. Her features were
solemn and composed. She took two careful handfuls, one after
the other, and, lifting one foot off the floor as if she were
spreading grass seed over a lawn, sprinkled them over the surface of the water. She stepped out of the way for me.

I slid both hands into the bag and brought them out cupped
together in a bowl. Before letting go, I looked at the knobby
pieces and saw they weren't flat, like shells, but rounded and
porous, like little ruins. I leaned way out and let them pour off
the ends of my fingers, watching them sink in the dark water,
thinking, This is just like anything else you throw overboard —
the way it falls in slow motion and then suddenly it's gone, so
gradually you can't tell the exact moment it disappears from
sight.

Caitlin followed. She was graceful, efficient, staring at the water afterward, her eyebrows peaked, her lips pressed tightly together.

Dad took a handful, quickly, gave it a toss, then held the bag upside down over the water and shook it out. A fine white dust swirled through the air, and he shook the bag and shook it again till the plastic was clean. Then he swiftly balled it up with two hands and shoved it into his pocket.

We kissed each other then, or some of us did. I kissed Minnie under her eye, and Gus gave me his hand and squeezed. Caitlin and I probably exchanged looks — I only sort of remember — but there was Sherman apart, up near the bow, and Chickie nervously trying to smile. Delilah moved up to Dad, and he took her kiss on his cheek while he started up the engine. The sky was breaking up, and white swirls shone through like marble.

We sped back to the inner thorofare. Caitlin turned around to Dad, her hair wrapping across her face, and shouted, "Do you think it will get nice?" She pointed ahead.

"I know it will," said Dad, steering straight, his eyes slitted against the wind.

When we got back to the dock, the light had become less opaque and the air was warmer. Sunlight showed up with the sharpening shadows. We unloaded onto the dock, wind-tousled and strangely exhilarated. Dad went into reverse — he was dropping us off — and putted out by himself to leave the boat at the mooring. Up the ramp we went, in single file, feeling something lofty in our procession, hearing flags billow and snap, following one another's heels, no one with the slightest idea, at the moment we raised our heads and looked around, of where to go next.

WRIGHT MORRIS

Glimpse Into Another Country

(FROM THE NEW YORKER)

HAZLITT'S WIFE CARRIED A BROOM to ward off the neighbor's dogs as she walked with her husband down the drive to the waiting taxi. Too old now to attack, the dogs barked hoarsely from behind a screen of bushes. "I'll outlive them if it kills me," she remarked, and she stooped for the morning paper, flattened by the garbage pickup. "No ethnic food," she told Hazlitt. "You hear me? You remember what happened in Phoenix." From his shoulders, as he stooped to kiss her, she removed the gray hairs.

Hazlitt was reluctant to fly, anywhere, but he wanted something in the way of assurance — of life assurance — that he hoped to get from a specialist in New York. "If that's what you want," his own doctor, in San Francisco, had advised him, "and you can afford it, go get it." Could he afford it? He had that assurance from his wife. "You're worth it," she said.

She had made considerable fuss to reserve Hazlitt a seat at one of the plane's windows, which turned out to be near the center of the right wing. A stewardess helped him out of his coat, and held it while he felt through the pockets for his glasses. A woman with quick searching eyes came along the aisle to stop at his row, then turned to hiss at her companion. The habit of hissing at people had always dismayed Hazlitt.

The woman's hair looked as if she had just blow-dried it. The man with her, by appearance a cultivated person, wore a smart suede cap and carried their coats. His rather abstracted manner led Hazlitt to feel he might be a teacher, off to an academic

meeting. As he reached her side, the woman slipped between
the seats to the one beside Hazlitt, without glancing at him.
She registered his presence, however, as she would a draft from
the window, by shifting in the seat toward her companion. She
wore knit gloves. With one hand she clutched a paperback
book.

Hazlitt had not flown enough to know if her indifference to
him was part of the etiquette of plane travel, where so many
strangers were jammed in together: why start up something
with a person who might well prove to be tiresome? He himself
was guarded even with his colleagues at the university. The
woman at his side had an appealing intactness, and her profile
seemed intelligent. A perfume, or it might be a powder, was
faintly scented with lilac.

Advised to buckle his seat belt, he observed that the palms of
his hands were clammy. At the takeoff he faced the window
with closed eyes. Perhaps the tilted wing spared him the vertigo
that might have been part of the lift-off, and as the plane set its
course he caught glimpses of the far blue horizon. The woman
beside him browsed in a copy of the *New York Times,* picked up
in the airport. Her interest seemed to be in the ads. At one
point, he was screened off behind the paper but able to check
the market quotations on his side. Finished with the paper, she
stuffed it between the seats on her left, away from Hazlitt. He
thought that rude, since he made it a point to share newspapers
with his traveling companions. As she relaxed for a moment,
closing her eyes, he was able to appraise her profile further —
a little sharp to his taste, but attractive. From the pink lobes of
her ears he received faintly erotic signals.

Suddenly, perhaps feeling his gaze, she turned to look directly past him, as if someone had tapped on the window. Now
she would speak, he thought, but she didn't. She turned away,
with a birdlike quickness, and leafed through the pages of her
paperback book. Idle riffling — the sort of thing Hazlitt found
irritating. At the back of the book, she paused to read a few
words about the author, then turned to read the book's conclud-
ing page. That done, she read the next-to-last page, then the
one before it. As she read, she nibbled at the corner of her
lip.

Hazlitt was flabbergasted. He had discovered that the book she chose to read backward was *The White Hotel*. He could not fully believe what he had seen, yet there was no question he had seen it. She did manage to read most of the final chapter before turning the book back to its opening page, which she placed face down in her lap. What did she want now? Something to drink. Her husband raised his hand to signal one of the stewards.

Surely a more worldly traveler than Hazlitt would not have been so appalled by what he had witnessed. How justify this scanning of a book in reverse? Could it not be argued that a sensible person, of a sensitive nature, might want to know what was in store before making a full commitment? Perhaps, but the practice was new to Hazlitt, a sworn and outspoken enemy of speed-reading.

At the announcement that they were passing over Lake Tahoe, the woman leaned toward the window as if she might see it. Her seeming unawareness of Hazlitt had a calming effect on him. He made way for her. He was at pains not to be there. Leaning forward, she had crushed several pages of her book, but this too was a matter of indifference to her. She put the book aside to accept, from her companion, a news magazine. She leafed through the pages, then stopped to consider an article on crime, with illustrations.

"Oh, my God!" she exclaimed, crumpling the page, and turned to fix Hazlitt with an intense, green-eyed stare. Did she think him a criminal? It seemed to him that her eyes moved closer together. "There's no place to go!" she cried. "Just imagine!" She had ignored Hazlitt; now he felt cornered by her. "Where would *you* go?" she barked.

His lips were dry. He wet them, and said, "My wife and I were recently in Oaxaca — "

"*Mexico?* Are you crazy?" She saw that he might be. "There is *nowhere* . . ." Her voice trailed off. Her husband had placed his hand on her lap to calm her.

"I was at a party in the forties — " Hazlitt began.

"In the forties!" she cried. "Who lives in the forties?"

Fortunately, he divined her meaning. "The *nineteen*-forties — the party was in the East Seventies. Musicians, writers, composers, and so on. Do you remember Luise Rainer?" Clearly she did not. "At the time," he continued, "she was an actress — "

"You write?" she asked him.

Hazlitt did write scholarly articles; he asked himself if she considered that writing. "I was with a friend," he said, "a painter. We all agreed there was nowhere to escape to. The war was everywhere, or soon would be. Then one of them said, 'You know what? There *is* no *where*. All the wheres have vanished.' "

Perhaps the woman felt there was more to the story. Her lips parted, but she said nothing.

"We have friends in Buenos Aires," he went on, "but I would never go so far as to recommend it."

"It's like no *air*. That's what it's like. It's like there's less air."

"As a matter of fact — " began Hazlitt, but she had turned from him to her crumpled magazine. Carefully, as if she meant to iron it, she smoothed it out on her lap. "That book you were reading," he continued. "I've met the author. A very respectable chap." (Everything he was saying was the purest hogwash.) "I know that he would consider it a personal favor if you read his book as it was printed, from the front to the back."

What had come over him? In her green, unblinking stare he caught the glimpse of a chill that might excite a lover. She turned from him to lean on her companion, who peered over her frizzly hair at Hazlitt. The man wore tinted bifocals. His expression was mild. "My wife said you had a question?"

Returning his gaze, Hazlitt knew he had been a fool. "It's just that I happen to know the author, and took the liberty of speaking for him."

"He's crazy," said the wife. "Don't rile him."

Calmly the man removed his glasses and polished the lenses with a fold of his tie. Unmistakably, Hazlitt recognized one of his own kind. A physicist, perhaps, with those hairy fingers. Or a member of a think tank. "Theoretically," the man said, breathing on a lens, "there is something in what you say, but, as a practical matter, having bought the book my wife is free to read it as she pleases, or to ignore it. Wouldn't you agree?"

Particularly galling to Hazlitt was the way the fellow had

turned the tables on him. It was usually he who was the cool one, the voice of reason in the tempest, the low-keyed soother of the savage breast. Worse yet, this fellow was about half his age.

"Of course! Of course! Stupid of me. My apologies to Mrs. — "

"Thayer. I'm Dr. Thayer."

Across the lap of Mrs. Thayer, who shrank back to avoid him, Hazlitt and Dr. Thayer clasped hands, exchanged the glances of complicit males. If there was a shred of solace in it for Hazlitt, it lay in Mrs. Thayer's full knowledge of this complicity.

"Take the filthy book!" she said, thrusting it at him. "And read it any way you like!"

Hazlitt let it fall to the floor between them. He fastened his gaze on the glare at the window. Some time later, the stewardess, serving his lunch, had to explain to him how to pull out the tray from the seat in front of him, and pry the lid from his salad dressing.

Hazlitt would say for this woman — when he discussed it with his wife — that she maintained to the last his nonexistence. He remained in his seat until the plane emptied, then wandered about the airport. He caught a glimpse of Dr. Thayer, on one of the escalators, helping his wife into her coat. The sharpness of her elbows troubled Hazlitt. Thin and intent as a cat, she reminded him of someone. Was it his wife? She groped in her purse for a piece of tissue, pressed it to her nose.

In the taxi to Manhattan, Hazlitt was moved to chat a bit with the driver, but the Plexiglas barrier between them seemed intimidating. Through the tinted windshield, as they approached the city, the October evening skyline was like the opening shot of a movie. Hazlitt had often told his wife that if the sun never rose he might like city living. In the car lights the streets glittered like enamel. It pleased him to note, as they drew near the Plaza Hotel, the horse-drawn hacks lined up along the curb. One of the drivers was a young woman with pigtails, frail as a waif. She held a leather feed bag to the muzzle of her horse, whose pelt shone like patent leather where the harness had worn off the hair.

The hotel porter, elderly himself, took a proprietary interest in Hazlitt. He led him into the bathroom to explain that the knobs on the faucets might confuse him if he got up at night for a drink of water: they turned contrary to the usual directions. A sign of the times, Hazlitt thought.

He thanked the porter, then stood at the window listening to the sounds of the street. A warm, moist breeze stirred the curtains. The tooting horns put him in mind of the radio plays of the forties. Turning to phone his wife, he saw his reflection in the mirror on the closet door. Something about the light, or the mirror, altered the impression he had of himself. A pity his wife couldn't see it. He would call her later; it was early still in California, and such talk could make her uneasy. What she feared the most when he traveled without her was that he might do something foolish, if not fatal, and end up hospitalized where she could not get at him. As he washed his hands — taking care with the faucets — he remembered her final caution: not to walk the streets at night, but if he did, not to be caught without money. She had given him a hundred dollars in twenties on the understanding he was not to spend it, so that when the muggers looked for money they would find it.

Hazlitt meant to stroll a bit — he needed the exercise — but when he left the hotel the young woman with the pigtails and her black spotted horse were still there. Frequent tosses of the horse's head had spread oats on the street and sidewalk. Jovially, Hazlitt inquired, "This rig for hire?"

"That depends where you're going." She spoke to him from her perch in a tone of authority.

"Bloomingdale's," he said, "before it closes."

"That's where I'm headed," she replied, ignoring his playful tone, and watched him climb into the cab. Hazlitt must have forgotten the leisurely pace of a weary horse. He leaned forward in the seat as if that might urge it along. As they approached Bloomingdale's, he saw that peddlers had spread their wares out on the sidewalks.

The girl stopped the horse so that the hack blocked the crosswalk, and a stream of pedestrians swirled around it. As Hazlitt arose to step down from the cab, it teetered slightly, and he peered about him for a helping hand. One of the peddlers — a tall, swarthy fellow wearing a pointed hat made of a folded newspaper — had taken a roll of bills from his pocket to make change for a customer. This person, lights reflected in her glasses, peered up at Hazlitt with a look of disbelief. Did he seem so strange? A moment passed before he recognized Mrs. Thayer. She wore tinted, horn-rimmed glasses, and a babushka-like scarf about her hair, tied beneath her chin. To take her change, while holding her purse, she gripped one of her knit gloves between her teeth, where it dangled like a third hand. The sight of Hazlitt had, in any case, left her speechless. He could think of nothing better to do than slip one hand into his coat front and strike the comical pose of a public figure welcomed by an admiring throng. The tilt of the carriage may have led him to misjudge the step down to the street. He toppled forward, both arms spread wide, and collapsed into the arms of the peddler, knocking off his paper hat. Over the man's broad shoulder he caught a glimpse of Mrs. Thayer, her hand clamped to her mouth now in either astonishment or laughter. She was gone by the time Hazlitt's feet were firmly planted on the street.

The peddler, after recovering his hat, was remarkably good-humored about it. "She knows you, eh?" he said, giving Hazlitt a leer as he smoothed the rumpled front of his coat. Hazlitt pondered the query as he selected, from the peddler's display, a French-type purse for his wife, a woman reluctant to buy such things for herself.

"Don't you worry!" the peddler added. "She'll be back. I still got her three dollars!" From his wad of bills he peeled off several and passed them to Hazlitt, giving him the smile of a collaborator. "You O.K.?" he said, and steadied the older man's arm as he stepped from the curb.

In Bloomingdale's foyer, where the doors revolved and Hazlitt felt well concealed by the darkness, he paused to spy on the peddler. There was something familiar about him — a big, rough fellow who turned out to be so gentle. In his sophomore year at college, Hazlitt had been intrigued by a swarthy, bearded giant, wearing a faded orange turban and a suit coat over what appeared to be his pajamas, who used to cross the campus di-

rectly below the dormitory window on his way to a shack in the
desert wash. He walked with a limp, and carried a sack of groceries over his shoulder. As he passed beneath Hazlitt's gaze he
would crook his head around, revealing his dark, hostile expression, and then beam directly at him the wide-eyed, toothy smile
of a child beholding a beloved object. These extremes of tem-
perament were like theatrical masks of contrary humors slipped
on and off his face. Hazlitt learned that the man was a Sikh, one
of a sect of fiercely independent warriors in India. What had
brought him to California? Everything about him was out of
scale and seemed disconcerting — even his smile. There were
rumors that he kept his wife captive, that he trapped and ate
coyotes. But what did all of that have to do with Hazlitt spying
on a peddler from Bloomingdale's foyer so many years later?

Nevertheless, the incident had aroused him, agreeably. This
state, he thought, might be what his younger colleagues called
"having a buzz on" — an expression that had previously mystified him. He wandered about the store's crowded aisles. In the
cosmetic section, the customers and the clerks chattered like
birds in an aviary. They leaned to peer into mirrors as if uncertain who they were. Hazlitt paused at a counter displaying
bracelets set with semiprecious stones. A young woman with
dark bangs to the edge of her eyes spoke to him. She opened
the case to lift out several of the items. In her opinion, they cost
practically nothing — a special purchase at seventy-nine dollars.
He would have guessed a price a third of that, but he showed
no surprise. One by itself was very nice, she advised him, but
two or more enhanced their beauty. To illustrate, she placed
two about her broad wrist, above a hand with blunt fingers and
cracked nails.

"Very well," Hazlitt said, feeling nothing at all, and waited as
she wrote up the order. Was it cash or card? Card, he replied,
and searched it out in his wallet.

"Oh, I'm so sorry," she said, "but we don't take Visa."

Hazlitt's astonishment was plain. He wondered if it might be
a cunning revenge of the East on California. Would they accept
his check? Of course. As he filled one out, his wife's face mate-
rialized suddenly, then receded. He wrote so few checks that
she had cautioned him to make certain he did it correctly.

His driver's license was also needed, the clerk told him. Ah, he was from San Francisco? She had spent a summer with a friend in Carmel, where she nearly froze. Hazlitt explained that the summers might run cooler than the winters, which was why some people found it so attractive. She did not follow his reasoning, her attention being on other matters. "I've got to get this O.K.'d," she said. "Would you just like to look around?"

Hazlitt looked around. Having already spent so much money, he could do without further temptations. To get out of the crowded aisles he wandered into an adjoining department. Against a pillar he saw a canvas chair, apparently meant for the lover of horses: it was made with stirrups, bridles, bits and strips of harness leather. He sagged into it. Nearby, a TV screen glowed like the sun at a porthole. He made out the image of a dense throng of people moving about in a large, dimly lit building. The flowing garments of the women, the density of the crowd suggested it was somewhere in India. As his eyes adjusted, Hazlitt saw that the floor seemed to be strewn with bodies, to which the passing crowd was indifferent. Some were alone. Others were gathered in crumpled heaps. The milling of the figures among these fallen creatures gave the scene an unreal, dreamlike aspect. Were they dead? No, they were sleeping. The film gave Hazlitt a glimpse into a strange country where the quick and the dormant were accustomed to mingle. Perhaps, he thought, it was not the walkers but the sleepers who would range the farthest in their travels.

He was distracted by a stream of jabbering, excited people, most of them young, who hurried down the store aisles toward the front exit. Then, rather suddenly, the place was quiet. He delayed a moment, expecting further excitement, then came out of the shadows and returned to the jewelry counter. The clerk was not there. Other departments also appeared to be abandoned. Through the glass doors of a side entrance he saw hurrying figures and flashing lights. A young man in shirtsleeves, with a perplexed expression, ran toward Hazlitt, waving a flashlight. He took him by the arm and steered him down the aisle. "Out! Out!" he cried. "We're emptying the building!"

"The clerk still has my driver's license," said Hazlitt, but in his agitation the man ignored him. He urged him along through the empty store to where several policemen stood at the exit.

"The clerk has my driver's license!" Hazlitt repeated.

"Don't drive," the man replied. "Take a cab."

Police vans and patrol cars blocked off the street. He stood for some time under one of the awnings waiting for something dramatic to happen. The revolving beacons on the cars lit up the faces of the crowd like torches. Several men in helmets and olive-drab uniforms entered the building carrying equipment. Hazlitt heard someone call them a bomb squad. The awareness that he had no driver's license, no positive identification, touched him with an obscure elation. He strolled along with a noisy group of young people who had just exited from a movie, and they seemed to take his presence for granted. When someone asked him the time, he said, "Nearly nine," and was reminded that he had not yet called his wife. "You won't believe this," he would say, knowing she would.

To get his call so early in her evening startled her. "Where are you?" she cried. It was his custom to report the events of the day — or the nonevents, if so they proved to be — and this time he really had a story to tell. But, hearing the note of concern in her voice, he changed his mind. Any mention of the bomb scare would disturb her rather than amuse her.

He explained — feeling the need to be explicit — that he was in his hotel room, seated on the bed, facing the partially opened window. A cool breeze stirred the curtain. He asked her if she could hear the car horns in the street below. If she had been with him, he said, they would have gone to a play — she loved the theater. As she spoke to him — how well he saw her — she would be seated at the kitchen table, behind the lazy Susan, with its clutter of vitamin bottles, and several of the squat candle glasses set out in anticipation of the first seasonal storms and blackouts. Hazlitt knew so exactly just how it all was that he could hear the sound of the wall clock — stuffed with a towel to mute the ticking — and he could read the pressure (falling) on the barometer at her shoulder. He continued to talk, in a way that soothed her, about his short ride in the horse-drawn hack (a thing they had done together), and about the swarthy peddler

selling his wares on the Bloomingdale's corner — for some reason, he avoided mention of Mrs. Thayer — until she spoke up
to remind him that he was phoning from New York, at his own
expense, and not from his office at the college. Before he replied she had hung up.

He was aware, with the lights switched off, how the sounds at
the window seemed magnified. In the play of reflections on the
ceiling he glimpsed, as through a canopy of leaves, the faraway
prospect he had seen on the Bloomingdale's TV — bustling figures swarming soundlessly among the bodies strewn about a
station lobby. Somehow the spectacle was full of mystery for
him. None of this was a dream — no, he was awake; he heard
the blast of the horns below his window — but the dreamlike
aura held him in its spell until those sleeping figures arose to
continue their journey.

In the doctor's waiting room the next morning, Hazlitt faced a
wall of brightly colored children's paintings, goblinlike creatures with popped eyes, short stumpy arms, stiltlike legs. It was
his wife who once remarked that this was probably how most
children saw the world — like specimens under the lens of a
microscope. In the suspended time that Hazlitt sat there, he
held and returned the gaze of a purple-faced goblin, preferring
it to the pale, ghostly image of the old man reflected in its
covering glass.

The specialist's assurance, spoken at Hazlitt's back between
thumps on his ribcage, drew more from its offhand manner
than from what the man said: he showed little real concern.
Every hour, Hazlitt gathered, the doctor saw patients more de-
serving of attention. His assistant, a well-coiffed matronly
woman with sinewy legs and the profile of a turkey, shared with
Hazlitt her opinion that "a reprieve is the best one can expect,
at our age."

He was down in the street, flowing north with the current,
before he sensed that he was free of a nameless burden, and
seemed lighter on his feet. He crossed to Park Avenue for a
leisurely stroll through the Waldorf lobby, for the pleasure of
its carpet and the creak of expensive Texas luggage. Approaching Bloomingdale's again, he paused to reconsider the previous

evening's scene: Hazlitt himself teetering in the hack, the dark-skinned peddler in his paper hat, and Mrs. Thayer reaching for her change, with one of her knit gloves still dangling from her teeth.

Back at Bloomingdale's jewelry counter, he found that the girl with the bangs had the morning off. In her place, an older and more professional clerk requested some further identification before she could give him his license back with the bracelets. She reminded him that one couldn't be too careful. Last night's bomb scare — a telephone call from the Bronx — proved to be without foundation, but the entire building had had to be vacated. What was this country coming to, she asked him.

Before Hazlitt could reply, his attention was distracted by a display in the case he was leaning on — a short strand of pearls on a headless bust. Was it some trick of the lighting that made them seem to glow? "These are real?" he asked the saleswoman. They were real. Would he like to see something less expensive? Her implication piqued him, because it was accurate. She took the strand from the case and let him hold it. He knew nothing about pearls, but he was dazzled. He saw them on his wife — he saw her wide-eyed astonishment, her look of disbelief. "If it's not too inconvenient," he said, "I'd like to return the bracelets and take the pearls."

He had not troubled to ask the price, and the clerk gave him a glance of puzzled admiration. "We'll just start all over," she said, "but I'm afraid I'll have to ask you once more for your driver's license."

Right at that point, Hazlitt might have reconsidered, but he did not. From his wallet he removed a second blank check, and waited for the woman to present him with the bill. The sum astounded but did not shock him. Writing the numbers, spelling the sum out gave him a tingling sense of exhilaration. Again he saw his wife, seated across the table from him, gaze at him openmouthed, as she would at a stranger.

"This will take a few minutes," the clerk said, and went off into the crowded aisles.

Hazlitt's elation increased. He drummed his nails on the case as he peered about him. One might have thought that he had propositioned the clerk, that she had accepted and gone off to pretty up a bit and get her wrap. His exhilaration persisted as he moseyed about. In the bakery department, he flirted with the clerk who served him a croissant he could eat on the spot. Back at the jewelry counter, he found everything in order. Was there anything else? His wife kept her jewels in pouches, he said — would they have a small pouch? The woman found one, of a suedelike material, into which the pearls nestled.

He was out of the building, under an awning that dramatized his own reflection in the shopwindow, before he again remembered the incident with the peddler on Fifty-ninth Street. He wanted to ask him if Mrs. Thayer had come back for her change, but the fellow was not there.

In the early years of their marriage, while he was doing his graduate work in the city, Hazlitt had loved to walk up Fifth Avenue with his wife for lunch at the Met. The museum itself confused and tired her; she did not like mummies, or tombs, or religious paintings. But Hazlitt liked to watch the people as they strolled about looking at objects, the stance they assumed when contemplating an artwork. Secret transactions were encouraged there, he felt, and a burden of culture was enlarged or diminished. An hour or so of this spectacle always left him so fatigued he was eager for the comforts of the dim Fountain Court lunchroom, the buzz of voices, and the splash of water.

Heading for the museum now, Hazlitt was already at Seventy-eighth Street before he was aware of the almost stalled bumper-to-bumper traffic. Passengers riding downtown in the buses and cabs made no faster progress than those who were walking. Some waved and exchanged remarks with the pedestrians. Hazlitt sauntered along, hardly caring that it had started to drizzle. Puddles had formed on the steps of the Met, and the sleeves and shoulders of his coat were wet. He checked the coat, then strolled about in a crowd like that in Grand Central Terminal. Just off the lobby, to the right, a new book department was jammed with shoppers. Hazlitt was attracted by the displays and the brilliant lights. On one of the tables, someone had opened, and left, a large volume — Fauve paintings, as bright as Christmas candy. Across the table another browser, sniffling slightly, her face partially veiled by the hood of a transparent slicker, had paused to dip into a collection of van Gogh's letters. She read the last in the book, which she seemed to like; she tried the next-to-last, then the next. Her slicker clearly revealed the unfortunate S-curve of her posture, and the purse that she clutched to her forward-thrusting abdomen. She pressed a wad of tissue to her nose as she sneezed.

Hazlitt wore a tweedy wool hat that concealed, his wife insisted, his best features. Mrs. Thayer passed so close behind him that he felt and heard the brush of her slicker. Was it possible that she found his reappearance as unsurprising as he found hers? Then he saw her at a distance, looking at cards, and her cheeks appeared flushed. It troubled him that she might have a fever. The short-sleeved dress she wore under her transparent raincoat exposed her thin arms. Later, in one of the admission lines, he watched her remove one of her knit gloves by gripping the tips of the fingers with her teeth, then tugging on them like a puppy. Hadn't her husband explained to her about germs?

Although it was still early, and Hazlitt was not fatigued, he made his way toward the Fountain Court lunchroom. He was standing at the entrance for a moment or two before he noticed the renovation. The dusky pool and its sculptured figures were gone. The basin was now a mere sunken pit, of a creamy color without shadows, and it was already bustling with diners crowding its tables. Instead of the refreshing coolness and splash of the water, there was the harsh clatter of plates and cutlery. Hazlitt just stood there, until he was asked to move. There was a bar to his right — he could have used a drink — but the flood of creamy light depressed him. He backed away, and out of long habit found the stairway that led down to the basement.

The dark and cool lavatory in this wing of the building used to be one of Hazlitt's regular stops. The high windows were near a playground, and he could often hear the shrill cries of the children outside. He thought he heard them again now as he opened the door, but the babble stopped as he entered the washroom. Six or seven small boys of assorted colors and sizes, their arms and faces smeared with gobs of white lather, stood facing the mirror at the row of washbowls. Their wide-eyed, soapy faces seemed to stare at Hazlitt from an adjoining room.

The stillness, like that of a silent movie, was broken only by the sound of lapping water. A thin film of water covered the tiles at Hazlitt's feet.

As if he found this circumstance more or less normal, he crossed the room to the nearest booth and pushed open the door. A youth, older than the others, was crouched on the rear of the fixture with his feet on the bowl's edge. With the thumb of his right hand he depressed the handle. The water spilled evenly from the rim of the clogged bowl to splash on the floor.

In the dark of the booth, Hazlitt saw little but the cupped whites of the boy's eyes. The youth raised his free hand slowly to his face as if to wipe away a lingering expression. Something in this gesture, like that of a mime, revealed to Hazlitt that the boy was stoned. In the deep void of his expanded pupils was all the *where* that the world was missing. The eyes did not blink. Hazlitt turned from him to face the mirror, and the boys, who had formed a circle around him. One had opened his shirt to expose his torso, creamy with lather. With the light behind them, all Hazlitt saw was the patches of white, like slush on pavement. Still, it pleased him to have their close attention.

The smallest boy thrust a hand toward him, its wet palm up. "Trick or treat," he said gravely. Two of those beside him hooted like crows.

"Well, let's see," Hazlitt said, and drew some coins from his pocket. He exposed them to the light, the silver coins glinting, just as the boy gave his hand a slap from the bottom. The coins flew up, scattering, then fell soundlessly into the film of water.

"Hey, man, that's no treat!" the boy scoffed, and he rolled his eyes upward.

From the pocket of his jacket Hazlitt withdrew the suede pouch; he loosened the noose and let the string of pearls fall into the boy's coral palm. How beautiful they were, as if just fished from the deep! The boy's hand closed on them like a trap; he made a movement toward the door as one of the others grabbed him. Down they both went, slippery as eels, with their companions kicking and pulling at them. They thrashed about silently at Hazlitt's feet like one writhing, many-limbed monster. He was able to leave unmolested and track down the hall in his squishy shoes.

In the gift shop off the lobby he bought a pin, of Etruscan design, that he felt his wife would consider a sensible value. Carrying his coat — the drizzle had let up, and the humid air seemed warm — he walked south under the trees edging the park to the Seventy-second Street exit. Held up by the traffic light, he stood breathing the fumes of a bus and listening to the throb of its motor. At a window level with his head, one of the riders tapped sharply on the glass. Hazlitt was hardly an arm's length away, but he saw the woman's face only dimly through the rain-streaked window. What appeared to be tears might have been drops of water. The close-set green eyes, as close together as ever, were remarkably mild, and gave him all the assurance he needed. As he stared, she put a wadded tissue to her nose, then raised her gloved hand, the palm toward him, to slowly wag the chewed fingertips. Its air brakes hissing, the bus carried her away.

JOYCE CAROL OATES

Nairobi

(FROM THE PARIS REVIEW)

EARLY SATURDAY AFTERNOON the man who had introduced himself as Oliver took Ginny to several shops on Madison Avenue above 70th Street to buy her what he called an appropriate outfit. For an hour and forty-five minutes she modeled clothes, watching with critical interest her image in the three-way mirrors, unable to decide if this was one of her really good days or only a mediocre day. Judging by Oliver's expression she looked all right, but it was difficult to tell. The salesclerks saw too many beautiful young women to be impressed, though one told Ginny she envied her her hair — not just that shade of chestnut red but the thickness too. In the changing room she told Ginny that her own hair was "coming out in handfuls" but Ginny told her it didn't show. It will begin to show one of these days, the salesgirl said.

Ginny modeled a green velvet jumpsuit with a brass zipper and oversized buckles, and an Italian knit dress with bunchy sleeves in a zigzag pattern of beige, brown, and cream, and a ruffled organdy "tea dress" in pale orange, and a navy-blue blazer made of Irish linen, with a pleated white linen skirt and a pale blue silk blouse. Assuming she could only have one costume, which seemed to be the case, she would have preferred the jumpsuit, not just because it was the most expensive outfit (the price tag read $475) but because the green velvet reflected in her eyes. Oliver decided on the Irish linen blazer and the skirt and blouse, however, and told the salesclerk to remove the tags and to pack up Ginny's own clothes, since she intended to wear the new outfit.

Strolling uptown, he told her that with her hair down like
that, and her bangs combed low on her forehead, she looked
like a "convent schoolgirl." In theory, that was. Tangentially.

It was a balmy, windy day in early April. Everyone was out.
Ginny kept seeing people she almost knew, Oliver waved hello
to several acquaintances. There were baby buggies, dogs being
walked, sports cars with their tops down. In shop windows —
particularly in the broad windows of galleries — Ginny's reflection in the navy-blue blazer struck her as unfamiliar and quirky
but not bad: the blazer with its built-up shoulders and wide
lapels was more stylish than she'd thought at first. Oliver too
was pleased. He had slipped on steel-frame tinted glasses. He
said they had plenty of time. A pair of good shoes — really good
shoes — might be an idea.

But first they went into a jewelry boutique at 76th Street,
where Oliver bought her four narrow silver bracelets, engraved
in bird and animal heads, and a pair of conch-shaped silver
earrings from Mexico. Ginny slipped her gold studs out and put
on the new earrings as Oliver watched. Doesn't it hurt to force
those wires through your flesh? He was standing rather close.

No, Ginny said. My earlobes are numb, I don't feel a thing.
It's easy.

When did you get your ears pierced? Oliver asked.

Ginny felt her cheeks color slightly — as if he were asking a
favor of her and her instinct wasn't clear enough, whether to
acquiesce or draw away just perceptibly. She drew away, still
adjusting the earrings, but said: I don't have any idea, maybe I
was thirteen, maybe twelve, it was a long time ago. We all went
out and had our ears pierced.

In a salon called Michel's she exchanged her chunky-heeled
red shoes for a pair of kidskin sandals that might have been the
most beautiful shoes she'd ever seen. Oliver laughed quizzically
over them: they were hardly anything but a few straps and a
price tag, he told the salesman, but they looked like the real
thing, they were what he wanted. The salesman told Oliver that
his taste was "unerring."

Do you want to keep your old shoes? Oliver asked Ginny.

Of course, Ginny said, slightly hurt, but as the salesman was
packing them she changed her mind. No, the hell with them,

she said. They're too much trouble to take along. — Which she
might regret afterward: but it was the right thing to say at that
particular moment.

In the cab headed west and then north along the park, Oliver
gave her instructions in a low, casual voice. The main thing was
that she should say very little. She shouldn't smile unless it was
absolutely necessary. While he and his friends spoke — if they
spoke at any length, he couldn't predict Marguerite's attitude
— Ginny might even drift away, pick up a magazine and leaf
through it if something appropriate was available, not nervously, just idly, for something to do, as if she were bored; better
yet, she might look out the window or even step out on the
terrace, since the afternoon was so warm. Don't even look at me,
Oliver said. Don't give the impression that anything I say —
anything the three of us say — matters very much to you.

Yes, said Ginny.

The important thing, Oliver said, squeezing her hand and
releasing it, is that you're basically not concerned. I mean
with the three of us. With Marguerite. With anyone. Do you
understand?

Yes, said Ginny. She was studying her new shoes. Kidskin in
a shade called "vanilla," eight straps on each shoe, certainly the
most beautiful shoes she'd ever owned. The price had taken her
breath away too. She hadn't any questions to ask Oliver.

When Ginny had been much younger — which is to say, a few
years ago, when she was new to the city — she might have had
some questions to ask. In fact she had had a number of questions to ask, then. But the answers had invariably disappointed.
The answers had contained so much less substance than her
own questions, she had learned, by degrees, not to ask.

So she told Oliver a second time, to assure *him:* Of course I
understand.

The apartment building they entered at Fifth and 88th was
older than Ginny might have guessed from the outside — the
mosaic murals in the lobby were in a quaint ethereal style unknown to her. Perhaps they were meant to be amusing, but she
didn't think so. It was impressive that the uniformed doorman
knew Oliver, whom he called "Mr. Leahy," and that he was so

gracious about keeping their package for them while they visited upstairs; it was impressive that the black elevator operator nodded and murmured hello in a certain tone. Smiles were measured and respectful all around, but Ginny didn't trouble to smile; she knew it wasn't expected of her.

In the elevator — which was almost uncomfortably small — Oliver looked at Ginny critically, standing back to examine her from her toes upward and finding nothing wrong except a strand of hair or two out of place. The Irish linen blazer was an excellent choice, he said. The earrings too. The bracelets. The shoes. He spoke with assurance though Ginny had the idea he was nervous, or excited. He turned to study his own reflection in the bronze-frosted mirror on the elevator wall, facing it with a queer childlike squint. This was his "mirror face," Ginny supposed, the way he had of confronting himself in the mirror so that it wasn't *really* himself but a certain habitual expression that protected him. Ginny hadn't any mirror face herself. She had gone beyond that, she knew better, those childish frowns and half-smiles and narrowed eyes and heads turned coyly or hopefully to one side — ways of protecting her from seeing "Ginny" when the truth of "Ginny" was that she required being seen head-on. But it would have been difficult to explain to another person.

Oliver adjusted his handsome blue-striped cotton tie and ran his fingers deftly through his hair. It was pale, fine, airily colorless hair, blond perhaps, shading into premature silver, rather thin, Ginny thought, for a man his age. (She estimated his age at thirty-four, which seemed "old" to her in certain respects, but she knew it was reasonably "young" in others.) Oliver's skin was slightly coarse; his nose wide at the bridge, and the nostrils disfigured by a few dark hairs that should have been snipped off; his lower jaw was somewhat heavy. But he was a handsome man. In his steel-rimmed blue-tinted glasses he was a handsome man, and Ginny saw for the first time that they made an attractive couple.

Don't trouble to answer any questions they might ask, Oliver said. In any case the questions won't be serious — just conversation.

I understand, Ginny said.

A Hispanic maid answered the door. The elevator and the corridor had been so dimly lit, Ginny wasn't prepared for the flood of sunlight in the apartment. They were on the eighteenth floor overlooking the park and the day was still cloudless.

Oliver introduced Ginny to his friends Marguerite and Herbert — the last name sounded like Crews — and Ginny shook hands with them unhesitatingly, as if it were a customary gesture with her. The first exchanges were about the weather. Marguerite was vehement in her gratitude since the past winter, January in particular, had been uncommonly long and dark and depressing. Ginny assented without actually agreeing. For the first minute or two she felt thrown off balance, she couldn't have said why, by the fact that Marguerite Crews was so tall a woman — taller even than Ginny. And she was, or had been, a very beautiful woman as well, with a pale olive-dark complexion and severely black hair parted in the center of her head and fixed in a careless knot at the nape of her neck.

Oliver was explaining apologetically that they couldn't stay. Not even for a drink, really: they were in fact already late for another engagement in the Village. Both the Crewses expressed disappointment. And Oliver's plans for the weekend had been altered as well, unavoidably. At this announcement the disappointment was keener, and Ginny looked away before Marguerite's eyes could lock with hers.

But Oliver was working too hard, Marguerite protested.

But he *must* come out to the Point as they'd planned, Herbert said, and bring his friend along.

Ginny eased discreetly away. She was aloof, indifferent, just slightly bored, but unfailingly courteous: a mark of good breeding. And the Irish linen blazer and skirt were just right.

After a brief while Herbert Crews came over to comment on the view and Ginny thought it wouldn't be an error to agree: the view of Central Park was, after all, something quite real. He told her they'd lived here for eleven years "off and on." They traveled a good deal, he was required to travel almost more than he liked, being associated with an organization Ginny might have heard of — the Zieboldt Foundation. He had just returned from Nairobi, he said. Two days ago. And still feeling the strain — the fatigue. Ginny thought that his affable talkative "social" manner showed not the least hint of fatigue but did not make this observation to Herbert Crews.

She felt a small pinprick of pity for the way Marguerite Crews's collarbones showed through her filmy muslin Indian blouse, and for the extreme thinness of her waist (cinched tight with a belt of silver coins or medallions), and for the faint scolding voice — so conspicuously a "voice" — with which she was speaking to Oliver. She saw that Oliver, though smiling nervously, and standing in a self-conscious pose with the thumb of his right hand hooked in his sports coat pocket, was enjoying the episode very much — she noted for the first time something vehement and cruel though at the same time unmistakably boyish in his face. Herbert Crews was telling her about Nairobi but she couldn't concentrate on his words. She was wondering if it might be proper to ask where Nairobi was — she assumed it was a country somewhere in Africa — but Herbert Crews continued, speaking now with zest of the wild animals, including great herds of "the most exquisitely beautiful gazelles," in the Kenya preserves. Had she ever been there, he asked. No, Ginny said. Well, said Herbert, nodding vigorously, it really *is* worth it. Next time Marguerite promised to come along.

Ginny heard Oliver explain again that they were already late for an appointment in the Village, unfortunately they couldn't stay for a drink, yes it was a pity but he hoped they might do it another time: with which Marguerite warmly agreed. Though it was clearly all right for Oliver and Ginny to leave now, Herbert Crews was telling her about the various animals he'd seen — elands, giraffes, gnus, hippopotami, crocodiles, zebras, "feathered monkeys," impalas — he had actually eaten impala and found it fairly good. But the trip was fatiguing and his business in Nairobi disagreeable. He'd discovered — as in fact the Foundation had known from certain clumsily fudged reports — that the microbiological research being subsidized there had not only come to virtually nothing, but that vast sums of money had "disappeared" into nowhere. Ginny professed to feel some sympathy though at the same time, as she said, she wasn't surprised. Well, she said, easing away from Herbert Crews's side, that seems to be human nature, doesn't it. All around the world.

Americans and Swedes this time, Herbert Crews said —
equally taken in.

It couldn't be avoided that Herbert tell Oliver what he'd been
saying — Oliver in fact seemed to be interested, he might have
had some indirect connection with the Foundation himself —
but unfortunately they were late for their engagement downtown, and within five minutes they were out of the apartment
and back in the elevator going down.

Oliver withdrew a handkerchief from his breast pocket, un-
folded it, and carefully wiped his forehead. Ginny was studying
her reflection in the mirror and felt a pinprick of disappointment — her eyes looked shadowed and tired, and her hair
wasn't really all that wonderful, falling straight to her shoulders.
Though she'd shampooed it only that morning, it was already
getting dirty — the wind had been so strong on their walk up
Madison.

On Fifth Avenue, in the gusty sunlight, they walked together
for several blocks. Ginny slid her arm through Oliver's as if they
were being watched, but at an intersection they were forced to
walk at different paces and her arm slipped free. It was time in
any case to say good-bye: she sensed that he wasn't going to ask
her, even out of courtesy, to have a drink with him: and she had
made up her mind not to feel even tangentially insulted. After
all, she hadn't been insulted.

He signaled a cab for her. He handed over the pink cardboard box with her denim jumper and sweater in it and shook
her hand vigorously. You were lovely up there, Oliver said —
just perfect. Look, I'll call you, all right?

She felt the weight, the subtle dizzying blow, of the "were."
But she thanked him just the same. And got into the cab. And
wasn't so stricken by a sudden fleeting sense of loss — of loss
tinged with a queer cold sickish knowledge — that, as the cab
pulled away into the traffic stream, she couldn't give him a final
languid wave of her hand, and even shape her mouth into a
puckish kiss. All she had really lost, in a sense, was her own pair
of shoes.

CYNTHIA OZICK

Rosa

(FROM THE NEW YORKER)

ROSA LUBLIN, A MADWOMAN and a scavenger, gave up her store
— she smashed it up herself — and moved to Miami. It was a
mad thing to do. In Florida she became a dependent. Her niece
in New York sent her money and she lived among the elderly,
in a dark hole, a single room in a "hotel." There was an ancient
dresser-top refrigerator and a one-burner stove. Over in a corner a round oak table brooded on its heavy pedestal, but it was
only for drinking tea. Her meals she had elsewhere, in bed or
standing at the sink — sometimes toast with a bit of sour cream
and half a sardine, or a small can of peas heated in a Pyrex mug.
Instead of maid service there was a dumbwaiter on a shrieking
pulley. On Tuesdays and Fridays it swallowed her meager bags
of garbage. Squads of dying flies blackened the rope. The sheets
on her bed were just as black — it was a five-block walk to the
laundromat. The streets were a furnace, the sun an executioner.
Every day without fail it blazed and blazed, so she stayed in her
room and ate two bites of a hard-boiled egg in bed, with a
writing board on her knees; she had lately taken to composing
letters.

She wrote sometimes in Polish and sometimes in English, but
her niece had forgotten Polish; most of the time Rosa wrote to
Stella in English. Her English was crude. To her daughter
Magda she wrote in the most excellent literary Polish. She wrote
on the brittle sheets of abandoned stationery that inexplicably
turned up in the cubbyholes of a blistered old desk in the lobby.
Or she would ask the Cuban girl in the receptionist's cage for a

piece of blank billing paper. Now and then she would find a clean envelope in the lobby bin; she would meticulously rip its seams and lay it out flat: it made a fine white square, the fresh face of a new letter.

The room was littered with these letters. It was hard to get them mailed — the post office was a block farther off than the laundromat, and the hotel lobby's stamp machine had been marked OUT OF ORDER for years. There was an oval tin of sardines left open on the sink counter since yesterday. Already it smelled vomitous. She felt she was in hell. "Golden and beautiful Stella," she wrote to her niece. "Where I put myself is in hell. Once I thought the worst was the worst, after that nothing could be the worst. But now I see, even after the worst there's still more." Or she wrote: "Stella, my angel, my dear one, a devil climbs into you and ties up your soul and you don't even know it."

To Magda she wrote: "You have grown into a lioness. You are tawny and you stretch apart your furry toes in all their power. Whoever steals you steals her own death."

Stella had eyes like a small girl's, like a doll's. Round, not big but pretty, bright skin underneath, fine pure skin above, tender eyebrows like rainbows, and lashes as rich as embroidery. She had the face of a little bride. You could not believe from all this beauty, these doll's eyes, these buttercup lips, these baby's cheeks, you could not believe in what harmless containers the bloodsucker comes.

Sometimes Rosa had cannibal dreams about Stella: she was boiling her tongue, her ears, her right hand, such a fat hand with plump fingers, each nail tended and rosy, and so many rings, not modern rings but old-fashioned junk-shop rings. Stella liked everything from Rosa's junk shop, everything used, old, lacy with other people's history. To pacify Stella, Rosa called her Dear One, Lovely, Beautiful; she called her Angel; she called her all these things for the sake of peace, but in reality Stella was cold. She had no heart. Stella, already nearly fifty years old, the Angel of Death.

The bed was black, as black as Stella's will. After a while Rosa had no choice, she took a bundle of laundry in a shopping cart and walked to the laundromat. Though it was only ten in the morning, the sun was killing. Florida, why Florida? Because here they were shells like herself, already fried from the sun. All the same she had nothing in common with them. Old ghosts, old socialists: idealists. The Human Race was all they cared for. Retired workers, they went to lectures, they frequented the damp and shadowy little branch library. She saw them walking with Tolstoy under their arms, with Dostoevsky. They knew good material. Whatever you wore they would feel between their fingers and give a name to: faille, corduroy, shantung, jersey, worsted, velours, crepe. She heard them speak of bias, grosgrain, the "season," the "length." Yellow they called mustard. What was pink to everyone else to them was sunset; orange was tangerine; red was hot tomato. They were from the Bronx, from Brooklyn, lost neighborhoods, burned out. A few were from West End Avenue. Once she met a former vegetable-store owner from Columbus Avenue; his store was on Columbus Avenue, his residence not far, on West Seventieth Street, off Central Park. Even in the perpetual garden of Florida, he reminisced about his flowery green heads of romaine lettuce, his glowing strawberries, his sleek avocados.

It seemed to Rosa Lublin that the whole peninsula of Florida was weighted down with regret. Everyone had left behind a real life. Here they had nothing. They were all scarecrows, blown about under the murdering sunball with empty ribcages.

In the laundromat she sat on a cracked wooden bench and watched the round porthole of the washing machine. Inside, the surf of detergent bubbles frothed and slapped her underwear against the pane.

An old man sat cross-legged beside her, fingering a newspaper. She looked over and saw that the headlines were all in Yiddish. In Florida the men were of higher quality than the women. They knew a little more of the world, they read newspapers, they lived for international affairs. Everything that happened in the Israeli Knesset they followed. But the women only recited meals they used to cook in their old lives — kugel, pirogen, latkes, blintzes, herring salad. Mainly the women thought about their hair. They went to hairdressers and came out into the brilliant day with plantlike crowns the color of zinnias. Sea-green paint on the eyelids. One could pity them: they were in love with rumors of their grandchildren, Katie at Bryn Mawr, Jeff at Princeton. To the grandchildren Florida was a slum, to Rosa it was a zoo.

She had no one but her cold niece in Queens, New York.

"Imagine this," the old man next to her said. "Just look, first he has Hitler, then he has Siberia, he's in a camp in Siberia! Next thing he gets away to Sweden, then he comes to New York and he peddles. He's a peddler, by now he's got a wife, he's got kids, so he opens a little store — just a little store, his wife is a sick woman, it's what you call a bargain store — "

"What?" Rosa said.

"A bargain store on Main Street, a place in Westchester, not even the Bronx. And they come in early in the morning, he didn't even hang out his shopping bags yet, robbers, muggers, and they choke him, they finish him off. From Siberia he lives for this day!"

Rosa said nothing.

"An innocent man alone in his store. Be glad you're not up there anymore. On the other hand, here it's no paradise neither. Believe me, when it comes to muggers and stranglers there's no utopia nowhere."

"My machine's finished," Rosa said. "I have to put in the dryer." She knew about newspapers and their evil reports: a newspaper item herself. WOMAN AXES OWN BIZ. Rosa Lublin, 59, owner of a secondhand furniture store on Utica Avenue, Brooklyn, yesterday afternoon deliberately demolished . . . The *News* and the *Post*. A big photograph, Stella standing near with her mouth stretched and her arms wild. In the *Times*, six lines.

"Excuse me, I notice you speak with an accent."

Rosa flushed. "I was born somewhere else, not here."

"I also was born somewhere else. You're a refugee? Berlin?"

"Warsaw."

"I'm also from Warsaw! Nineteen-twenty I left. Nineteen-six I was born."

"Happy birthday," Rosa said. She began to pull her things out of the washing machine. They were twisted into each other like mixed-up snakes.

"Allow me," said the old man. He put down his paper and

helped her untangle. "Imagine this," he said. "Two people from Warsaw meet in Miami, Florida. In nineteen-ten I didn't dream of Miami, Florida."

"My Warsaw isn't your Warsaw," Rosa said.

"As long as your Miami, Florida, is my Miami, Florida." Two whole rows of glinting dentures smiled at her; he was proud to be a flirt. Together they shoved the snarled load into the dryer. Rosa put in two quarters and the thundering hum began. They heard the big snaps on the belt of her dress with the blue stripes, the one that was torn in the armpit, under the left sleeve, clanging against the caldron's metal sides.

"You read Yiddish?" the old man said.

"No."

"You can speak a few words maybe?"

"No." My Warsaw isn't your Warsaw. But she remembered her grandmother's cradle-croonings: her grandmother was from Minsk. *Unter Reyzls vigele shteyt a klor-vays tsigele.* How Rosa's mother despised those sounds! When the drying cycle ended, Rosa noticed that the old man handled the clothes like an expert. She was ashamed for him to touch her underpants. *Under Rosa's cradle there's a clear-white little goat . . .* But he knew how to find a sleeve, wherever it might be hiding.

"What is it," he asked, "you're bashful?"

"No."

"In Miami, Florida, people are more friendly. What," he said, "you're still afraid? Nazis we ain't got, even Ku Kluxers we ain't got. What kind of person are you, you're still afraid?"

"The kind of person," Rosa said, "is what you see. Thirty-nine years ago I was somebody else."

"Thirty-nine years ago I wasn't so bad myself. I lost my teeth without a single cavity," he bragged. "Everything perfect. Periodontal disease."

"*I* was a chemist almost. A physicist," Rosa said. "You think I wouldn't have been a scientist?" The thieves who took her life! All at once the landscape behind her eyes fell out of control: a bright field flashed; then a certain shadowy corridor leading to the laboratory-supplies closet. The closet opened in her dreams also. Retorts and microscopes were ranged on the shelves. Once, walking there, she was conscious of the coursing of her own ecstasy — her new brown shoes, laced and sober, her white coat, her hair cut short in bangs: a serious person of seventeen, ambitious, responsible, a future Marie Curie! One of her teachers in the high school praised her for what he said was a "literary style" — oh, lost and kidnapped Polish! — and now she wrote and spoke English as helplessly as this old immigrant. From Warsaw! Born 1906! She imagined what bitter ancient alley, dense with stalls, cheap clothes strung on outdoor racks, signs in jargoned Yiddish. Anyhow they called her refugee. The Americans couldn't tell her apart from this fellow with his false teeth and his dewlaps and his rakehell reddish toupee bought God knows when or where — Delancey Street, the lower East Side. A dandy. Warsaw! What did he know? In school she had read Tuwim: such delicacy, such loftiness, such *Polishness*. The Warsaw of her girlhood: a great light: she switched it on, she wanted to live inside her eyes. The curve of the legs of her mother's bureau. The strict leather smell of her father's desk. The white tile tract of the kitchen floor, the big pots breathing, a narrow tower stair next to the attic . . . the house of her girlhood laden with a thousand books. Polish, German, French; her father's Latin books; the shelf of shy literary periodicals her mother's poetry now and then wandered through, in short lines like heated telegrams. Cultivation, old civilization, beauty, history! Surprising turnings of streets, shapes of venerable cottages, lovely aged eaves, unexpected and gossamer turrets, steeples, the gloss, the antiquity! Gardens. Whoever speaks of Paris has never seen Warsaw. Her father, like her mother, mocked at Yiddish; there was not a particle of ghetto left in him, not a grain of rot. Whoever yearns for an aristocratic sensibility, let him switch on the great light of Warsaw.

"Your name?" her companion said.

"Lublin, Rosa."

"A pleasure," he said. "Only why backwards? I'm an application form? Very good. You apply, I accept." He took command of her shopping cart. "Wherever is your home is my direction that I'm going anyhow."

"You forgot to take your laundry," Rosa said.

"Mine I did day before yesterday."

"So why did you come here?"

"I'm devoted to nature. I like the sound of a waterfall. Wherever it's cool it's a pleasure to sit and read my paper."

"What a story!"

"All right, so I go to have a visit with the ladies. Tell me, you like concerts?"

"I like my own room, that's all."

"A lady what wants to be a hermit!"

"I got my own troubles," Rosa said.

"Unload on me."

In the street she plodded beside him dumbly, a led animal. Her shoes were not nice; she should have put on the other ones. The sunlight was smothering — cooked honey dumped on their heads: one lick was good, too much could drown you. She was glad to have someone to pull the cart.

"You got internal warnings about talking to a stranger? If I say my name, no more a stranger. Simon Persky. A third cousin to Shimon Peres, the Israeli politician. I have different famous relatives, plenty of family pride. You ever heard of Betty Bacall, who Humphrey Bogart the movie star was married to, a Jewish girl? Also a distant cousin. I could tell you the whole story of my life experience, beginning with Warsaw. Actually it wasn't Warsaw, it was a little place a few miles out of town. In Warsaw I had uncles."

Rosa said again, "Your Warsaw isn't my Warsaw."

He stopped the cart. "What is this? A song with one stanza? You think I don't know the difference between generations? I'm seventy-one, and you, you're only a girl."

"Fifty-eight." Though in the papers, when they told how she smashed up her store, it came out fifty-nine. Stella's fault, Stella's black will, the Angel of Death's arithmetic.

"You see? I told you! A girl!"

"I'm from an educated family."

"Your English ain't better than what any other refugee talks."

"Why should I learn English? I didn't ask for it, I got nothing to do with it."

"You can't live in the past," he advised. Again the wheels of the cart were squealing. Like a calf, Rosa followed. They were approaching a self-service cafeteria. The smells of eggplant, fried potatoes, mushrooms blew out as if pumped. Rosa read the sign: KOLLINS KOSHER KAMEO: EVERYTHING ON YOUR PLATE AS PRETTY AS A PICTURE: REMEMBRANCES OF NEW YORK AND THE PARADISE OF YOUR MATERNAL KITCHEN: DELICIOUS DISHES OF AM-BROSIA AND NOSTALGIA: AIR CONDITIONED THRU-OUT.

"I know the owner," Persky said. "He's a big reader. You want tea?"

"Tea?"

"Not iced. The hotter the better. This is physiology. Come in, you'll cool off. You got some red face, believe me."

Rosa looked in the window. Her bun was loose, strings dangling on either side of her neck. The reflection of a ragged old bird with worn feathers. Skinny, a stork. Her dress was missing a button, but maybe the belt buckle covered this shame. What did she care? She thought of her room, her bed, her radio. She hated conversation.

"I got to get back," she said.

"An appointment?"

"No."

"Then have an appointment with Persky. So come, first tea. If you take with an ice cube, you're involved in a mistake."

They went in and chose a tiny table in a corner — a sticky disc on a wobbly plastic pedestal. "You'll stay, I'll get," Persky said.

She sat and panted. Silverware tapped and clicked all around. No one here but old people. It was like the dining room of a convalescent home. Everyone had canes, dowager's humps, acrylic teeth, shoes cut out for bunions. Everyone wore an open collar showing mottled skin, ferocious clavicles, the wrinkled foundations of wasted breasts. The air conditioning was on too high; she felt the cooling sweat licking from around her neck down, down her spine into the crevice of her bottom. She was afraid to shift; the chair had a wicker back and a black plastic seat. If she moved even a little, an odor would fly up: urine, salt, old woman's fatigue. She left off panting and shivered. What do I care? I'm used to everything. Florida, New York, it doesn't matter. All the same, she took out two hairpins and caught up the hanging strands; she shoved them into the core of her gray knot and pierced them through. She had no mirror, no comb, no pocketbook; not even a handkerchief. All she had was a

Kleenex pushed into her sleeve and some coins in the pocket of her dress.

"I came out only for the laundry," she told Persky. With a groan he set down a loaded tray: two cups of tea, a saucer of lemon slices, a dish of eggplant salad, bread on what looked like a wooden platter but was really plastic, another plastic platter of Danish. "Maybe I didn't bring enough to pay."

"Never mind, you got the company of a rich retired taxpayer. I'm a well-off man. When I get my Social Security, I spit on it."

"What line of business?"

"The same what I see you got one lost. At the waist. Buttons. A shame. That kind's hard to match, as far as I'm concerned we stopped making them around a dozen years ago. Braided buttons is out of style."

"Buttons?" Rosa said.

"Buttons, belts, notions, knickknacks, costume jewelry. A factory. I thought my son would take it over but he wanted something different. He's a philosopher, so he became a loiterer. Too much education makes fools. I hate to say it, but on account of him I had to sell out. And the girls, whatever the big one wanted, the little one also. The big one found a lawyer, that's what the little one looked for. I got one son-in-law in business for himself, taxes, the other's a youngster, still on Wall Street."

"A nice family," Rosa bit off.

"A loiterer's not so nice. Drink while it's hot. Otherwise it won't reach to your metabolism. You like eggplant salad on top of bread and butter? You got room for it, rest assured. Tell me, you live alone?"

"By myself," Rosa said, and slid her tongue into the tea. Tears came from the heat.

"My son is over thirty, I still support him."

"My niece, forty-nine, not married, she supports me."

"Too old. Otherwise I'd say let's make a match with my son, let her support him too. The best thing is independence. If you're able-bodied, it's a blessing to work." Persky caressed his chest. "I got a bum heart."

Rosa murmured, "I had a business, but I broke it up."

"Bankruptcy?"

"Part with a big hammer," she said meditatively, "part with a piece of construction metal I picked up from the gutter."

"You don't look that strong. Skin and bones."

"You don't believe me? In the papers they said an axe, but where would I get an axe?"

"That's reasonable. Where would you get an axe?" Persky's finger removed an obstruction from under his lower plate. He examined it: an eggplant seed. On the floor near the cart there was something white, a white cloth. Handkerchief. He picked it up and stuffed it in his pants pocket. Then he said, "What kind of business?"

"Antiques. Old furniture. Junk. I had a specialty in antique mirrors. Whatever I had there, I smashed it. See," she said, "*now* you're sorry you started with me!"

"I ain't sorry for nothing," Persky said. "If there's one thing I know to understand, it's mental episodes. I got it my whole life with my wife."

"You're not a widower?"

"In a manner of speaking."

"Where is she?"

"Great Neck, Long Island. A private hospital, it don't cost me peanuts." He said, "She's in a mental condition."

"Serious?"

"It used to be once in a while, now it's a regular thing. She's mixed up that she's somebody else. Television stars. Movie actresses. Different people. Lately my cousin, Betty Bacall. It went to her head."

"Tragic," Rosa said.

"You see? I unloaded on you, now you got to unload on me."

"Whatever I would say, you would be deaf."

"How come you smashed up your business?"

"It was a store. I didn't like who came in it."

"Spanish? Colored?"

"What do I care who came? Whoever came, they were like deaf people. Whatever you explained to them, they didn't understand." Rosa stood up to claim her cart. "It's very fine of you to treat me to the Danish, Mr. Persky. I enjoyed it. Now I got to go."

"I'll walk you."

"No, no, sometimes a person feels to be alone."

"If you're alone too much," Persky said, "you think too much."

"Without a life," Rosa answered, "a person lives where they can. If all they got is thoughts, that's where they live."

"You ain't got a life?"

"Thieves took it."

She toiled away from him. The handle of the cart was a burning rod. A hat, I ought to have worn a hat! The pins in her bun scalded her scalp. She panted like a dog in the sun. Even the trees looked exhausted: every leaf face downward under a powder of dust. Summer without end, a mistake!

In the lobby she waited before the elevator. The "guests" — some had been residents for a dozen years — were already milling around, groomed for lunch, the old women in sundresses showing their thick collarbones and the bluish wells above them. Instead of napes they had rolls of wide fat. They wore no stockings. Brazen blue-marbled sinews strangled their squarish calves; in their reveries they were again young women with immortal pillar legs, the white legs of strong goddesses; it was only that they had forgotten about impermanence. In their faces, too, you could see everything they were not noticing about themselves — the red gloss on their drawstring mouths was never meant to restore youth. It was meant only to continue it. Flirts of seventy. Everything had stayed the same for them: intentions, actions, even expectations — they had not advanced. They believed in the seamless continuity of the body. The men were more inward, running their lives in front of their eyes like secret movies.

A syrup of cologne clogged the air. Rosa heard the tearing of envelopes, the wing-shudders of paper sheets. Letters from children: the guests laughed and wept, but without seriousness, without belief. Report-card marks, separations, divorces, a new coffee table to match the gilt mirror over the piano, Stuie at sixteen learning to drive, Millie's mother-in-law's second stroke, rumors of the cataracts of half-remembered acquaintances, a cousin's kidney, the rabbi's ulcer, a daughter's indigestion, burglary, perplexing news of East Hampton parties, psychoanalysis . . . the children were rich, how was this possible from such poor parents? It was real and it was not real. Shadows on a wall; the shadows stirred, but you could not penetrate the wall. The

guests were detached; they had detached themselves. Little by
little they were forgetting their grandchildren, their aging children. More and more they were growing significant to themselves. Every wall of the lobby a mirror. Every mirror hanging
thirty years. Every table surface a mirror. In these mirrors the
guests appeared to themselves as they used to be, powerful
women of thirty, striving fathers of thirty-five, mothers and
fathers of dim children who had migrated long ago, to other
continents, inaccessible landscapes, incomprehensible vocabu-
laries. Rosa made herself brave; the elevator gate opened, but
she let the empty car ascend without her and pushed the cart
through to where the black Cuban receptionist sat, maneuver-
ing clayey sweat balls up from the naked place between her
breasts with two fingers.

"Mail for Lublin, Rosa," Rosa said.

"Lublin, you lucky today. Two letters."

"Take a look where you keep packages also."

"You a lucky dog, Lublin," the Cuban girl said, and tossed an
object into the pile of wash.

Rosa knew what was in that package. She had asked Stella to
send it; Stella did not easily do what Rosa asked. She saw immediately that the package was not registered. This angered
her: Stella the Angel of Death! Instantly she plucked the package out of the cart and tore the wrapping off and crumpled it
into a standing ashtray. Magda's shawl! Suppose, God forbid, it
got lost in the mail, what then? She squashed the box into her
breasts. It felt hard, heavy; Stella had encased it in some terrible
untender rind; Stella had turned it to stone. She wanted to kiss
it, but the maelstrom was all around her, pressing toward the
dining room. The food was monotonous and sparse and often
stale; still, to eat there increased the rent. Stella was all the time
writing that she was not a millionaire; Rosa never ate in the
dining room. She kept the package tight against her bosom and
picked through the crowd, a sluggish bird on ragged toes, dragging the cart.

In her room she breathed noisily, almost a gasp, almost a
squeal, left the laundry askew in the tiny parody of a vestibule,
and carried the box and the two letters to the bed. It was still
unmade, fish-smelling, the covers knotted together like an um-

bilical cord. A shipwreck. She let herself down into it and
knocked off her shoes — oh, they were scarred; that Persky
must have seen her shame, first the missing button, afterward
the used-up shoes. She turned the box round and round — a
rectangular box. Magda's shawl! Magda's swaddling cloth. Magda's shroud. The memory of Magda's smell, the holy fragrance
of the lost babe. Murdered. Thrown against the fence, barbed,
thorned, electrified; grid and griddle; a furnace; the child on
fire! Rosa put the shawl to her nose, to her lips. Stella did not
want her to have Magda's shawl all the time, she had such funny
names for having it — trauma, fetish, God knows what: Stella
took psychology courses at the New School at night, looking for
marriage among the flatulent bachelors in her classes.

One letter was from Stella and the other was one of those
university letters, still another one, another sample of the disease. But in the box, Magda's shawl! The box would be last,
Stella's fat letter first (fat meant trouble), the university letter
did not matter. A disease. Better to put away the laundry than
to open the university letter.

Dear Rosa [Stella wrote]:
    All right, I've done it. Been to the post office and mailed it. Your
idol is on its way, separate cover. Go on your knees to it if you want.
You make yourself crazy, everyone thinks you're a crazy woman.
Whoever goes by your old store still gets glass in their soles. You're
the older one, I'm the niece, I shouldn't lecture, but my God! It's
thirty years, forty, who knows, give it a rest. It isn't as if I don't know
just exactly how you do it, what it's like. What a scene, disgusting!
You'll open the box and take it out and cry, and you'll kiss it like a
crazy person. Making holes in it with kisses. You're like those people
in the Middle Ages who worshipped a piece of the True Cross, a
splinter from some old outhouse as far as anybody knew, or else they
fell down in front of a single hair supposed to be some saint's. You'll
kiss, you'll pee tears down your face, and so what? Rosa, by now,
believe me, it's time, you have to have a life.

Out loud Rosa said, "Thieves took it."
And she said, "And you, Stella, *you* have a life?"

    If I were a millionaire I'd tell you the same thing: get a job. Or else, come back and move in here. I'm away the whole day, it will be like living alone if that's what you want. It's too hot to look around down there, people get like vegetables. With everything you did for me I don't mind keeping up this way maybe another year or so, you'll think I'm stingy for saying it like that, but after all I'm not on the biggest salary in the world.

Rosa said, "Stella! Would you be alive if I didn't take you out from there? Dead. You'd be dead! So don't talk to me how much an old woman costs! I didn't give you from my store? The big gold mirror, you look in it at your bitter face — I don't care how pretty, even so it's bitter — and you forget who gave you presents!"

And as far as Florida is concerned, well, it doesn't solve anything. I don't mind telling you now that they would have locked you up if I didn't agree to get you out of the city then and there. One more public outburst puts you in the bughouse. No more public scandals! For God's sake, don't be a crazy person! Live your life!

Rosa said again, "Thieves took it," and went, scrupulously, meticulously, as if possessed, to count the laundry in the cart.

A pair of underpants was missing. Once more Rosa counted everything: four blouses, three cotton skirts, three brassieres, one half-slip and one regular, two towels, eight pairs of underpants . . . nine went into the washing machine, the exact number. Degrading. Lost bloomers — dropped God knows where. In the elevator, in the lobby, in the street even. Rosa tugged, and the dress with the blue stripes slid like a coarse colored worm out of twisted bedsheets. The hole in the armpit was bigger now. Stripes, never again anything on her body with stripes! She swore it, but this, fancy and with a low collar, was Stella's birthday present, Stella bought it. As if innocent, as if ignorant, as if *not there*. Stella, an ordinary American, indistinguishable! No one could guess what hell she had crawled out of until she opened her mouth and up coiled the smoke of accent.

Again Rosa counted. A fact, one pair of pants lost. An old woman who couldn't even hang on to her own underwear.

She decided to sew up the hole in the stripes. Instead she put water on to boil for tea and made the bed with the clean sheets from the cart. The box with the shawl would be the last thing. Stella's letter she pushed under the bed next to the telephone. She tidied all around. Everything had to be nice when the box was opened. She spread jelly on three crackers and deposited a Lipton's tea bag on the Welch's lid. It was grape jelly, with a picture of Bugs Bunny elevating an officious finger. In spite of Persky's Danish, empty insides. Always Stella said: Rosa eats little by little, like a tapeworm in the world's belly.

Then it came to her that Persky had her underpants in his pocket.

Oh, degrading. The shame. Pain in the loins. Burning. Bending in the cafeteria to pick up her pants, all the while tinkering with his teeth. Why didn't he give them back? He was embarrassed. He had thought a handkerchief. How can a man hand a woman, a stranger, a piece of her own underwear? He could have shoved it right back into the cart, how would that look? A sensitive man, he wanted to spare her. When he came home with her underpants, what then? What could a man, half a widower, do with a pair of female bloomers? Nylon-plus-cotton, the long-thighed kind. Maybe he had filched them on purpose, a sex maniac, a wife among the insane, his parts starved. According to Stella, Rosa also belonged among the insane, Stella had the power to put her there. Very good, they would become neighbors, confidantes, she and Persky's wife, best friends. The wife would confess all of Persky's sexual habits. She would explain how it is that a man of this age comes to steal a lady's personal underwear. Whatever stains in the crotch are nobody's business. And not only that: a woman with children, Persky's wife would speak of her son and her married lucky daughters. And Rosa too, never mind how Stella was sour over it, she would tell about Magda, a beautiful young woman of thirty, thirty-one: a doctor married to a doctor; large house in Mamaroneck, New York; two medical offices, one on the first floor, one in the finished basement. Stella was alive, why not Magda? Who was Stella, coarse Stella, to insist that Magda was not alive? Stella the Angel of Death. Magda alive, the pure eyes, the bright hair. Stella, never a mother, who was Stella to mock the kisses Rosa put in Magda's shawl? She meant to crush it into her mouth. Rosa, a mother the same as anyone, no different from Persky's wife in the crazy house.

This disease! The university letter, like all of them — five, six postmarks on the envelope. Rosa imagined its pilgrimage: first to the *News*, the *Post*, maybe even the *Times*, then to Rosa's old store, then to the store's landlord's lawyers, then to Stella's apartment, then to Miami, Florida. A Sherlock Holmes of a letter. It had struggled to find its victim, and for what? More eating alive.

DEPARTMENT OF CLINICAL SOCIAL PATHOLOGY
UNIVERSITY OF KANSAS-IOWA
April 17, 1977
Dear Ms. Lublin:

Though I am not myself a physician, I have lately begun to amass survivor data as rather a considerable specialty. To be concrete: I am presently working on a study, funded by the Minew Foundation of the Kansas-Iowa Institute for Humanitarian Context, designed to research the theory developed by Dr. Arthur R. Hidgeson and known generally as Repressed Animation. Without at this stage going into detail, it may be of some preliminary use to you to know that investigations so far reveal an astonishing generalized minimalization during any extended period of stress resulting from incarceration, exposure, and malnutrition. We have turned up a wide range of neurological residues (including, in some cases, acute cerebral damage, derangement, disorientation, premature senility, etc.), as well as hormonal changes, parasites, anemia, thready pulse, hyperventilation, etc.; in children especially, temperatures as high as 108°, ascitic fluid, retardation, bleeding sores on the skin and in the mouth, etc. What is remarkable is that these are all *current conditions* in survivors and their families.

Disease, disease! Humanitarian Context, what did it mean? An excitement over other people's suffering. They let their mouths water up. Stories about children running blood in America from sores, what muck. Consider also the special word they used: *survivor*. Something new. As long as they didn't have to say *human being*. It used to be *refugee*, but by now there was no such creature, no more refugees, only survivors. A name like

a number — counted apart from the ordinary swarm. Blue dig-
its on the arm, what difference? They don't call you a woman
anyhow. *Survivor.* Even when your bones get melted into the
grains of the earth, still they'll forget *human being.* Survivor and
survivor and survivor; always and always. Who made up these
words, parasites on the throat of suffering!

For some months teams of medical paraphrasers have been con-
ducting interviews with survivors, to contrast current medical para-
phrase with conditions found more than three decades ago, at the
opening of the camps. This, I confess, is neither my field nor my
interest. My own concern, both as a scholar of social pathology and
as a human being . . .

Ha! For himself it was good enough, for himself he didn't
forget this word *human being!*

. . . is not with medical nor even with psychological aspects of survivor data.

Data. Drop in a hole!

What particularly engages me for purposes of my own participa-
tion in the study (which, by the way, is intended to be definitive, to
close the books, so to speak, on this lamentable subject) is what I can
only term the "metaphysical" side of Repressed Animation (R.A.). It
begins to be evident that prisoners gradually came to Buddhist posi-
tions. They gave up craving and began to function in terms of non-
functioning, i.e., nonattachment. The Four Noble Truths in
Buddhist thought, if I may remind you, yield a penetrating summary
of the fruit of craving: pain. "Pain" in this view is defined as ugliness,
age, sorrow, sickness, despair, and, finally, birth. Nonattachment is
attained through the Eightfold Path, the highest stage of which is the
cessation of all human craving, the loftiest rapture, one might say, of
consummated indifference.

It is my hope that these speculations are not displeasing to you.
Indeed, I further hope that they may even attract you, and that you
would not object to joining our study by means of an in-depth inter-
view to be conducted by me at, if it is not inconvenient, your home.
I should like to observe survivor syndroming within the natural setting.

Home! Where, where?

As you may not realize, the national convention of the American Association of Clinical Social Pathology has this year, for reasons of fairness to our East Coast members, been moved from Las Vegas to Miami Beach. The convention will take place at a hotel in your vicinity about the middle of next May, and I would be deeply grateful if you could receive me during that period. I have noted via a New York City newspaper (we are not so provincial out here as some may think!) your recent removal to Florida; consequently you are ideally circumstanced to make a contribution to our R.A. study. I look forward to your consent at your earliest opportunity.

Very sincerely yours,
James W. Tree, Ph.D.

Drop in a hole! Disease! It comes from Stella, everything! Stella saw what this letter was, she could see from the envelope — Dr. Stella! Kansas-Iowa Clinical Social Pathology, a fancy hotel, this is the cure for the taking of a life! Angel of Death!

With these university letters Rosa had a routine: she carried the scissors over the toilet bowl and snipped little bits of paper and flushed. In the bowl going down, the paper squares whirled like wedding rice.

But this one: drop in a hole with your Four Truths and your Eight Paths together! Nonattachment! She threw the letter into the sink; also its crowded envelope ("Please forward," Stella's handwriting instructed, pretending to be American, leaving out the little stroke that goes across the 7); she lit a match and enjoyed the thick fire. Burn, Dr. Tree, burn up with your Repressed Animation! The world is full of Trees! The world is full of fire! Everything, everything is on fire! Florida is burning!

Big flakes of cinder lay in the sink: black foliage, Stella's black will. Rosa turned on the faucet, and the cinders spiraled down and away. Then she went to the round oak table and wrote the first letter of the day to her daughter, her healthy daughter, her daughter who suffered neither from thready pulse nor anemia, her daughter who was a professor of Greek philosophy at Columbia University in New York City, a stone's throw — the phi-

losophers' stone that prolongs life and transmutes iron to gold
— from Stella in Queens!

Magda, my Soul's Blessing [Rosa wrote],
   Forgive me, my yellow lioness. Too long a time since the last writing. Strangers scratch at my life; they pursue, they break down the
bloodstream's sentries. Always there is Stella. And so half a day
passes without my taking up my pen to speak to you. A pleasure, the
deepest pleasure, home bliss, to speak in our own language. Only to
you. I am always having to write to Stella now, like a dog paying
respects to its mistress. It's my obligation. She sends me money. She,
whom I plucked out of the claws of all those Societies that came to us
with bread and chocolate after the liberation! Despite everything,
they were selling sectarian ideas; collecting troops for their armies.
If not for me they would have shipped Stella with a boatload of
orphans to Palestine, to become God knows what, to live God knows
how. A field worker jabbering Hebrew. It would serve her right.
Americanized airs. My father was never a Zionist. He used to call
himself a "Pole by right." The Jews, he said, didn't put a thousand
years of brains and blood into Polish soil in order to have to prove
themselves to anyone. He was the wrong sort of idealist, maybe, but
he had the instincts of a natural nobleman. I could laugh at that now
— the whole business — but I don't, because I feel too vividly what
he was, how substantial, how not given over to any light-mindedness
whatever. He had Zionist friends in his youth. Some left Poland early
and lived. One is a bookseller in Tel Aviv. He specializes in foreign
texts and periodicals. My poor little father. It's only history — an ad
hoc instance of it, you might say — that made the Zionist solution.
My father's ideas were more logical. He was a Polish patriot on a
temporary basis, he said, until the time when nation should lie down
beside nation like the lily and the lotus. He was at bottom a prophetic
creature. My mother, you know, published poetry. To you all these
accounts must have the ring of pure legend.
   Even Stella, who *can* remember, refuses. She calls me a parable-
maker. She was always jealous of you. She has a strain of dementia,
and resists you and all other reality. Every vestige of former existence
is an insult to her. Because she fears the past she distrusts the future
— it, too, will turn into the past. As a result she has nothing. She sits
and watches the present roll itself up into the past more quickly than
she can bear. That's why she never found the one thing she wanted
more than anything, an American husband. I'm immune to these
pains and panics. Motherhood — I've always known this — is a pro-

found distraction from philosophy, and all philosophy is rooted in
suffering over the passage of time. I mean the *fact* of motherhood,
the physiological fact. To have the power to create another human
being, to be the instrument of such a mystery. To pass on a whole
genetic system. I don't believe in God, but I believe, like the Catho-
lics, in mystery. My mother wanted so much to convert; my father
laughed at her. But she was attracted. She let the maid keep a statue
of the Virgin and Child in the corner of the kitchen. Sometimes she
used to go in and look at it. I can even remember the words of a
poem she wrote about the heat coming up from the stove, from the
Sunday pancakes —

> Mother of God, how you shiver
> in these heat-ribbons!
> Our cakes rise to you
> and in the trance of His birthing
> you hide.

Something like that. Better than that, more remarkable. Her Polish
was very dense. You had to open it out like a fan to get at all the
meanings. She was exceptionally modest, but she was not afraid to
call herself a symbolist.

I know you won't blame me for going astray with such tales. After
all, you're always prodding me for these old memories. If not for
you, I would have buried them all, to satisfy Stella. Stella Columbus!
She thinks there's such a thing as the New World. Finally — at last,
at last — she surrenders this precious vestige of your sacred baby-
hood. Here it is in a box right next to me as I write. She didn't take
the trouble to send it by registered mail! Even though I told her and
told her. I've thrown out the wrapping paper, and the lid is plastered
down with lots of Scotch tape. I'm not hurrying to open it. At first
my hunger was unrestrained and I couldn't wait, but nothing is nice
now. I'm saving you; I want to be serene. In a state of agitation one
doesn't split open a diamond. Stella says I make a relic of you. She
has no heart. It would shock you if I told you even one of the horrible
games I'm made to play with her. To soothe her dementia, to keep
her quiet, I pretend you died. Yes! It's true! There's nothing, however crazy, I wouldn't say to her to tie up her tongue. She slanders.
Everywhere there are slanders, and sometimes — my bright lips, my
darling! — the slanders touch even you. My purity, my snow queen!

I'm ashamed to give an example. Pornography. What Stella, that
pornographer, has made of your father. She thieves all the truth, she
robs it, she steals it, the robbery goes unpunished. She lies, and it's
the lying that's rewarded. The New World! That's why I smashed up

my store! Because here they make up lying theories. Even the professors — they take human beings for specimens. In Poland there used to be justice; here they have social theories. Their system inherits almost nothing from the Romans, that's why. Is it a wonder that the lawyers are no better than scavengers who feed on the droppings of thieves and liars? Thank God you followed your grandfather's bent and studied philosophy and not law.

Take my word for it, Magda, your father and I had the most ordinary lives — by "ordinary" I mean respectable, gentle, cultivated. Reliable people of refined reputation. His name was Andrzej. Our families had status. Your father was the son of my mother's closest friend. She was a converted Jew married to a Gentile: you can be a Jew if you like, or a Gentile, it's up to you. You have a legacy of choice, and they say choice is the only true freedom. We were engaged to be married. We would have been married. Stella's accusations are all Stella's own excretion. Your father was not a German. I was forced by a German, it's true, and more than once, but I was too sick to conceive. Stella has a naturally pornographic mind, she can't resist dreaming up a dirty sire for you, an SS man! Stella was with me the whole time, she knows just what I know. They never put me in their brothel either. Never believe this, my lioness, my snow queen! No lies come out of me to you. You are pure. A mother is the source of consciousness, of conscience, the ground of being, as philosophers say. I have no falsehoods for you. Otherwise I don't deny some few tricks: the necessary handful. To those who don't deserve the truth, don't give it. I tell Stella what it pleases her to hear. My child, perished. Perished. She always wanted it. She was always jealous of you. She has no heart. Even now she believes in my loss of you: and you a stone's throw from her door in New York! Let her think whatever she thinks; her mind is awry, poor thing; in me the strength of your being consumes my joy. Yellow blossom! Cup of the sun!

What a curiosity it was to hold a pen — nothing but a small pointed stick, after all, oozing its hieroglyphic puddles: a pen that speaks, miraculously, Polish. A lock removed from the tongue. Otherwise the tongue is chained to the teeth and the palate. An immersion into the living language: all at once this cleanliness, this capacity, this power to make a history, to tell, to explain. To retrieve, to reprieve!

To lie.

The box with Magda's shawl was still on the table. Rosa left it there. She put on her good shoes, a nice dress (polyester, "wrinkle-free" on the inside label); she arranged her hair, brushed her teeth, poured mouthwash on the brush, sucked it up through the nylon bristles, gargled rapidly. As an afterthought she changed her bra and slip; it meant getting out of her dress and into it again. Her mouth she reddened very slightly — a smudge of lipstick rubbed on with a finger.

Perfected, she mounted the bed on her knees and fell into folds. A puppet, dreaming. Darkened cities, tombstones, colorless garlands, a black fire in a gray field, brutes forcing the innocent, women with their mouths stretched and their arms wild, her mother's voice calling. After hours of these pitiless tableaux, it was late afternoon; by then she was certain that whoever put her underpants in his pocket was a criminal capable of every base act. Humiliation. Degradation. Stella's pornography!

To retrieve, to reprieve. Nothing in the elevator; in the lobby, nothing. She kept her head down. Nothing white glimmered up.

In the street a neon dusk was already blinking. Gritty mixture of heat and toiling dust. Cars shot by like large bees. It was too early for headlights: in the lower sky two strange competing lamps — a scarlet sun, round and brilliant as a blooded egg yolk; a silk-white moon, gray-veined with mountain ranges. These hung simultaneously at either end of the long road. The whole day's burning struck upward like a moving weight from the sidewalk. Rosa's nostrils and lungs were cautious: burning molasses air. Her underpants were not in the road.

In Miami at night no one stays indoors. The streets are clogged with wanderers and watchers; everyone in search, bedouins with no fixed paths. The foolish Florida rains spray down — so light, so brief and fickle, no one pays attention. Neon alphabets, designs, pictures, flashing undiminished right through the sudden small rain. A quick lick of lightning above one of the balconied hotels. Rosa walked. Much Yiddish. Caravans of slow old couples, linked at the elbows, winding down to the cool of the beaches. The sand never at rest, always churning, always inhabited; copulation under blankets at night, beneath neon-radiant low horizons.

She had never been near the beach; why should her underpants be lost in the sand?

On the sidewalk in front of the KOLLINS KOSHER KAMEO, nothing. Shining hungry smell of boiled potatoes in sour cream. The pants were not necessarily in Persky's pocket. Dented garbage barrels, empty near the curb. Pants already smoldering in an ash heap, among blackened tomato cans, kitchen scrapings, conflagrations of old magazines. Or: a simple omission, an accident, never transferred from the washing machine to the dryer. Or, if transferred, never removed. Overlooked. Persky unblemished. The laundromat was locked up for the night, with a metal accordion gate stretched across the door and windows. What marauders would seek out caldrons, giant washtubs? Property misleads, brings false perspectives. The power to smash her own. A kind of suicide. She had murdered her store with her own hands. She cared more for a missing pair of underpants, lost laundry, than for business. She was ashamed; she felt exposed. What was her store? A cave of junk.

On the corner across the street from the laundromat a narrow newspaper store, no larger than a stall. Persky might have bought his paper there. Suppose later in the day he had come down for an afternoon paper, her pants in his pocket, and dropped them?

Mob of New York accents. It was a little place, not air-conditioned.

"Lady? You're looking for something?"

A newspaper? Rosa had enough of the world.

"Look, it's like sardines in here. Buy something or go out."

"My store used to be six times the size of this place," Rosa said.

"So go to your store."

"I don't have a store." She reconsidered. If someone wanted to hide — to hide, not destroy — a pair of underpants, where would he put them? Under the sand. Rolled up and buried. She thought what a weight of sand would feel like in the crotch of her pants, wet heavy sand, still hot from the day. In her room it was hot, hot all night. No air. In Florida there was no air, only this syrup seeping into the esophagus. Rosa walked; she saw everything, but as if out of invention, out of imagination; she was unconnected to anything. She came to a gate; a mottled beach spread behind it. It belonged to one of the big hotels. The latch opened. At the edge of the waves you could look back and see black crenelated forms stretching all along the shore. In the dark, in silhouette, the towered hotel roofs held up their merciless teeth. Impossible that any architect pleasurably dreamed these teeth. The sand was only now beginning to cool. Across the water the sky breathed a starless black; behind her, where the hotels bit down on the city, a dusty glow of brownish red lowered. Mud clouds. The sand was littered with bodies. Photograph of Pompeii: prone in the volcanic ash. Her pants were under the sand; or else packed hard with sand, like a piece of torso, a broken statue, the human groin detached, the whole soul gone, only the loins left for kicking by strangers. She took off her good shoes to save them and nearly stepped on the sweated faces of two lovers plugged into a kiss. A pair of water animals in suction. The same everywhere, along the rim of every continent, this gurgling, foaming, trickling. A true smasher, a woman whose underpants have been stolen, a woman who has murdered her business with her own hands, would know how to step cleanly into the sea. A horizontal tunnel. You can fall into its pull just by entering it upright. How simple the night sea; only the sand is unpredictable, with its hundred burrowings, its thousand buryings.

When she came back to the gate, the latch would not budge. A cunning design, it trapped the trespasser.

She gazed up, and thought of climbing; but there was barbed wire on top.

So many double mounds in the sand. It was a question of choosing a likely sentinel: someone who would let her out. She went back down onto the beach again and tapped a body with the tip of her dangling shoe. The body jerked as if shot: it scrambled up.

"Mister? You know how to get out?"

"Room key does it," said the second body, still flat in the sand. It was a man. They were both men, slim and coated with sand; naked. The one lying flat — she could see what part of him was swollen.

"I'm not from this hotel," Rosa said.

"Then you're not allowed here. This is a private beach."

"Can you let me out?"

"Lady, please. Just buzz off," the man in the sand said.

"I can't get out," Rosa pleaded.

The man who was standing laughed.

Rosa persisted. "If you have a key — "

"Believe me, lady, not for you" — muffled from below.

She understood. Sexual mockery. "Sodom!" she hissed, and
stumbled away. Behind her their laughter. They hated women.
Or else they saw she was a Jew; they hated Jews; but no, she had
noticed the circumcision, like a jonquil, in the dim sand. Her
wrists were trembling. To be locked behind barbed wire! No
one knew who she was; what had happened to her; where she
came from. Their gates, the terrible ruse of their keys, wire
brambles, men lying with men . . . She was afraid to approach
any of the other mounds. No one to help. Persecutors. In the
morning they would arrest her.

She put on her shoes again, and walked along the cement
path that followed the fence. It led her to light; voices of black
men. A window. Vast deep odors: kitchen exhaust, fans stirring
soup smells out into the weeds. A door wedged open by a milk-
can lid. Acres of counters, stoves, steamers, refrigerators, per-
colators, bins, basins. The kitchen of a castle. She fled past the
black cooks in their meat-blooded aprons, through a short corridor; a dead end facing an elevator. She pushed the button and
waited. The kitchen people had seen her; would they pursue?
She heard their yells, but it was nothing to do with her — they
were calling Thursday, Thursday. On Thursday no more new
potatoes. A kind of emergency maybe. The elevator took her to
the main floor, to the lobby; she emerged, free.

This lobby was the hall of a palace. In the middle a real fountain. Water springing out of the mouths of emerald-green dol-
phins. Skirted cherubs, gilded. A winged mermaid spilling gold
flowers out of a gold pitcher. Lofty plants — a forest — palms
sprayed dark blue and silver and gold, leafing out of masses of
green marble vessels at the lip of the fountain. The water flowed
into a marble channel, a little indoor brook. A royal carpet for
miles around, woven with crowned birds. Well-dressed men and

women sat in lion-clawed gold thrones, smoking. A golden babble. How happy Stella would be, to stroll in a place like this!
Rosa kept close to the walls.

She saw a man in a green uniform.

"The manager," she croaked. "I have to tell him something."

"Office is over there." He shrugged toward a mahogany desk
behind a glass wall. The manager, wearing a red wig, was making a serious mark on a crested letterhead. Persky, too, had
a red wig. Florida was glutted with fake fire, burning false
hair! Everyone a piece of impostor. "Ma'am?" the manager
said.

"Mister, you got barbed wire by your beach."

"Are you a guest here?"

"I'm someplace else."

"Then it's none of your business, is it?"

"You got barbed wire."

"It keeps out the riffraff."

"In America it's no place for barbed wire on top of fences."

The manager left off making his serious marks. "Will you
leave?" he said. "Will you please just leave?"

"Only Nazis catch innocent people behind barbed wire," Rosa
said.

The red wig dipped. "My name is Finkelstein."

"Then you should know better!"

"Listen, walk out of here if you know what's good for you."

"Where were you when we was there?"

"Get out. So far I'm asking nicely. Please get out."

"Dancing in the pool in the lobby, that's where. Eat your
barbed wire, Mr. Finkelstein, chew it and choke on it!"

"Go home," Finkelstein said.

"You got Sodom and Gomorrah in your back yard! You got
gays and you got barbed wire!"

"You were trespassing on our beach," the manager said. "You
want me to call the police? Better leave before. Some important
guests have come in, we can't tolerate the noise and I can't spare
the time for this."

"They write me letters all the time, your important guests.
Conventions," Rosa scoffed. "Clinical Social Pathology, right?
You got a Dr. Tree staying?"

"Please go," Finkelstein said.

"Come on, you got a Dr. Tree? No? I'll tell you, if not today you'll get him later on, he's on the way. He's coming to investigate specimens. I'm the important one! It's me he's interviewing, Finkelstein, not you! I'm the study!"

The red wig dipped again.

"Aha!" Rosa cried. "I see you got Tree! You got a whole bunch of Trees!"

"We protect the privacy of our guests."

"With barbed wire you protect. It's Tree, yes? I can see I'm right! It's Tree! You got Tree staying here, right! Admit you got Tree! Finkelstein, you SS, admit it!"

The manager stood up. "Out," he said. "Get out now. Immediately."

"Don't worry, it's all right. It's my business to keep away. Tree I don't need. With Trees I had enough, you don't have to concern yourself — "

"Leave," said the red wig.

"A shame," Rosa said, "a Finkelstein like you." Irradiated, triumphant, cleansed, Rosa marched through the emerald glitter, toward the illuminated marquee in front. HOTEL MARIE LOUISE, in green neon. A doorman like a British admiral, gold braid cascading from his shoulders. They had trapped her, nearly caught her; but she knew how to escape. Speak up, yell. The same way she saved Stella, when they were pressing to take her on the boat to Palestine. She had no fear of Jews; sometimes she had — it came from her mother, her father — a certain contempt. The Warsaw swarm, shut off from the grandeur of the true world. Neighborhoods of a particular kind. Persky and Finkelstein. "Their" synagogues — balconies for the women. Primitive. Her own home, her own upbringing — how she had fallen. A loathsome tale of folk sorcery: nobility turned into a small dun rodent. Cracking her teeth on the poison of English. Here they were shallow, they knew nothing. Light-minded. Stella looking, on principle, to be light-minded. Blue stripes, barbed wire, men embracing men . . . whatever was dangerous and repugnant they made prevalent, frivolous.

Lost. Lost. Nowhere. All of Miami Beach, empty; the sand, empty. The whole wild hot neon night city: an empty search. In someone's pocket.

Persky was waiting for her. He sat in the torn brown plastic wing chair near the reception desk, one leg over the side, reading a newspaper.

He saw her come in and jumped up. He wore only a shirt and pants; no tie, no jacket. Informal.

"Lublin, Rosa!"

Rosa said, "How come you're here?"

"Where you been the whole night? I'm sitting hours."

"I didn't tell you where I stay," Rosa accused.

"I looked in the telephone book."

"My phone's disconnected, I don't know nobody. My niece, she writes, she saves on long distance."

"All right. You want the truth? This morning I followed you, that's all. A simple walk from my place. I sneaked in the streets behind you. I found out where you stay, here I am."

"Very nice," Rosa said.

"You don't like it?"

She wanted to tell him he was under suspicion; he owed her a look in his jacket pocket. A self-confessed sneak who follows women. If not his jacket, his pants. But it wasn't possible to say a thing like this. Her pants in his pants. Instead she said, "What do you want?"

He flashed his teeth. "A date."

"You're a married man."

"A married man what ain't got a wife."

"You got one."

"In a manner of speaking. She's crazy."

Rosa said, "I'm crazy, too."

"Who says so?"

"My niece."

"What does a stranger know?"

"A niece isn't a stranger."

"My own son is a stranger. A niece definitely. Come on, I got my car nearby. Air-conditioned, we'll take a spin."

"You're not a kid, I'm not a kid," Rosa said.

"You can't prove it by me," Persky said.

"I'm a serious person," Rosa said. "It isn't my kind of life, to run around noplace."

"Who said noplace? I got a place in mind." He reflected. "My Senior Citizens. Very nice pinochle."

"Not interested," Rosa said. "I don't need new people."

"Then a movie. You don't like new ones, we'll find dead ones. Clark Gable. Jean Harlow."

"Not interested."

"A ride to the beach. A walk on the shore, how about it?"

"I already did it," Rosa said.

"When?"

"Tonight. Just now."

"Alone?"

Rosa said, "I was looking for something I lost."

"Poor Lublin, what did you lose?"

"My life."

She was all at once not ashamed to say this outright. Because of the missing underwear she had no dignity before him. She considered Persky's life: how trivial it must always have been: buttons, himself no more significant than a button. It was plain he took her to be another button like himself, battered now and out of fashion, rolled into Florida. All of Miami Beach, a box for useless buttons!

"This means you're tired. Tell you what," Persky said. "Invite me upstairs. A cup of tea. We'll make a conversation. You'll see, I got other ideas up my sleeve — tomorrow we'll go someplace and you'll like it."

Her room was miraculously ready: tidy, clarified. It was sorted out: you could see where the bed ended and the table commenced. Sometimes it was all one jumble, a highway of confusion. Destiny had clarified her room just in time for a visitor. She started the tea. Persky put his newspaper down on the table, and on top of it an oily paper bag. "Crullers!" he announced. "I bought them to eat in the car, but this is very nice, cozy. You got a cozy place, Lublin."

"Cramped," Rosa said.

"I work from a different theory. For everything there's a bad way of describing, also a good way. You pick the good way, you get along better."

"I don't like to give myself lies," Rosa said.

"Life is short, we all got to lie. Tell me, you got paper napkins? Never mind, who needs them. Three cups! That's a lucky thing, usually when a person lives alone they don't keep so many.

Look, vanilla icing, chocolate icing. Two plain also. You prefer with icing or plain? Such fine tea bags, they got style. Now, you see, Lublin? Everything's nice!"

He had set the table. To Rosa this made the corner of the room look new, as if she had never seen it before.

"Don't let the tea cool off. Remember what I told you this morning, the hotter the better," Persky said; he clanged his spoon happily. "Here, let's make more elbow room — "

His hand, greasy from the crullers, was on Magda's box.

"Don't touch!"

"What's the matter? It's something alive in there? A bomb? A rabbit? It's squashable? No, I got it — a lady's hat!"

Rosa hugged the box; she was feeling foolish, trivial. Everything was frivolous here, even the deepest property of being. It seemed to her someone had cut out her life organs and given them to her to hold. She walked the little distance to the bed — three steps — and set the box down against the pillow. When she turned around, Persky's teeth were persisting in their independent bliss.

"The fact is," he said, "I didn't expect nothing from you tonight. You got to work things through, I can see that. You remind me of my son. Even to get a cup of tea from you is worth something, I could do worse. Tomorrow we'll have a real appointment. I'm not inquiring, I'm not requesting. I'll be the boss, what do you say?"

Rosa sat. "I'm thinking, I should get out and go back to New York to my niece — "

"Not tomorrow. Day after tomorrow you'll change your life, and tomorrow you'll come with me. We got six meetings to pick from."

Rosa said doubtfully, "Meetings?"

"Speakers. Lectures for fancy people like yourself. Something higher than pinochle."

"I don't play," Rosa acknowledged.

Persky looked around. "I don't see no books neither. You want me to drive you to the library?"

A thread of gratitude pulled in her throat. He almost understood what she was: no ordinary button. "I read only Polish," she told him. "I don't like to read in English. For literature you need a mother tongue."

"*Li*terature, my my. Polish ain't a dime a dozen. It don't grow
on trees neither. Lublin, you should adjust. Get used to it!"

She was wary: "I'm used to everything."

"Not to being a regular person."

"My niece Stella," Rosa slowly gave out, "says that in America
cats have nine lives, but we — we're less than cats, so we got
three. The life before, the life during, the life after." She saw
that Persky did not follow. She said, "The life after is now. The
life before is our *real* life, at home, where we was born."

"And during?"

"This was Hitler."

"Poor Lublin," Persky said.

"You wasn't there. From the movies you know it." She recognized that she had shamed him; she had long ago discovered
this power to shame. "After, after, that's all Stella cares. For me
there's one time only, there's no after."

Persky speculated. "You want everything the way it was before."

"No, no, no," Rosa said. "It can't be. I don't believe in Stella's
cats. Before is a dream. After is a joke. Only during stays. And
to call it a life is a lie."

"But it's over," Persky said. "You went through it, now you
owe yourself something."

"This is how Stella talks. Stella — " Rosa halted; then she
came on the word. "Stella is self-indulgent. She wants to wipe
out memory."

"Sometimes a little forgetting is necessary," Persky said, "if
you want to get something out of life."

"Get something! Get *what?*"

"You ain't in a camp. It's finished. Long ago it's finished. Look
around, you'll see human beings."

"What I see," Rosa said, "is bloodsuckers."

Persky hesitated. "Over there, they took your family?"

Rosa held up all the fingers of her two hands. Then she said,
"I'm left. Stella's left." She wondered if she dared to tell him
more. The box on the bed. "Out of so many, three."

Persky asked, "Three?"

"Evidence," Rosa said briskly. "I can show you."

She raised the box. She felt like a climber on the margin of a
precipice. "Wipe your hands."

Persky obeyed. He rubbed the last of the cruller crumbs on his shirt front.

"Unpack and look in. Go ahead, lift up what's inside."

She did not falter. What her own hands longed to do she was yielding to a stranger, a man with pockets; she knew why. To prove herself pure: a madonna. Supposing he had vile old man's thoughts: let him see her with the eye of truth. A mother.

But Persky said, "How do you count three — "

"Look for yourself."

He took the cover off and reached into the box and drew out a sheet of paper and began to skim it.

"That has to be from Stella. Throw it out, never mind. More scolding, how I'm a freak — "

"Lublin, you're a regular member of the intelligentsia! This is quite some reading matter. It ain't in Polish neither." His teeth danced. "On such a sad subject, allow me a little joke. Who came to America was one, your niece Stella; Lublin, Rosa, this makes two; and Lublin's brain — three!"

Rosa stared. "I'm a mother, Mr. Persky," she said, "the same as your wife, no different." She received the paper between burning palms. "Have some respect," she commanded the bewildered glitter of his plastic grin. And read:

Dear Ms. Lublin:

I am taking the liberty of sending you, as a token of my good faith, this valuable study by Hidgeson (whom, you may recall, I mentioned in passing in my initial explanatory letter), which more or less lays the ethological groundwork for our current structures. I feel certain that — in preparation for our talks — you will want to take a look at it. A great deal of our work has been built on these phylogenetic insights. You may find some of the language a bit too technical; nevertheless I believe that simply having this volume in your possession will go far toward reassuring you concerning the professionalism of our endeavors, and of your potential contribution toward them.

Of special interest, perhaps, is Chapter Six, entitled "Defensive Group Formation: The Way of the Baboons."

Gratefully in advance,
James W. Tree, Ph.D.

Persky said, "Believe me, I could smell with only one glance it wasn't from Stella."

She saw that he was holding the thing he had taken out of the box. "Give me that," she ordered.

He recited, "By A. R. Hidgeson. And listen to the title, something fancy — 'Repressed Animation: A Theory of the Biological Ground of Survival.' I told you fancy! This isn't what you wanted?"

"Give it to me."

"You didn't want? Stella sent you what you didn't want?"

"Stella sent!" She tore the book from him — it was heavier than she had guessed — and hurled it at the ceiling. It slammed down into Persky's half-filled teacup. Shards and droplets flew. "The way I smashed up my store, that's how I'll smash Tree!"

Persky was watching the tea drip to the floor.

"Tree?"

"Dr. Tree! Tree the bloodsucker!"

"I can see I'm involved in a mistake," Persky said. "I'll tell you what, you eat up the crullers. You'll feel better and I'll come tomorrow when the mistake is finished."

"I'm not your button, Persky! I'm nobody's button, not even if they got barbed wire everywhere!"

"Speaking of buttons, I'll go and push the elevator button. Tomorrow I'll come back."

"Barbed wire! You took my laundry, you think I don't know that? Look in your dirty pockets, you thief Persky!"

In the morning, washing her face — it was swollen, nightmares like weeds, the bulb of her nose pale — Rosa found, curled inside a towel, the missing underwear.

She went downstairs to the desk; she talked over having her phone reconnected. Naturally they would charge more, and Stella would squawk. All the same, she wanted it.

At the desk they handed her a package; this time she examined the wrapping. It had come by registered mail and it was from Stella. It was not possible to be hoodwinked again, but Rosa was shocked, depleted, almost as if yesterday's conflagration hadn't been Tree but really the box with Magda's shawl.

She lifted the lid of the box and looked down at the shawl; she was indifferent. Persky too would have been indifferent. The colorless cloth lay like an old bandage; a discarded sling.

For some reason it did not instantly restore Magda, as usually happened, a vivid thwack of restoration, like an electric jolt. She was willing to wait for the sensation to surge up whenever it would. The shawl had a faint saliva smell, but it was more nearly imagined than smelled.

Under the bed the telephone vibrated: first a sort of buzz, then a real ring. Rosa pulled it out.

The Cuban's voice said, "Missus Lublin, you connected now."

Rosa wondered why it was taking so long for Magda to come alive. Sometimes Magda came alive with a brilliant swoop, almost too quickly, so that Rosa's ribs were knocked on their insides by copper hammers, clanging and gonging.

The instrument, still in her grip, drilled again. Rosa started: it was as if she had squeezed a rubber toy. How quickly a dead thing can come to life! Very tentatively, whispering into a frond, Rosa said, "Hello?" It was a lady selling frying pans.

"No," Rosa said, and dialed Stella. She could hear that Stella had been asleep. Her throat was softened by a veil. "Stella," Rosa said, "I'm calling from my own room."

"Who is this?"

"Stella, you don't recognize me?"

"Rosa! Did anything happen?"

"Should I come back?"

"My God," Stella said, "is it an emergency? We could discuss this by mail."

"You wrote me I should come back."

"I'm not a millionaire," Stella said. "What's the point of this call?"

"Tree's here."

"Tree? What's that?"

"*Doctor* Tree. You sent me his letter, he's after me. By accident I found out where he stays."

"No one's after you," Stella said grimly.

Rosa said, "Maybe I should come back and open up again."

"You're talking nonsense. You *can't.* The store's finished. If you come back it has to be a new attitude absolutely, recuperated. The end of morbidness."

"A very fancy hotel," Rosa said. "They spend like kings."

"It's none of your business."

"A Tree is none of my business? He gets rich on our blood! Prestige! People respect him! A professor with specimens! He wrote me baboons!"

"You're supposed to be recuperating," Stella said; she was wide awake. "Walk around. Keep out of trouble. Put on your bathing suit. Mingle. How's the weather?"

"In that case you come here," Rosa said.

"Oh my God, I can't afford it. You talk like I'm a millionaire. What would I do down there?"

"I don't like it alone. A man stole my underwear."

"Your *what?*" Stella squealed.

"My panties. There's plenty perverts in the streets. Yesterday in the sand I saw two naked men."

"Rosa," Stella said, "if you want to come back, come back. I wrote you that, that's all I said. But you could get interested in something down there for a change. If not a job, a club. If it doesn't cost too much, I wouldn't mind paying for a club. You could join some kind of group, you could walk, you could swim — "

"I already walked."

"Make friends." Stella's voice tightened. "Rosa, this is long *dis*tance."

On that very phrase, "long *dis*tance," Magda sprang to life. Rosa took the shawl and put it over the knob of the receiver: it was like a little doll's head then. She kissed it, right over Stella's admonitions. "Good-bye," she told Stella, and didn't care what it had cost. The whole room was full of Magda: she was like a butterfly, in this corner and in that corner, all at once. Rosa waited to see what age Magda was going to be: how nice, a girl of sixteen, girls in their bloom move so swiftly that their blouses and skirts balloon, they are always butterflies at sixteen. There was Magda, all in flower. She was wearing one of Rosa's dresses from high school. Rosa was glad: it was the sky-colored dress, a middling blue with black buttons seemingly made of round chips of coal, like the unlit shards of stars. Persky could never have been acquainted with buttons like that, they were so black and so sparkling; original, with irregular facets like bits of true coal from a vein in the earth or some other planet. Magda's hair was still as yellow as buttercups, and so slippery and fine that her two barrettes, in the shape of cornets, kept sliding down toward the sides of her chin — that chin which was the marvel of her face; with a different kind of chin it would have been a much less explicit face. The jaw was ever so slightly too long, a deepened oval, so that her mouth, especially the lower lip, was not crowded but rather made a definite mark in the middle of spaciousness. Consequently the mouth seemed as significant as a body arrested in orbit, and Magda's sky-filled eyes, nearly rectangular at the corners, were like two obeisant satellites. Magda could be seen with great clarity. She had begun to resemble Rosa's father, who had also had a long oval face anchored by a positive mouth. Rosa was enraptured by Magda's healthy forearms. She would have given everything to set her before an easel, to see whether she could paint in watercolors; or to have her seize a violin, or a chess queen; she knew little about Magda's mind at this age, or whether she had any talents; even what her intelligence tended toward. And also she was always a little suspicious of Magda, because of the other strain, whatever it was, that ran in her. Rosa herself was not truly suspicious, but Stella was, and that induced perplexity in Rosa. The other strain was ghostly, even dangerous. It was as if the peril hummed out from the filaments of Magda's hair, those narrow bright wires.

My Gold, my Wealth, my Treasure, my Hidden Sesame, my Paradise, my Yellow Flower, my Magda! Queen of Bloom and Blossom!

When I had my store I used to "meet the public," and I wanted to tell everybody — not only our story but other stories as well. Nobody knew anything. This amazed me, that nobody remembered what happened only a little while ago. They didn't remember because they didn't know. I'm referring to certain definite facts. The tramcar in the Ghetto, for instance. You know they took the worst section, a terrible slum, and they built a wall around it. It was a regular city neighborhood, with rotting old tenements. They pushed in half a million people, more than double the number there used to be in that place. Three families, including all their children and old folks, into one apartment. Can you imagine a family like us — my father who had been the director-general of the Bank of Warsaw, my sheltered mother, almost Japanese in her shyness and refinement, my two young brothers, my older brother, and me — all of us, who had lived in a tall house with four floors and a glorious attic (you could touch the top of the house by sticking your arm far out its window; it was like pulling the whole green ribbon of summer indoors) — imagine confining *us* with teeming Mockowiczes and Rabinowiczes and Perskys and Finkelsteins, with all their bad-smelling grandfathers and their hordes of feeble children! The children were half-dead, always sitting on boxes in tatters with such sick eyes, pus on the lids and the pupils too wildly lit up. All these families used up their energies with walking up and down, and bowing, and shaking and quaking over old rags of prayer books, and their children sat on the boxes and yelled prayers, too. We thought they didn't know how to organize themselves in adversity, and, besides that, we were furious: because the same sort of adversity was happening to *us* — my father was a person of real importance, and my tall mother had so much delicacy and dignity that people would bow automatically, even before they knew who she was. So we were furious in every direction, but most immediately we were furious because we had to be billeted with such a class, with these old Jew peasants worn out from their rituals and superstitions, phylacteries on their foreheads sticking up so stupidly, like unicorn horns, every morning. And in the most repulsive slum, deep in slops and vermin and a toilet not fit for the lowest criminal. We were not of a background to show our fury, of course, but my father told my brothers and me that my mother would not be able to live through it, and he was right.

In my store I didn't tell this to everyone; who would have the patience to hear it all out? So I used to pick out one little thing here, one little thing there, for each customer. And if I saw they were in a hurry — most of them were, after I began — I would tell just about the tramcar. When I told about the tramcar, no one ever understood that it ran on tracks! Everybody always thought of buses. Well, they couldn't tear up the tracks, they couldn't get rid of the overhead electric wire, could they? The point is they couldn't reroute the whole tram system; so, you know, they didn't. The tramcar came right through the middle of the Ghetto. What they did was build a sort of overhanging pedestrian bridge for the Jews — they couldn't get near the tramcar to escape on it into the other part of Warsaw. The other side of the wall.

The most astounding thing was that the most ordinary streetcar, bumping along on the most ordinary trolley tracks, and carrying the most ordinary citizens going from one section of Warsaw to another, ran straight into the place of our misery. Every day, and several times a day, we had these witnesses. Every day they saw us — women with shopping sacks, and once I noticed a head of lettuce sticking up out of the top of a sack. Green lettuce! I thought my salivary glands would split with aching for that leafy greenness. And girls wearing hats. They were all the sort of plain people of the working class with slovenly speech who ride tramcars, but they were considered better than we, because no one regarded us as Poles anymore. And we, my father, my mother — we had so many pretty jugs on the piano and shining little tables, replicas of Greek vases, and one an actual archeological find that my father had dug up on a school vacation in his teens, on a trip to Crete — it was all pieced together, and the missing parts, which broke up the design of a warrior with a javelin, filled in with reddish clay. And on the walls, up and down the corridors and along the stairs, we had wonderful ink drawings, the black so black and miraculous, how it measured out a hand and then the shadow of the hand. And with all this — especially our Polish, the way my parents enunciated Polish in soft calm voices with the most precise articulation, so that every syllable struck its target — the people in the tramcar were regarded as Poles — well, they *were*, I don't take it away from them, though they took it away from us — and we were not! They, who couldn't read one line of Tuwim, never mind Virgil, and my father, who knew nearly the whole first half of the Aeneid by heart. And in this place now I am like the woman who held the lettuce in the tramcar. I said all this in my store, talking to the deaf. How I became like the woman with the lettuce.

Rosa wanted to explain to Magda still more about the jugs and the drawings on the walls, and the old things in the store, things that nobody cared about, broken chairs with carved birds, long strings of glass beads, gloves and wormy muffs abandoned in drawers. But she was tired from writing so much, even though this time she was not using her regular pen, she was writing inside a blazing flying current, a terrible beak of light bleeding out a kind of cuneiform on the underside of her brain. The drudgery of reminiscence brought fatigue, she felt glazed, lethargic. And Magda! Already she was turning away. Away. The blue of her dress was now only a speck in Rosa's eye. Magda did not even stay to claim her letter: there it flickered, unfinished, like an ember, and all because of the ringing from the floor near the bed. Voices, sounds, echoes, noise — Magda collapsed at any stir, fearful as a phantom. She behaved at these moments as if she were ashamed, and hid herself. Magda, my beloved, don't be ashamed! Butterfly, I am not ashamed of your presence: only come to me, come to me again, if no longer now, then later, always come. These were Rosa's private words; but she was stoic, tamed; she did not say them aloud to Magda. Pure Magda, head as bright as a lantern.

The shawled telephone, little grimy silent god, so long comatose — now, like Magda, animated at will, ardent with its cry. Rosa let it clamor once or twice and then heard the Cuban girl announce — oh, "announce"! — Mr. Persky: should he come up or would she come down? A parody of a real hotel! — of, in fact, the MARIE LOUISE, with its fountains, its golden thrones, its thorned wire, its burning Tree!

"He's used to crazy women, so let him come up," Rosa told the Cuban. She took the shawl off the phone.

Magda was not there. Shy, she ran from Persky. Magda was away.

LOWRY PEI

The Cold Room

(FROM STORIES)

THE DOGS WERE THE WORST. He found it hard to work up much
sympathy for rats, and he was thankful they were the only animals he had to work with — injecting them, sticking tubes into
them, changing their plumbing, draining their blood for analysis. Some technicians had to deal with cows or pigs, which were
too big to be moved from place to place, and usually ended up
imprisoned in a lab built around them, where no one ever saw
them but the people who tended their cables and tubes. Bats
were too small and strange to care about, and laboratory rab-
bits were almost too stupid. But the cats bothered him, and the
dogs were the worst. Especially when at the end of the day he
took the dead rats — bulges in bloody plastic bags, their dead
tails no longer pink but white like the rest of them — down to
the cold room. He opened the heavy door, like that on a meat
locker, and threw the sack toward one of the garbage cans inside, trying not to see the fifty-five-gallon drums of dead dogs.
The dogs that wouldn't fit into the drums lay stiffening in transparent green bags on the floor. He held his breath while doing
this, and if the rats missed the garbage can he didn't go inside
to pick them up.

The rat room stank, but Jackson was used to it. The first time
he had come down to inject the rats at 8:10 on a Monday morning he had thought the smell would drive him out of the room.
It was still bad on Mondays, if the weekend crew hadn't bothered to clean that particular room, but in general the rat room
was bearable. Perhaps he was learning how to turn off his nose.

Sometimes Jackson and the other technicians would even hang around for a few minutes after they'd finished weighing and feeding and injecting, just to get away from the Chief and his post-docs, and look at other people's rats to pass the time — especially the huge old slow ones, weighing over half a kilo, that lived one to a cage like solitary pets.

On this particular day Jackson left the rat room by himself, having come down in midmorning to see if the previous day's surgical work had survived. As he passed down the dingy hallway, toward the double doors that led to the hospital proper, he heard shouting and scuffling behind him. Turning, he saw a furry gray dog bounding at him, away from two technicians and a wheeled cage. The dog ran straight to him, happy and friendly, unlike the sullen curs who filled most of the cages; it seemed half-grown, still puppyish in its reactions. Apparently it had already forgotten the other two technicians and the cage. He hunkered down and clicked his tongue to the dog, holding out his hands; it ran around him, wagging its hindquarters, while he petted it on the run. Then he stopped the dog, putting an arm around its chest, and it jumped up on him, licking at his face. Jackson stood up, lifting the dog off the floor, and handed it to the two technicians, who had approached with the cage. "Thanks," they said, threw the dog in, and trundled it off.

After they had banged through the double doors, Jackson stood still in the hallway, fingering the bottles and syringes in his lab coat pockets, frowning at the floor. Giving back the dog had been an automatic response. Been here too long, he thought. But what choice did he have? Refuse to give it back, run off with it across the parking lot, lose his job, leave town to avoid the police — all for one dog?

The scene returned to him over and over, throughout the day. The gray dog had approached him with the joy of discovering a new friend — and he had given it back, to be taken upstairs and have clever anastomoses made in its circulatory system that would eventually mean liver failure, hypertension, a heart attack. The incident seemed like a message he ought not to ignore, as if words had been spoken to him about the urgency of loving — how there might be only a moment to make the choice, and never a second chance. It was a hot day, and the air conditioner in the lab worked poorly; heat radiated from the dissecting lamp, and on a counter behind him the dead rats faintly stank.

The Chief's graduate student, whom they had all come to hate, was driving the technicians to finish his thesis experiments — as he had done for weeks — so they did not get out of the lab until nearly 5:30. Jackson took down two heavy plastic bags of dead rats and threw them into the cold room on the way out, taking a quick, reluctant look to find out if the gray dog was there yet. He didn't see it.

It was hot outside, and still a couple of hours until sunset. Jackson had never known what hot was until he had moved to Kentucky. The low sun was an inexorable presence, beating into his face as he walked across the parking lot to his car.

Home, he said hello to the cat (imagining it briefly, as usual, with a tube in its neck), made himself a drink of cheap gin and cheap tonic, turned on his hi-fi (watching the exposed tubes of the amplifier glow into life), put on a record of Satie he had nearly played to death. The simple chords of the "Gymnopedies" crossed the air of the room. His lifeline. There was no mail. He picked up the book he was halfway through and began reading, about being a warrior, about waiting for one's will, about acquiring patience.

In a few minutes he made another gin-and-tonic and put a pot of leftover stew on the stove. He turned the record over. It was hot in the apartment, but he refused to turn on the air conditioner; that processed air smelled too much like the hospital. He sweated and chewed on ice cubes.

He continued to read while he ate dinner.

He put his plate on the floor for the cat.

The dishes were beginning to pile up. Not that he had many.

He wanted another gin-and-tonic, but he was afraid of getting in the habit of drinking too much, and besides, gin was expensive.

It was finally beginning to cool off. The crickets were loud outside.

He was bored, but there was no one he wanted to call, and in any case, he was waiting for Debbie to call and say when she was coming in from Boston. Out the open window he watched the lights blink on the smokestack of the power plant, wondering if they had ever prevented a plane from crashing into it. Expecting the phone to ring put him on edge — he dreaded the sound. Even when the phone sat silent he had the feeling it was watching him, that through it Debbie could monitor his thoughts as precisely as he could a rat's blood pressure. She knew when he was attracted to another woman before he did. But what rat ever unhooked himself, got up off the workbench and walked away?

He drank another gin-and-tonic and went to bed; lying there, he thought of what the telephone, and therefore Debbie, must know.

He had met Janet at a party in Lexington. They were sitting in a circle of eight or ten, making conversation with different people; they had talked to each other for a few minutes an hour earlier. She had a delicate face and yet her mouth could widen humorously in a way that convinced him she knew more than she was telling. The room crowded in on him, full of people who took up more space in the world than he felt entitled to. He sat in a chair, she on the floor at his left, and when she bent forward, exposing the nape of her neck, Jackson felt a tenderness that overpowered him and made him reach toward her. He gave himself up for a fool as his hand covered that vulnerable spot, but she did not flinch, or move away. As if she had understood before he did, she looked at him once. Her eyes were open and so were his; then she went on with her conversation. After living alone in a strange town for a year, working in a rat lab, waiting for the mail, Jackson felt life start up in him again, something other than endurance take over the controls.

They kept talking to other people, and his hand kept caressing her neck; awareness of that touch drowned out every word, and yet it was a secret. Then those other people moved away, and they turned to each other. They squeezed themselves into the chair and held hands, and felt their legs touching, and talked. Later, when the crowd had thinned out, they leaned against a wall in the hallway, kissing. Some people passed by and smirked, but Jackson hardly noticed. Her wanting him filled him with huge surprise, as if a secret order of things were being revealed to him for the first time.

When they left into the frosty night it was nearly first light. Jackson lived seventy miles away, in Louisville, but he could not leave her. She said he could come over for a while.

When they reached her apartment it was dawn, and he wanted her absolutely. He knelt, face against her body, his hands under her sweater touching her breasts, her back.

No, she said, she could not go to bed with him. He picked her up and carried her to the bed a few feet away, laid her on it, lay down beside her.

"If someone had told me last night that I'd be lying in bed with you this morning, I'd have said they were crazy," she said, but she made no resistance as he drew her sweater over her head, she slid her fingers onto his chest as he unbuttoned his shirt, and neither of them said anything more.

When they got up it was Sunday afternoon. Bright sun beat against a windowful of plants so thick they almost blocked the light. On an impulse of hers, they went out to Lexington's dinky, antiquated airport and watched the infrequent traffic come and go. She said she liked to stand at the windows of the little terminal and think about leaving, about how she could go from there to any place she could afford, fast, and all he could think was, Don't go.

When it began to get dark and cold, they went back to her apartment and made love again, this time in darkness, with the alcohol out of their bodies; afterwards, Jackson felt so at home he was afraid to notice the feeling in case it might go away.

"I've got to go have dinner at my parents'," she said, when they were getting dressed again. "Want to come? I'd love for them to meet you." ·

He had been profoundly uninterested in everyone but her since the night before; now the social world came back all at once and scared him.

"I really have to go back. But thank you."

"Come on, there'll be lots of people there, we do it every couple of weeks."

Lots of people — no, there had to be some excuse. "Do you really think it's a good idea? I mean, you just picked me up at a party last night," he said with a lame smile, trying to pass it off as a joke.

"Suit yourself," she said, turning around sharply and going to the closet.

"I'm sorry," Jackson said to her back. The flash of anger had seemed to wake him from a half-dream he had been in all day, and, waking, he remembered for the first time that it had seemed crazy to hope they could be joined. He thought of the lab, taking orders from the Chief, the evenings silent except for the record player. Something amazing had happened. All at once he was uncertain what to do. She stepped into her shoes. "It doesn't matter," she said, turning around and coming back to him. "You can come over some other time."

After that they saw each other every couple of weeks. At first they parted each time with nothing arranged except that they would be together again; then they began to write to each other and plan their next weekend. She never mentioned the Sunday dinners at her family's house again; when it came to be late Sunday afternoon, Jackson drove home, and ate dinner by himself.

The fourth time they were together she told him that his lovemaking was not as gentle as it had been, there was something rough and distant about it. He knew it was true. They had never, either of them, spoken the word *love* to the other, but Jackson thought of saying it every day. He thought of how her shoulders felt, or the red in her hair under strong sunlight, or the way her eyes would mock him and then go serious, letting him in again. Without expecting to, he admired her, he could not hear her voice enough. For hours he would forget everything but her. He did not want to be reminded that when he went home to the apartment he never dared take her to, the telephone would be there, watching him and listening. The harshness was for that, and she felt it. She didn't ask him what caused it; he didn't ask her what she did on the weekends when she couldn't see him.

One night he put a letter to her and a letter to Debbie in the mailbox at the same time; as they tumbled in together, he was seized with a sudden fear that he might have put them in the wrong envelopes, and then he realized that something had to change.

Debbie was thirty-six, divorced, eleven years older than Jackson. They had gone to the same graduate school; by the end of a year they were living together. For Jackson, it had been like walking in on a marriage at the five-year mark. Ceremonies of intimacy waited in the rooms of her house like furniture. How to have a drink before dinner (he toasting, "Happy days"; she, "and happy nights"); how to have elegant Sunday breakfasts; how to celebrate holidays — she taught him these things. To Jackson it was like being transported overnight to some part of the future. He hardly knew what was happening to him, except that he was in over his head, and that much of the time he was happy. He was both frightened and proud that he lived with a grown woman, a whole being, unlike the younger women his friends went out with. He never had to invent something to do.

But he wanted to do the starting of things, that was the point. When he saw that Debbie avoided single men her own age, he felt more trapped than relieved. The sensation ate at him, isolated him with her. After a year and a half he knew it was time for them to give it up; he felt sure she knew it too, and he expected her to take the initiative, but she did not. His moving away did not seem enough to tip the balance. He tried to tell himself that being with Janet made no difference to him and Debbie, but apparently he had to choose one or the other, and the one he had to choose was Debbie. He could not be the one to say "the end"; she had handed him a life, and if he could not go on loving her, what was he?

"Look, you don't just write somebody and say, 'I've got this other girlfriend,' " Janet said, late on a Saturday afternoon. "How am I supposed to know what you really mean in a letter? I spent the last four days wondering what the secret message is."

"There isn't one."

"Come on, there is, of course there is. All it takes is the nerve to say it." It was dusk, and they hadn't turned a lamp on yet; in the dimness of her living room her eyes flashed angrily at him and away from him.

"I've got a secret too," she said in a different tone, after a silence. "I was almost thinking of marrying him last winter, right before we met."

Fear and astonishment shot through Jackson; an abyss seemed to open behind his heels. His own audacity, in retrospect, was staggering.

"And now?" he said, in place of all the other questions he wanted to ask, that would have involved the word *love.*

"I don't know. I used to see him every weekend when you weren't here. I don't like that — being divided. For a while I thought about not seeing you anymore."

He remembered what his life had been like before they had met, how often she entered his mind as he endured the routine of the lab. He touched her arm hesitantly, wanting to hold her.

"Does she know about me?" Janet said.

"No."

"George knows about you." But she turned toward him.

Gradually, unwillingly, he ceased to call her; he wrote less and less. He thought of her every day. Debbie, to whom his love was due, was coming in the middle of July, as had been planned for months.

On the Fourth of July, as Jackson sat listening to a baseball game and drinking his third gin-and-tonic of the afternoon, the phone rang. For a moment he entertained the thought that Debbie might not be coming.

"Hello, Jackson," Janet said.

How could he not have known that this would happen someday, that there would be pain? He was half-drunk and glad of it.

"I've missed you," he said, hating himself.

"All you have to do is call."

Silence.

"I know," he mumbled, miserable.

"What is going on in your head, anyway? Don't you think I'm worth talking to long enough to say, 'This is it'? Or what *is* the message?"

"It's about Debbie," he said with great reluctance. "It's about what you said, about being divided . . ."

"I didn't stop seeing you, did I?"

"It's a thing about loyalty, I don't know what else to say."

He could hear her crying angrily, and wished that he were dead, that anything had happened but this.

"I never said it was easy — do you think it's been easy for me the last six months? I've been waiting to hear from you for weeks, do you know that?"

He forced words out one by one. "I felt like I owed it to her."

"Owed her what? To hurt me?"

Silence.

"Well, what's all this been about, then? Look, I don't give a damn about her or how you feel about her, I just need you over here right now."

"I want to be there, you must know that. I've never been more sorry about anything in my whole damn life."

"I don't want you to be sorry," she said in a barely audible voice, "I want you to come over."

"I don't think I can."

"Jackson," she cried, "who the hell is living your *life?*" but before he even understood the question, the line went dead.

Debbie got off the plane in a white suit, elegant, self-possessed; as always he had partly forgotten how she looked, the quality of her being, and was surprised for a moment, like a spectator, at the idea of this woman flying a thousand miles to be in the arms of a twenty-five-year-old lab technician.

The eating and drinking and talking were the same; the lovemaking was not. After the first time he hardly wanted her. He worked hard to hide it; she wanted him very much.

"God, it's been forever," she said on Saturday night. "For some reason all the men I meet are singularly unattractive."

"That's too bad," he said.

"And you?"

He hesitated. "Oh — I hardly meet anyone, you know."

She said nothing. Like the telephone.

In the morning, when he did not want to lie in bed once they were awake, she said, "Jackson, are you in love with someone else?"

His heart pounded. "What?" he said, hopping on one foot as he pulled on his pants. "No, of course not." He hurried into the bathroom.

Sunday breakfast dragged uncomfortably.

Driving in his car in the afternoon, she said, "Why don't you just tell me and get it over with?"

"Nothing to tell." He kept his eyes on the road.

After dinner she said, "Jackson, there's no point in playing games. You've been acting peculiar ever since I got here and I want to know what's going on."

"What do you mean, peculiar?"

"You're just not interested. It's like I'm taking up time you want for something else. Which is a hell of a welcome after all our letters, and not seeing each other since Christmas."

He was silent, staring into his third drink. It had been two weeks since he had spoken to Janet.

"If you didn't want me here you could have said so and saved me a lot of time and money."

"That's not true, it's not true I don't want you here, it's just that — "

"That what?"

"Nothing."

"You've been seeing somebody," she said with dreadful sadness, like a rejected child.

"Sort of," he muttered, looking away.

"Look, just tell me the truth. Can you manage that much consideration for my feelings?"

"Yes. I was seeing somebody for a while."

"And?"

"And I stopped."

"What's the matter, did the novelty wear off?"

He looked straight at her for a moment. "Stopped because of you."

"What's her name?"

"What difference does it make?"

"Where'd you meet her, at the hospital? How old is she?"

"I met her at a party."

"So you met her at a party — after writing me you're so lonely and sad, and me wasting all kinds of sympathy on you — and then what happened?"

"How much difference does it make exactly what happened? What do you think happened?" He heard his own cynical tone and despised himself.

"And who took the initiative?"

"We both did."

"No. Somebody had to start first."

"Okay, it was me — does that satisfy you? — it was me." He got up and went to the refrigerator, made another gin-and-tonic, keeping his back to her.

"Satisfy me?" she burst out suddenly. "Satisfy me that I've been up in Boston writing you letters about how much I miss you when you're down here screwing some . . ." Jackson stood by the divider between the kitchen and the living room, watching her work up her anger, trying to stifle his own rage. He took two gulps out of his drink.

"That's it, drink it up, have another one, then you won't have to think about it. That's what Rick always did." The way she pronounced the name made Jackson think he didn't ever want to hate anybody that much. He sat down on the table at which they had eaten dinner and stared at the floor, sweating. The cat, crouched beneath the table, stared back at him. This was what he got, he thought, for not having the courage to tell her months before.

"Can't you even say anything?"

No, he thought. After a long while he said, "What's the point?"

She stood up and walked past him toward the bedroom. "The point is that if there was an airplane out of this dump tonight I'd be on it, and the point is that there is one tomorrow and I will." As she passed him, her body shrank from him in a melodramatic way he could scarcely believe. She slammed the door, and through it he heard her fall on the bed and start to cry.

Jackson sat slumped, drink in hand, while the ice melted and she cried. He had made two women, at least one of whom he loved, desperately unhappy within the space of two weeks. He deserved some sort of medal, he thought, paralyzed.

He stayed there, blankly wretched, for over an hour, trying to get up the resolve to go in the bedroom, to do his duty, whatever in the world that might be. Finally he turned out the lights in the front room. There was silence from within. As soundlessly as possible he opened the door and entered the bedroom. Debbie lay face down on the bed, her head turned away from him, her feet over the side. She still had her shoes on. Thinking of the discomfort of waking that way, Jackson approached her and began to ease one of them off.

"Don't touch me," she said, wide awake. He almost jumped back. She kicked the shoes off, hard, and curled up on her side facing the wall.

For five minutes Jackson stood listening to himself breathe and trying not to make even that sound. Then gingerly he sat down on the bed, and, a minute or two later, put his hand on her shoulder. There was no response.

"Debbie — "

"Don't talk to me. If you want the other half of the bed, you can have it, but I'd prefer it if you'd leave me in peace."

She twitched his hand off her shoulder violently. As if in slow motion, cringing at every creak of the bedsprings, he stretched himself out on the bed.

He could not imaginably sleep. It was hot and he was still fully dressed. The silence was unendurable.

An hour later she said, in the same cold, wide-awake voice, "I don't think you know what it means to love anybody."

He lay still, his head over the edge of the bed, one hand grasping the metal frame.

"I think you're right," he finally said. It was a superhuman effort to say anything. If what she said was true, why should he bother to move, to speak at all?

"You think you can just give in like that and get some sympathy — 'poor me, I'm so awful' — I know that game."

He wanted to vomit out the guilt, expel it in one black pile, or have it cut out, like taking a core through a geological sample. "I'm — "

" 'I'! All the time 'I'! Can't you even talk without saying 'I' all the time?"

He did not want to talk, ever again, most particularly never to talk to the woman who lay beside him. He hated her, and that proved that she was right. He must not hate her. If he were not to go on being the heartless bastard she had proved him to be, he must say something, and yet what could he say that would prove him to be otherwise?

"Are you just going to lie there? Or are you going to go to sleep again, like you usually do when somebody starts telling you the truth about yourself? Why don't you get up and drink the rest of that bottle of gin, so you won't have to think about it?"

He lay for a long time contemplating that possibility, that he should do it, flauntingly, admitting that he was hateful. He could not do it because he could not move, and because he wanted to do it, and because he could not face the notion of abandoning decency altogether. And yet finally he did move, swinging one leg out of bed, then the other, letting himself slide down off the bed onto hands and knees on the floor, heavy, slack, his mouth open in the dark. He stayed there on all fours for what seemed a long time before he could muster the ability to stand up and move toward the bedroom door. He could feel the force of her hatred against his back.

The gin bottle stood on a narrow counter between the kitchen and the rest of the front room. He picked it up and looked at it in the dim light from outside. It was over half full. He put his hand to the top as if to unscrew it, but did not; instead, he took hold of the bottle by the neck, holding it like a club. His eyes wandered over the room. He was a hateful person, self-centered; self-centered even in thinking he was hateful. He walked to the stereo and brought the bottle down on its amplifier, smashing its tubes; the bottle broke against its transformers, and gin poured over the chassis. He dropped the neck of the bottle on top of the wreckage, breathing cold ginsmell, and stood over it in silence, eyes closed in the dark.

"And what was that?"

He almost fell asleep standing up before he answered.

"The record player."

"I suppose you think that proves something," she muttered, and began to cry again. Jackson was more exhausted than he had ever been in his life; he returned to the bedroom and lay on the bed, as close to the edge as possible.

At seven the alarm went off. Jackson got up, still dressed, his shoes still on, barely able to stand, and left the bedroom.

While he ate breakfast he cried, and part of his mind watched him do both these things at once and dully said, Get on with it.

There had not been a sound from the bedroom by the time he left.

All day, by the hot glare of the dissecting lamp, he cut away a patch of skin from an anesthetized rat's neck, dug down with a pair of hemostats between two muscles, found the carotid artery, occluded it so that the blood would not spurt out when he cut into it, made a tiny hole with a pair of eye-surgery scissors, worked a saline-filled cannula into the artery, tied it in, turned on the strip-chart recorder, took a twenty-minute record of the rat's systolic, diastolic, and mean pressure, its heart rate and body temperature, turned off the recorder, tied off the artery, pulled the cannula out and flushed it, gave the rat an overdose of anesthetic and put it on a counter to die out of the way. Over and over. He drank burned-tasting coffee that felt as though it were poisoning him. His hands shook slightly. He was too tired to sweat. He worked. The clock hands crawled. He didn't care.

At five o'clock he took the dead rats down in the service elevator and threw them in the cold room. Holding the door open, he was too exhausted to feel the usual repulsion. He stepped in and let the heavy door close behind him; the hair rose slightly on the back of his neck. The dead dog on the top of the drum was still limp; the ones under it had stiffened into a three-dimensional jigsaw puzzle. He pulled them out, one by one, by their rigid legs, looking dispassionately at the holes in their sides, their forced-open chests. He made himself continue, even when he had to reach all the way to the bottom, so that his head was inside the drum. All the dogs were on the floor. The gray dog was not among them. So that meant it was still alive, unless it had died already and been hauled off to the rendering plant. He didn't know how often they were taken away. Jackson sat down with his back to the wall and thought, Tomorrow, if the dog's still alive, I'll steal it and move to Lexington. It was pleasant to think so. As he sat there the cold floor warmed under his hand until its temperature reminded him of the fine dust of the softball field at his grade school, which he had once loved to sift through his fingers like cool water. Then he fell into a kind of daze, a quiet blankness, until a technician from another lab, coming in with a dead rabbit, looked wild-eyed at the scattered dogs and sent him out, half-frozen, into the summer dusk.

The warmth of the air was incomprehensible, the smell of it perfection after the air of the cold room. The low sun felt like a hot shower. Even the heat of his car, closed up all day in the sun, was momentarily tolerable. He rolled down the windows and began to drive.

A block from home it occurred to him that Debbie might still be there. He turned in the opposite direction and drove aimlessly until he came to a phone booth.

The sound of long-distance, electronic wind. What in God's name would his explanation be? Through the smudged glass, as the phone began to ring, he could see motorists driving their cars with purposeful faces, with determination, as if getting home were a matter of life or death. She had looked at him only once, when he had touched the back of her neck with his hand, and that had been enough. If only he could knock at her door immediately, be present and let her see him, then she would know. But somehow he would have to say.

"Hello?"

He was not quite ready; but relief rose in him like vertigo, sent him spinning past everything that would be difficult, in the moment before he could begin.

JONATHAN PENNER

Things To Be Thrown Away

(FROM THE YALE REVIEW)

THIS IS THE SHELL of a horseshoe crab. It came from near here,
some May or June — the season they hit the Connecticut
beaches, coupling in the shallow water, spawning in mud, often
getting stranded by the withdrawing tide. My father and mother
brought Howard and me to see them.

Most that we found high on the beach were still alive, helpless
on their backs. My father and Howard lifted the great horny
things by their tails: the ten legs wiggling wildly in air, the ab-
dominal gills flapping and rippling in such desperate thirst
that I ran to my mother. She lifted me by my armpits. Leave
them, I yelled, but they carried them down to the water, holding
them away from their bodies at rigid arm's length. You're heartless, Adam, shouted my father. They swung them in with
smacking plops, Howard jumping back to avoid the splashes.
The beach stank, and I thought this shell would fill the basement with it — the dust must seal it up.

We walked by the water at low tide and saw them gliding,
searching for mates. Look, said my mother, pointing: a couple,
the male hooked to the larger female, scudding across the bottom. We kept pace along the shore. From those hideous lovers
there sometimes rose a milky cloud of tiny bubbles. When they
swerved off into the deep, my mad father galloped into the sea,
trying to herd them toward shore, stamping out glistening
sheets of spray, and Howard backed higher up the beach. He
has always been cautious, extremely cautious, about getting wet.

Always, at the pediatrician's, it was I, the younger brother, who sat first on the examining table, legs dangling, holding the kidney-shaped pan against my neck, so Dr. Zorn could shoot an amazing invasion of warm water into my ear. That feels nice, I would announce, as they all expected me to.

Adam says it's nice, Howard, my mother said, reaching around to stroke behind her at the level of his head. Howard was silent. He peered and cringed. See how gentle Dr. Zorn is being? she asked him. Now the other one, said Dr. Zorn, meaning ear. Transferring the sloshing pan, I dropped a casual glance to it: practically nothing. If Howard envied my courage now — and he never said so, if he did — I would envy him in a few minutes, as he sat with eyes screwed shut, a thin whimper escaping his grinning mouth, while great clots of wax were flushed from him. To be so productive, so cleansed.

This stopwatch is from Woolworth's. Mornings, my father got his blood going by snapping his fingers until the sound was like firecrackers. Then he'd go jogging with this stopwatch, so many times around the block that Howard and I would forget him as we played, and he seemed not to circle but simply to appear, like a tropical fish at the front of the tank. In summer he came back very red, and we flanked him where he flopped on the bottom step, elbows on spread knees, smelling hot and acrid as some process of heavy industry, dripping so much sweat onto the cracked cement walk that the big black ants of our neighborhood had to detour around the puddle.

And this too, this string of Ivy League pennants — we bought this at Woolworth's, too. For my father, who loved buying things, price was no object: a screwdriver with a magnetic tip, or a perfect hand of bananas, pleased him as much as a rich new suit of Harris tweed. Times when my mother wasn't with us, my father and I would rage through the store, calling to each other from aisle to aisle, fingering artificial flowers and student lamps and netlike bags of miniature candy bars, while Howard stood in the pet section as though tethered there, watching the fish swim in their silence. At the checkout counter my father and I would pile our pillage. Howard would have nothing, unless it was a card for our mother — he got them when Mother's Day or Valentine's Day had just gone by, at half price. I would try to explain the error in this. But on the ride home my father would nudge me and whisper, Have a heart, until I turned around and told my unhappy brother, riding in back with our purchases, that I was only jealous, his card was terrific. He would squint in doubt, wiping an already gleaming wrist across his nostrils.

This is a garden rake of very superior design. Nothing like it in Woolworth's or anywhere: my father made them himself, down by the river in a tiny factory that he convinced his draft board was a defense plant. He drove his black box of a Hudson to real defense plants for hundreds of miles around, offering to subcontract, bringing home blueprints of weapons systems. These were marked CONFIDENTIAL and SECRET, and he loved to unroll them on our speckled linoleum floor and study them for hours, though he couldn't understand them in the least. Anyone who ran a defense plant didn't have to go to war. I called him a coward, but my mother and Howard disagreed. Some men won't march, she told me. Your father can't even dance with a partner. I thought she was wrong but maybe she was right, because when they found out that his factory was making garden rakes and not bombsights, as he'd claimed, he ran away, leaving us.

Our basement filled with garden rakes: our only asset, my mother said calmly. Howard blubbered. It's okay, I told him. We can sell those, they're top quality. My mother took me aside and said, Adam. I need you to help Howard, now. He doesn't understand things as quickly as you do.

This well-sealed box, which must be full of mildew anyway, is labeled DIPLOMAS, REPORT CARDS — H & A. By junior high school we were in the same grade, but how could I protect him? He'd stayed back two years. I had skipped a year and was practically a midget. If the bullies came after him I'd charge like crazy, but they were never impressed. Howard would let them do to him what they wanted, but if they came after me he would pull them off, and in a minute I would be running for a teacher while he lay quietly, pinned to the floor.

Dr. Zorn, who obviously liked our mother a lot, said I would grow, though maybe never very big. He said that for a mind like Howard's, none of the regular tests were valid, that Howard was probably just preoccupied with sex. If Howard was, he never

said so. When pictures were passed around on the playground
— pictures that I felt guilty and honored to hold in my hand —
he'd frown over them the way he did over algebra problems.
But he had hair, his voice had changed, and before I even had
a wet dream he was masturbating every night, soaking so many
Kleenex tissues that I would have felt intimidated if it had been
anyone but Howard.

His genitals were well developed and would have been re-
spected in the showers, where mine were ridiculed. But Howard, who hated getting wet, never showered even at home, and
on Tuesdays and Thursdays came to our mother with ailments
that might excuse him from gym. In this department Howard
was gifted. His afflictions told the seasons: hay fever in spring,
infected pores in summer, leaf mold allergy in fall, cracked and
peeling fingertips in winter. Dr. Zorn thought gym class was
exactly what Howard needed — gym had been fun for him, he
told us, the trampoline especially. When he came to visit, he'd
take miserable Howard into a room and shut the door to counsel
him, but after exclamations that mounted in volume out he'd
stalk, ruffling his hair. When I went in, Howard would be
slumped in a chair, as limp as the freshly killed. Always, Dr.
Zorn wrote the note that got Howard through the next few
weeks.

When we were in high school, our mother got a judge to
annul her marriage to our father. Then she married Dr. Zorn.
I tried to understand why, and explained it to Howard as well
as I could: she was lonely. It might be mostly platonic. But
Howard, who was sure that our father was still alive and would
someday return, never forgave our mother until, I guess, the
end of her life.

This bedpan, though I handled it then, is the one thing here
I will not touch: this, and this shell of a horseshoe crab, maybe
because they're shaped the same. I went to college, the state
university — that was when I took down from my wall this string
of Ivy League pennants — because Howard, who couldn't finish
high school, was spending a year in the state training school, in
the same town. At the start of the summer we came home and
found our mother a skeleton, almost. Anybody could see what
was coming. She hadn't wanted us to be distracted from our

studies, Dr. Zorn explained. He looked exhausted from nursing her, and I envied him that. But my brother couldn't bear to be in her room.

At her funeral, I saw Howard looking over the small crowd, again and again, as if through sheer determination he could make our father be there. He even had me looking, making allowances for changes the years could have brought. Then the funeral was over. Howard was in tears, grinning, making sounds. I put my arms around him, and in a moment I was soaking. He was heaving violently, like a water-breather dragged into the air. His tears were stinging my eyes; he held me tighter and my ear grew wet. It's just us two, I said. We'll take care of each other. But he just stood there crying and gasping until I felt his tears on my neck, and I knew I had to push him away before the tide of him reached my heart.

NORMAN RUSH

Bruns

(FROM THE NEW YORKER)

POOR BRUNS. They hated him so much it was baroque. But then so is Keteng baroque, everything about it.

Probably the Boers were going to hate Bruns no matter what. Boers run Keteng. They've been up there for generations, since before the Protectorate. When independence came, it meant next to nothing to them. They ignored it. They're all citizens of Botswana, but they are Boers underneath forever, really unregenerate. Also, in Keteng you're very close to the border with South Africa. They still mostly use rands for money instead of pula. Boers slightly intrigue me. For a woman, I'm somewhat an elitist, and hierarchy always interests me. I admit these things. The Boers own everything in Keteng, including the chief. They wave him to the head of the queue for petrol, which he gets for free, naturally, just like the cane liquor they give him. They own the shops. Also they think they really know how to manage the Bakorwa, which actually they do. You have to realize that the Bakorwa have the reputation of being the most violent and petulant tribe in the country, which is about right. All the other tribes say so. And in fact the Boers do get along with them. In fact, the original whites in Keteng — that would be the Vissers, Du Toits, Pieterses . . . seven families altogether — were all rescued by the Bakorwa when their ox wagons broke down in the desert when they were trekking somewhere. They started out as bankrupts and now they own the place. It's so feudal up there you cannot conceive. That is, it has been until now.

I know a lot about Keteng. I got interested in Keteng out of boredom with my project. Actually, my project collapsed. My thesis adviser at Stanford talked me into my topic anyway, so it wasn't all that unbearable when it flopped. At certain moments I can even get a certain vicious satisfaction out of it. Frankly, the problem is partly too many anthropologists in one small area. We are thick on the ground. And actually we hate each other. The problem is that people are contaminating one another's research, so hatred is structural and I don't need to apologize. At any rate, I was getting zero. I was supposed to be showing a relationship between diet and fertility among the Bakorwa up near Tsopong, in the hills. The theory was that fertility would show some seasonality because the diet in the deep bush was supposedly ninety percent hunting-gathering, which would mean sharp seasonal changes in diet content. But the sad fact is you go into the middle of nowhere and people are eating Simba chips and cornflakes and drinking Castle lager. The problem is Americans, partly. Take the hartebeest domestication project, where they give away so much food and scraps and things that you have a kind of permanent beggar settlement outside the gate. And just to mention the other research people you have encumbering the ground — you have me, you have the anthropologists from the stupid Migration Study and the census, and you have people from some land-grant college someplace following baboons around. By the way, there were some baboon attacks on Bakorwa gathering firewood around Keteng, which they blame on the Americans for pestering the baboons. Or Imiricans, as the Boers would say. America gets the blame.

The other thing is that Keteng is remote. It's five hours from the rail line, over unspeakable roads, through broiling-hot empty thornveldt. In one place there's no road and you just creep over red granite swells for a kilometer, following a little line of rocks. So the Boers got used to doing what they wanted, black government or not. They still pay their farm labor in sugar and salt and permission to crawl underneath their cows and suck fresh milk. It is baroque. So I got interested in Keteng and started weekending. At my project site, camping was getting uncomfortable, I should mention, with strange figures hanging around my perimeter. Nobody did anything, but it makes you nervous. In Keteng I can always get a room from the sisters at the mission hospital and a bath instead of washing my armpits under my shirt because you never know who's watching.

The place I stay when I descend into Keteng is interesting and is one reason I keep going back. I can see everything from the room the sisters give me. The hospital is up on the side of a hill, and the sisters' hostel is higher than that, on the very top. My room is right under the roof, the second story, where there's a water tank and therefore a perpetual sound of water gurgling down through pipes, a sound you get famished for in a place so arid. Also, in tubs on the roof they have vines growing that drape down over the face of the building, so you have this green-curtain effect over your window. The sisters have a little tiny enclosed locked-up courtyard where they hang their under-things to dry, which is supposed to be secret and sacrosanct, which you can see into from my room. You can also see where Bruns stayed — a pathetic bare little shack near the hospital with gravel around the stoop and a camp stool so he could sit in the sun and watch his carrots wither. At the foot of the hill the one street in Keteng begins at the hospital gate and runs straight to the chief's court at the other end of town. Downtown amounts to a dozen one-story buildings — shops — with big houses behind them. You can see the Bakorwa wards spreading away from the center of Keteng — log kraals, mud rondavels with thatch, mostly, although cement-block square houses with sheet-metal roofs held down by cobbles are infiltrating the scene. Sometimes I think anthropology should be considered a form of voyeurism rather than a science, with all the probing into reproductive life and so forth we do. I'm voyeuristic. I like to pull my bed up to the window and lie there naked, studying Keteng. Not that the street life is so exotic. Mostly it's goats and cattle. I did once see a guy frying a piece of meat on a shovel. The nuns have really hard beds, which I happen to prefer.

Poor Bruns. The first thing I ever heard about him was that there was somebody new in Keteng who was making people as nervous as poultry, as they put it. That's an Afrikaans idiom. They meant Bruns. He was a volunteer from some Netherlands

religious outfit and a conscientious objector like practically all
the Dutch and German volunteers are. He was assigned to be
the fleet mechanic at the mission hospital. He was a demon
mechanic, it turned out, who could fix anything. Including the
X-ray machine, for example, which was an old British Army
World War I field unit, an antique everybody had given up on.
Of course, what do the Boers care, because when they get even
just a little cut it's into the Cessna and over the border into the
Republic to Potgietersrust or even Pretoria. But other people
were ecstatic. Bruns was truly amazing. People found out. A few
of the Bakorwa farmers have tractors or old trucks, and Bruns,
being hyper-Christian, of course started fixing them up for free
in his spare time. On Saturdays you'd see Bakorwa pushing
these old wrecks, hordes of them pushing these three or four
old wrecks toward Keteng for Bruns. So, number one, right
away that made Bruns less than popular around Du Toit's garage. Du Toit didn't like it. It even got a little mean, with some
of Bruns's tools disappearing from his workroom at the hospital
until he started really locking things up.

The other thing that fed into making people nervous right
away was Bruns physically. He was very beautiful, I don't know
how else to put it. He was very Aryan, with those pale-blue eyes
that are apparently so de rigueur for male movie stars these
days. He had a wonderful physique. At some point possibly he
had been a physical culturist, or maybe it was just the effect of
constant manual work and lifting. Also I can't resist mentioning
a funny thing about Boer men. Or, rather, let me back into it:
there is a thing with black African men called the African Physiological Stance, which means essentially that men, when they
stand around, don't bother to hold their bellies in. It might seem
like a funny cultural trait to borrow, but Boer men picked it up.
It doesn't look so bad with blacks because the men stay pretty
skinny, usually. But in whites, especially in Boers, who run to
fat anyway, it isn't so enthralling. They wear their belts underneath their paunches, somewhat on the order of a sling. Now
consider Bruns strictly as a specimen walking around with his
nice flat belly, a real waist, and, face it, a very compact nice little
behind, and also keep in mind that he's Dutch, so in a remote
way he's the same stock as the Boer men there, and the contrast

was not going to be lost on the women, who are another story. The women have nothing to do. Help is thick on the ground. They get up at noon. They consume bales of true-romance magazines from Britain and the Republic, so incredibly crude. They do makeup. And they can get very flirtatious in an incredibly heavy-handed way after a couple of brandies. Bruns was the opposite of flirtatious. I wonder what the women thought it meant. He was very scrupulous when he was talking to you — it was nice. He never seemed to be giving you ratings on your secondary sex characteristics when he was talking to you, unlike everybody else. He kept his eyes on your face. As a person with large breasts I'm sensitized on this. Boer men are not normal. They think they're a godsend to any white woman who turns up in this wilderness. Their sex ideas are derived from their animals. I've heard they just unbanned "Love Without Fear" in South Africa this year, which says something. The book was published in 1941.

On top of that, the Dutch-Boer interface is so freakish and tense anyway. The Dutch call Afrikaans "baby Dutch." Boers are a humiliation to the Dutch, like they are their ids set free in the world or something similar. The Dutch Parliament keeps almost voting to get an oil boycott going against South Africa.

Also it wasn't helpful that Bruns was some kind of absolute vegetarian, which he combined with fasting. He was whatever is beyond lactovegetarian in strictness. You have never seen people consume meat on the scale of the Boers. As a friend of mine says, Boers and meat go together like piss and porcelain. Biltong, sausages, any kind of meat product, pieces of pure solid fat — they love meat. So there was another rub.

Bruns was so naive. He apparently had no idea he was coming to live in a shame culture. Among the Bakorwa, if you do something wrong and somebody catches you, they take you to the customary court and give you a certain number of strokes with a switch in public. They wet it first so it hurts more. This is far from being something whites thought up and imposed. It's the way it is. The nearest regular magistrate is — where? Bobonong? Who knows? Bakorwa justice is based on beatings and the fear of beatings and shame, full stop. It's premodern. But here comes Bruns wearing his crucifix and wondering what is going on. The problem was he had an unfortunate introduction to the culture. You could call wife beating among the Bakorwa pretty routine. I think he saw an admission to the hospital related to that. Also he himself was an ex–battered child, somebody said. I'm thinking of setting up a course for people who get sent here. I can give you an example of the kind of thing people should know about and not think twice about. The manager of the butchery in one of the towns caught two women shoplifting and he made them stand against the wall while he whipped them with an extension cord instead of calling the police. This shamed them and was probably effective and they didn't lose time from work or their families. You need anthropologists to prepare people for the culture here. Bruns needed help. He needed information.

Bruns belonged to some sect. It was something like the people in England who jump out and disrupt fox hunts. Or there was a similar group, also in England, of people who were interposing themselves between prizefighters, to stop prizefighting. Bruns was from some milieu like that. I think he felt like he'd wandered into something by Hieronymus Bosch which he was supposed to do something about.

The fact is that the amount of fighting and beating there is in Bakorwa culture is fairly staggering to a person at first. Kids get beaten at school and at home, really hard sometimes. Wives naturally get beaten. Animals. Pets. Donkeys. And of course the whole traditional court process, the *kgotla*, is based on it. I think he was amazed. Every Wednesday at the *kgotla* the chief hears charges and your shirt comes off and you get two to twenty strokes, depending. Then there's the universal recreational punching and shoving that goes on when the locals start drinking. So it's not something you can afford to be sensitive about if you're going to work here for any length of time.

Bruns decided to do something. The first thing he tried was absurd and made everything worse.

He started showing up at the *kgotla* when they were giving judgment and just stood there watching them give strokes. He was male, so he could get right up in the front row. I understand he never said anything, the idea being just to be a sorrowful witness. I guess he thought it would have some effect. But the Bakorwa didn't get it and didn't care. He was welcome.

Maybe I'm just a relativist on corporal punishment. Our own wonderful culture is falling apart with crime, more than Keteng is, and you could take the position that substituting imprisonment for the various kinds of rough justice there used to be has only made things worse. Who knows if there was less crime when people just formed mobs in a cooperative spirit and rode people out of town on a rail or horsewhipped them, when that was the risk you were running rather than plea bargaining and courses in basket weaving or some other fatuous kind of so-called rehabilitation? I don't.

Bruns convinced himself that the seven families were to blame for all the violence — spiritually to blame at least. He was going to ask them to do something about it, take some kind of stand, and he was going to the center of power, Deon Du Toit.

There's some disagreement as to whether Bruns went once to Du Toit's house or twice. Everybody agrees Du Toit wasn't home and that Bruns went in and stayed, however many times he went, stayed talking with Marika, Du Toit's slutty wife. The one time everybody agrees on was at night. Bruns started to turn away when the maid told him Du Toit wasn't there. But then somehow Bruns was invited in. That's established. Then subsequently there was one long afternoon encounter, supposedly.

Bruns was going to blame the families for everything — for making money off liquor, which leads to violence, for doing nothing about violence to women and not even appearing in *kgotla* for women who worked for them when they were brutalized by their husbands or boyfriends, for corrupting the chief, who was an incompetent anyway, for doing nothing about conditions at the jail. I can generate this list out of my own knowledge of Bruns's mind: everything on it is true. Finally there was something new he was incensed about. The drought had been bad and Du Toit had just started selling water for three pula a drum. You know a drought is bad when cattle come into town and bite the brass taps off cisterns. A wildebeest charged an old woman carrying melons and knocked her down so it could get the moisture in the melons.

We know what Du Toit did when he came back and found out Bruns had been there. First he punched the housemaid, Myriad Gofetile (her twin sister also works for Du Toit), for letting Bruns in or for not telling him about it, one or the other. And Marika wasn't seen outside the house for a while, although the Boers usually try not to mark their women where it shows when they beat them.

Those are two people I would love to see fighting, Deon and Marika Du Toit, tooth and nail. It would be gorgeous. Both of them are types. He's fairly gigantic. Marika has skin like a store dummy's. She's proud of it. She's one of those people who are between twenty-five and forty but you can't tell where. She has high cheekbones you can't help envying, and these long eyes, rather Eurasian-looking. She wears her hair like a fool, though — lacquered, like a scoop around her head. Her hair is yellow-ish. She hardly says anything. But she doesn't need to because she's so brilliant with her cigarette, smoking and posing.

Deon was away hunting during the time or times Bruns visited. The inevitable thing happened, besides beating up on his household, when Deon found out. This was the day he got back, midmorning. He sent a yard boy to the hospital with a message to the effect that Bruns is ordered to drop whatever he's doing and come immediately to see Deon at the house.

Bruns is cool. He sends back the message that he's engaged on work for the hospital and regrets he isn't free to visit.

So that message went back, and the yard boy comes back with a new command that Bruns should come to Du Toit's at tea, which would be at about eleven. Bruns sends the message back that he doesn't break for tea, which was true.

Suddenly you have Deon himself materializing in the hospital garage, enraged, still covered with gore from hauling game out of his pickup. He had shot some eland.

"You don't come by my wife when I am away!" He ended up screaming this at Bruns, who just carried on fixing some vehicle.

He now orders Bruns to come to his house at lunch, calling him a worm and so on, which was apropos Bruns being a pacifist.

Bruns took the position that he had authority over who was present in the garage and ordered Du Toit to leave.

Then there was a stupid exchange to the effect that Bruns would come only if Du Toit was in actual fact inviting him to a meal at noon.

Throughout all this Bruns is projecting a more and more sorrowful calmness. Also, everything Bruns says is an aside, since he keeps steadily working. Deon gets frantic. The sun is pounding down. You have this silent chorus of Africans standing around. There is no question but that they are loving every moment.

It ends with Deon telling Bruns he had better be at his house at noon if he expects to live to have sons.

Of course, after the fact everybody wanted to know why somebody didn't intervene.

Bruns did go at lunchtime to Deon's.

The whole front of Deon's place is a screened veranda he uses for making biltong. From the street it looks like red laundry. There are eight or nine clotheslines perpetually hung with rags of red meat turning purple, air-drying. This is where they met. Out in the road you had an audience of Bakorwa pretending to be going somewhere, slowly.

Meat means flies. Here is where the absurd takes a hand. Deon comes into the porch from the house. Bruns goes into the porch from the yard. The confrontation is about to begin. Deon is just filling his lungs to launch out at Bruns when the absurd thing happens: he inhales a fly. Suddenly you have a farce going. The fly apparently got rather far up his nostril. Deon goes into a fit, stamping and snorting. He's in a state of terror. You inhale a fly and the body takes over. Also you have to remember that there are certain flies that fly up the nostrils of wildebeests and lay eggs that turn into maggots that eat the brains of the animals, which makes them gallop in circles until they die of exhaustion. Deon has seen this, of course.

The scene is over before it begins. Deon crashes back into his living room screaming for help. It is total public humiliation. The Bakorwa see Bruns walk away nonchalantly and hear Du Toit thrashing and yelling.

Marika got the fly out with tweezers, I heard. By then Bruns was back at work.

Here is my theory of the last act. Deon's next move was inevitable — to arrange for a proxy to catch Bruns that same night and give him a beating. For symbolic and other reasons, it had to be one of the Bakorwa. At this point both Bruns and Deon are deep in the grip of the process of the Duel, capital D. Pragmatically, there would be no problem for Deon in getting one of the Bakorwa to do the job and probably even take the blame for it in the unlikely event he got caught. This is not to say there was no risk to Deon, because there was, some. But if you dare a Boer to do something, which is undoubtedly the way Deon perceived it, he is lost. An example is a man who was dared to kiss a rabid ox on the lips, at the abattoir in Cape Town. It was in the *Rand Daily Mail.* By the way, the point of kissing the ox on the lips is that it gives rabies its best chance of getting directly to your brain. So he did it. Not only that, he defaulted on the course of rabies injections the health department was frantically trying to get him to take. Here is your typical Boer folk hero. Add to that the Duel psychology, which is like a spell that spreads out and paralyzes people who might otherwise be expected to step in and put a stop to something so weird. Still, when someone you know personally like Bruns is found dead, it shocks you. I had cut this man's hair.

I'm positive two things happened the last night, although the official version is that only one did.

The first is that Deon sent somebody, a local, to beat Bruns up. When night falls in Keteng it's like being under a rock. There's no street lighting. The stores are closed. The whites pull their curtains. Very few Bakorwa can afford candles or paraffin lamps. It can seem unreal, because the Bakorwa are used to getting out and about in the dark and you can hear conversations and deals going down and so on, all in complete blackness. They even have parties in the dark where you can hear *bojalwa* being poured and people singing and playing those one-string tin-can violins. There was no moon that night and it was cloudy.

Bruns would often go out after dinner and sit on one of the big rocks up on the hill and do his own private vespers. He'd go out at sunset and sit there into the night thinking pure thoughts. He had a little missal he took with him, but what he could do with it in the dark except fondle it I have no idea.

So I think Bruns went out, got waylaid and beaten up as a lesson, and went back to his hut. I think the point of it was mainly just to humiliate him and mark him up. Of course, because of his beliefs, he would feel compelled just to endure the beating. He might try to shield his head or kidneys, but he couldn't fight back. He would not be in the slightest doubt that it was Bakorwa doing it and that they had been commissioned by Du Toit. So he comes back messed up, and what is he supposed to do?

Even very nice people find it hard to resist paradox. For example, whenever somebody who knows anything about it tells the story of poor Bruns, they always begin with the end of the story, which is that he drowned, their little irony being that of course everybody knows Botswana is a desert and Keteng is a desert. So poor Bruns, his whole story and what he did is reduced to getting this cheap initial sensation out of other people.

As I reconstruct the second thing that happened, it went like this: Bruns wandered back from his beating and possibly went into his place with the idea of cleaning himself up. His state of mind would have to be fairly terrible at this point. He has been abused by the very people he is trying to champion. At the same time, he knows Du Toit is responsible and that he can never prove it. And also he is in the grip of the need to retaliate. And he is a pacifist. He gets an idea and slips out again into the dark.

They found Bruns the next morning, all beaten up, drowned, his head and shoulders submerged in the watering trough in Du Toit's side yard. The police found Deon still in bed, in his clothes, hung over and incoherent. Marika was also still in bed, also under the weather, and she also was marked up and made a bad exhibit. They say Deon was struck dumb when they took him outside to show him the body.

Here's what I see. Bruns goes to Deon's, goes to the trough and plunges his head underwater and fills his lungs. I believe he could do it. It would be like he was beaten and pushed under. He was capable of this. He would see himself striking at the center of the web and convicting Du Toit for a thousand unrecorded crimes. It's self-immolation. It's nonviolent.

Deon protested that he was innocent, but he made some serious mistakes. He got panicky. He tried to contend he was with one of the other families that night, but that story collapsed when somebody else got panicky. Also it led to some perjury charges against the Vissers. Then Deon changed his story, saying how he remembered hearing some noises during the night, going out to see what they were, seeing nothing, and going back in and to bed. This could be the truth, but by the time he said it nobody believed him.

The ruin is absolute. It is a real Götterdämmerung. Deon is in jail, charged, and the least he can get is five years. He will have to eat out of a bucket. The chief is disgraced and they are discussing a regency. Bruns was under his protection, formally, and all the volunteer agencies are upset. In order to defend himself the chief is telling everything he can about how helpless he is in fact in Keteng, because the real power is with the seven families. He's pouring out details, so there are going to be charges against the families on other grounds, mostly about bribery and taxes. Also, an election is coming, so the local member of Parliament has a chance to be zealous about white citizens acting like they're outside the law. Business licenses are getting suspended. Theunis Pieters is selling out. There's a new police compound going up and more police coming in. They're posting a magistrate.

There is ruin. It's perfect.

JAMES SALTER

Foreign Shores

(FROM ESQUIRE)

MRS. PENCE AND HER WHITE SHOES were gone. She had left the week before, and the room at the top of the stairs was empty, cosmetics no longer littering the dresser, the ironing board finally taken down. Only a few scattered hairpins and a trace of talcum remained. The next day Truus arrived with two suitcases and splotched cheeks. It was March and cold. Christopher met her in the kitchen as if by accident. "Do you shoot people?" he asked.

She was Dutch and had no work permit, it turned out. The house was a mess. "I can pay you a hundred and thirty-five dollars a week," Gloria told her.

Christopher didn't like her at first, but soon the dishes piled on the counter were washed and put away, the floor was swept, and things were more or less returned to order — the cleaning girl came only once a week. Truus was slow but diligent. She did the laundry, which Mrs. Pence, who was a registered nurse, had always refused to do, shopped, cooked meals, and took care of Christopher. She was a hard worker, nineteen, and in sulky bloom. Gloria sent her to Elizabeth Arden's in Southampton to get her complexion cleared up and gave her Mondays and one night a week off.

Gradually Truus learned about things. The house, which was a large converted carriage house, was rented. Gloria, who was twenty-nine, liked to sleep late, and burned spots sometimes appeared in the living room rug. Christopher's father lived in California, and Gloria had a boyfriend named Ned. "That son of a bitch," she often said, "might as well forget about seeing Christopher again until he pays me what he owes me."

"Absolutely," Ned said.

When the weather became warmer, Truus could be seen in the village in one shop or another or walking along the street with Christopher in tow. She was somewhat drab. She had met another girl by then, a French girl, also an au pair, with whom she went to the movies. Beneath the trees with their new leaves the expensive cars glided along, more of them every week. Truus began taking Christopher to the beach. Gloria watched them go off. She was often still in her bathrobe. She waved and drank coffee. She was very lucky. All her friends told her and she knew it herself: Truus was a prize. She had made herself part of the family.

"Truus knows where to get pet mices," Christopher said.

"To get what?"

"Little mices."

"Mice," Gloria said.

He was watching her apply makeup, which fascinated him. Face nearly touching the mirror, intent, she stroked her long lashes upward. She had a great mass of blond hair, a mole on her upper lip with a few untouched hairs growing from it, a small blemish on her forehead, but otherwise a beautiful face. Her first entrance was always stunning. Later you might notice the thin legs, aristocratic legs she called them, her mother had them, too. As the evening wore on she lost her perfection. The gloss disappeared from her lips, she misplaced earrings. The highway patrol all knew her. A few weeks before she had driven into a ditch on the way home from a party and walked down Georgica Road at three in the morning, breaking two panes of glass to get in the kitchen door.

"Her friend knows where to get them," Christopher said.

"Which friend?" Truus said.

"We met him."

Gloria's eyes shifted from their own reflection to rest for a moment on that of Truus, who was watching, no less absorbed.

"Can I have some mices?" Christopher pleaded.

"Hmm?"

"Please."

"No, darling."

"Please!"

"No, we have enough of our own as it is."

"Where?"

"All over the house."

"Please!"

"No. Now stop it." To Truus she remarked casually, "Is it a boyfriend?"

"It's no one," Truus said. "Just someone I met."

"Well, just remember you have to watch yourself. You never know who you're meeting, you have to be careful." She drew back slightly and examined her eyes, large and black-rimmed. "Just thank God you're not in Italy," she said.

"Italy?"

"You can't even walk out on the street there. You can't even buy a pair of shoes, they're all over you, touching and pawing."

It had happened outside Dean & DeLuca's when Christopher insisted on carrying the bag and just past the door had dropped it.

"Oh, look at that," Truus said in irritation. "I told you not to drop it."

"I didn't drop it. It slipped."

"Don't touch it," she warned. "There's broken glass."

Christopher stared at the ground. He had a sturdy body, bobbed hair, and a cleft in his chin like his banished father's. People were walking past them. Truus was annoyed. It was hot, the store was crowded, she would have to go back inside.

"Looks like you had a little accident," a voice said. "Here, what'd you break? That's all right, they'll exchange it. I know the cashier."

When he came out again a few moments later, he said to Christopher, "Think you can hold it this time?"

Christopher was silent.

"What's your name?"

"Well, tell him," Truus said. After a moment, "His name is Christopher."

"Too bad you weren't with me this morning, Christopher. I

went to a place where they had a lot of tame mice. Ever seen any?"

"Where?" Christopher said.

"They sit right in your hand."

"Where is it?"

"You can't have a mouse," Truus said.

"Yes, I can." He continued to repeat it as they walked along. "I can have anything I want," he said.

"Be quiet." They were talking above his head. Near the corner they stopped for a while. Christopher was silent as they went on talking. He felt his hair being tugged but did not look up.

"Say good-bye, Christopher."

He said nothing. He refused to lift his head.

In midafternoon the sun was like a furnace. Everything was dark against it, the horizon lost in haze. Far down the beach in front of one of the prominent houses a large flag was waving. With Christopher following her, Truus trudged through the sand. Finally she saw what she had been looking for. Up in the dunes a figure was sitting.

"Where are we going?" Christopher asked.

"Just up here."

Christopher soon saw where they were headed.

"I have mices" was the first thing he said.

"Is that right?"

"Do you want to know their names?" In fact, they were two frantic gerbils in a tank of wood shavings. "Catman and Batty," he said.

"Catman?"

"He's the big one." Truus was spreading a towel. "Do we have to stay here?" he asked.

"Yes."

"Why?" he asked. He wanted to go down near the water. Truus finally agreed.

"But only if you stay where I can see you," she said.

The shovel fell out of his bucket as he ran off. She had to call him to make him come back. He went off again and she pretended to watch him.

"I'm really glad you came," the young man said. "You know, I don't know your name. I know his, but I don't know yours."

"Truus."

"I've never heard that name before. What is it, French?"

"It's Dutch."

"Oh, yeah?"

His name was Robbie Werner — "Not half as nice," he said. He had an easy smile and pale-blue eyes. There was something spoiled about him, like a student who has been expelled and is undisturbed by it. The sun was roaring down and striking Truus's shoulders beneath her shirt. She was wearing a blue one-piece bathing suit underneath. She was aware of being too heavy, of the heat, and of the thick, masculine legs stretched out near her.

"Do you live here?" she said.

"I'm just here on vacation."

"From where?"

"Try and guess."

"I don't know," she said. She was never good at that.

"Saudi Arabia," he said. "It's about three times this hot."

He worked there, he explained. He had an apartment of his own and a free telephone. At first she did not believe him. She glanced at him as he talked and realized he was telling the truth. He got two months of vacation a year, he said, usually in Europe. She imagined it as sleeping in hotels and getting up late and going out to lunch. She did not want him to stop talking. She could not think of anything to say.

"How about you?" he said. "What do you do?"

"Oh, I'm just taking care of Christopher."

"Where's his mother?"

"She lives here. She's divorced," Truus said.

"It's terrible the way people get divorced," he said.

"I agree with you."

"I mean, why get married?" he said. "Are your parents still married?"

"Yes," she said, although they did not seem to be a good example. They had been married for nearly twenty-five years. They were worn out from marriage, her mother especially.

Suddenly Robbie raised himself slightly. "Oh-oh," he said.

"What is it?"

"Your kid. I don't see him."

Truus jumped up quickly, looked around, and began to run

toward the water. There was a kind of shelf the tide had made that hid the ocean's edge. As she ran she finally saw, beyond it, the little blond head. She was calling his name.

"I told you to stay up where I could see you," she cried, out of breath, when she reached him. "I had to run all the way. Do you know how much you frightened me?"

Christopher slapped aimlessly at the sand with his shovel. He looked up and saw Robbie. "Do you want to build a castle?" he asked innocently.

"Sure," Robbie said after a moment. "Come on, let's go down a little further, closer to the water. Then we can have a moat. Do you want to help us build a castle?" he said to Truus.

"No," Christopher said, "she can't."

"Sure, she can. She's going to do a very important part of it for us."

"What?"

"You'll see." They were walking down velvety sand dampened by the tide.

"What's your name?" Christopher asked.

"Robbie. Here's a good place." He knelt and began scooping out large handfuls.

"Do you have a penis?"

"Sure."

"I do, too," Christopher said.

She was preparing his dinner while he played outside on the terrace, banging on the slate with his shovel. It was hot. Her clothes were sticking to her and there was moisture on her upper lip, but afterward she would go up and shower.

She had a room on the second floor — not the one Mrs. Pence had had, but a small guest room painted white with a crude patch on the door where the original lock had been removed. Just outside the window were trees and the thick hedge of the neighbor. The room faced south and caught the breeze. Often in the morning Christopher would crawl into her bed, his legs cool and hair a little sour-smelling. The room was filled with molten light. Sunlight shimmered on the blue floor. She could feel sand in the sheets, the merest trace of it. She turned her head sleepily to look at her watch on the night table. Not yet six.

The first birds were singing. Beside her, eyes closed, mouth parted to reveal a row of small teeth, lay this perfect boy.

He had begun digging in the border of flowers. He was piling dirt on the edge of the terrace.

"Don't, you'll hurt them," Truus said. "If you don't stop, I'm going to put you up in the tree, the one by the shed."

The telephone was ringing. Gloria picked it up in the other part of the house.

"It's for you," she called.

"Hello?" Truus said.

"Hi." It was Robbie.

"Hello," she said. She couldn't tell if Gloria had hung up. Then she heard a click.

"Are you going to be able to meet me tonight?"

"Yes, I can meet you," she said. Her heart felt extraordinarily light.

Christopher had begun to scrape his shovel across the screen. "Excuse me," she said, putting her hand over the mouthpiece. "Stop that," she commanded.

She had turned to him after she hung up. He was watching from the door. "Are you hungry?" she asked.

"No."

"Come, let's wash your hands."

"Why are you going out?"

"Just for fun. Come on."

"Where are you going?"

"Oh, stop, will you!"

That night the air was still. The heat spread over one immediately, like a flush. In the thunderous cool of the Laundry, past the darkened station, they sat near the bar, which was lined with men. It was noisy and crowded. Every so often someone passing by would say hello.

"Some zoo, eh?" Robbie said.

Gloria came there often, Truus knew.

"What do you want to drink?"

"Beer," she said.

There were at least twenty men at the bar. She was aware of occasional glances.

"You know, you don't look bad in a bathing suit," Robbie said.
The opposite, she felt, was true.

"Have you ever thought of taking off a few pounds?" he
asked. He had a calm, unhurried way of speaking. "It could
really help you."

"Yes, I know," she said.

"Have you ever thought of modeling?"

She would not look at him.

"I'm serious," he said. "You have a nice face."

"I'm not quite a model," she murmured.

"That's not the only thing. You also have a very nice ass. You
don't mind me saying that?"

She shook her head.

Later they drove past large, dark houses and down a road
that unexpectedly opened at the end like the vista she knew was
somehow opening to her. There were gently rolling fields and
distant lights. A scrap of yellow cloth hung from a pole. A street
sign saying EGYPT LANE — she was too dizzy to read it — floated
for an instant in the headlights.

"Do you know where we are?"

"No," she said.

"That's the Maidstone Club."

They crossed a small bridge and went on. Finally they turned
into a driveway. She could hear the ocean when he shut off the
ignition. There were two other cars parked nearby.

"Is someone here?"

"No, they're all asleep," he whispered.

They walked on the grass to the other side of the house. His
room was in a kind of annex. There was a smell of dampness.
The dresser was strewn with clothes, shaving gear, magazines.
She saw all this vaguely when he struck a match to light a candle.

"Are you sure no one's here?" she said.

"Don't worry."

It was all a little clumsy. Afterward they showered together.

There was almost nothing on the menu Gloria was interested in
eating.

"What are you going to have?" she said.

"Crab salad," Ned said.

"I think I'll have the avocado," she decided.

The waiter took the menus.

"A pharmaceutical company, you say?"

"I think he works for some big one," she said.

"Which one?"

"I don't know. It's in Saudi Arabia."

"Saudi Arabia?" he said doubtfully.

"That's where all the money is, isn't it?" she said. "It certainly isn't here."

"How'd she meet this fellow?"

"Picked him up, I think."

"Typical," he said. He pushed his rimless glasses higher on his nose with one finger. He was wearing a string sweater with the sleeves pulled up. His hair was faded by the sun. He looked very boyish and handsome. He was thirty-three and had never been married. There were only two things wrong with him: his mother had all the money in a trust, and his back. Something was wrong with it. He had terrible spasms and sometimes had to lie for hours on the floor.

"Well, I'm sure he knows she's just a baby sitter. I hope he doesn't break her heart," Gloria said. "Actually, I'm glad he showed up. It's better for Christopher. She's less likely to return the erotic feelings he has for her."

"The what?"

"Believe me, I'm not imagining it."

"Oh, come on, Gloria."

"There's something going on. Maybe she doesn't know it. He's in her bed all the time."

"He's only five."

"They can have erections at five," Gloria said.

"Oh, really."

"Darling, I've seen him with them."

"At five?"

"You'd be surprised," she said. "They're born with them. You just don't remember, that's all."

She did not become lovesick, she did not brood. She was more silent for a while but also more settled, not particularly sad. In the flat-heeled shoes that gave her a slightly dumpy appearance she went shopping as usual. The thought even crossed Gloria's mind that she might be pregnant.

"Is everything all right?" she asked.

"Pardon?"

"Darling, do you feel all right? You know what I mean."

There were times, when the two of them came back from the beach and Truus was patiently brushing the sand from Christopher's feet, that Gloria felt great sympathy for her and understood why she was quiet. How much of fate lay in one's appearance! Truus's face seemed empty, without expression, except when she was playing with Christopher, and then it brightened. She was so like a child anyway, a bulky child, an unimaginative playmate who in the course of things would be forgotten. And the foolishness of her dreams! She wanted to become a fashion designer, she announced one day. She was interested in designing clothes.

What she actually felt in the weeks after her boyfriend left, no one knew. She came in carrying the groceries, the screen door banged behind her. She answered the phone, took messages. In the evening she sat on the worn couch with Christopher watching television upstairs. Sometimes they both laughed. The shelves were piled with games, plastic toys, children's books. Once in a while Christopher was told to bring one down so his mother could read him a story. It was very important that he like books, Gloria said.

It was a pale-blue envelope with Arabic printing in the corner. Truus opened it standing at the kitchen counter and began to read the letter. The handwriting was childish and small. *Dear Truus*, it said, *Thank you for your letter. I was glad to receive it. You don't have to put so many stamps on letters to Saudi Arabia though. One U.S. airmail is enough. I'm glad to hear you miss me.* She looked up. Christopher was banging on something in the doorway.

"This won't work," he said.

He was dragging a toy car that had to be pumped up with air to run.

"Here, let me see," she said. He seemed on the verge of tears. "This fits here, doesn't it?" She attached the small plastic hose. "There, now it will work."

"No, it won't," he said.

"No, it won't," she mimicked.

He watched gloomily as she pumped. When the handle grew stiff she put the car on the floor, pointed it, and let it go. It leapt across the room and crashed into the opposite wall. He went over and nudged it with his foot.

"Do you want to play with it?"

"No."

"Then pick it up and put it away."

He didn't move.

"Put . . . it . . . away . . ." she said in a deep voice, coming toward him one step at a time. He watched from the corner of his eye. Another tottering step. "Or I eat you," she growled.

He ran for the stairs, shrieking. She continued to shuffle slowly toward him. The dog was barking. Gloria came in the door, reaching down to pull off her shoes and kick them to one side. "Hi, any calls?" she asked.

Truus abandoned her performance. "No. No one."

Gloria had been visiting her mother, which was always tiresome. She looked around. Something was going on, she realized. "Where's Christopher?"

A glint of blond hair appeared above the landing.

"Hello, darling," she said. There was a pause. "Mummy said hello. What's wrong? What's happening?"

"We're just playing a game," Truus explained.

"Well, stop playing for a moment and come and kiss me."

She took him into the living room. Truus went upstairs. Sometime later she heard her name being called. She folded the letter which she had been reading for the fifth or sixth time, and went to the head of the stairs. "Yes?"

"Can you come down?" Gloria called. "He's driving me crazy."

"He's impossible," she said when Truus arrived. "He's spilled his milk, he's kicked over the dog water. Look at this mess!"

"Let's go outside and play a game," Truus said to him, reaching for his hand, which he pulled away. "Come. Or do you want to go on the pony?"

He stared at the floor. As if she were alone in the room, she got down on her hands and knees. She shook her hair and made a curious sound, a faint neigh, pure as the tinkle of glass. She turned to gaze indifferently at him over her shoulder. He was watching.

"Come," she said calmly. "Your pony is waiting."

After that, when the letters arrived Truus would fold them and slip them into her pocket while Gloria went through the mail: bills, gallery openings, urgent requests for payment, occasionally a letter. She wrote very few herself but always complained when she did not receive them. Comments on the logic of this only served to annoy her.

The fall was coming. Everything seemed to deny it. The days were still warm, the great, terminal sun poured down. The leaves, more luxuriant than ever, covered the trees. Behind the hedges, lawn mowers made a final racket. On the warm slate of the terrace, left behind, a grasshopper, a veteran in dark green and yellow, limped along. The birds had torn off one of his legs.

One morning Gloria was upstairs when something happened to catch her eye. The door to the little guest room was open and on the night table, folded, was a letter. It lay there in the silence, half of it raised like a wing in the air. The house was empty. Truus had gone to shop and pick up Christopher at nursery school. With the curiosity of a schoolgirl, Gloria sat down on the bed. She opened the envelope and took out the pages. The first thing her eye fell upon was a line just above the fold. It stunned her. For a moment she was dazed. She read the letter through nervously. She opened the drawer. There were others. She read them as well. Like love letters they were repetitious, but they were not love letters. He did more than work in an office, this man, much more. He went through Europe, city after city, looking for young people who in hotel rooms and cheap apartments — she was horrified by the images of it — stripped and were immersed in a river of sordid acts. The letters were like those of a high-school boy, that was the most terrible part. They were letters of recruitment, so simple they might have been copied out by an illiterate.

Sitting there framed in the doorway, her hand nearly trembling, she could not think what to do. She felt deeply upset, frightened, betrayed. She glanced out the window. She wondered if she should go immediately to the nursery school — she could be there in minutes — and take Christopher somewhere where he would be safe. No, that would be foolish. She hurried downstairs to the telephone.

"Ned," she said when she reached him — her voice was shaking. She was looking at a letter that asked a number of matter-of-fact questions.

"What is it? Is anything wrong?"

"Come right away. I need you. Something's happened."

For a while then she stood there with the letters in her hand. Looking around hurriedly, she put them in a drawer where garden seeds were kept. She began to calculate how long it would be before he would be there, driving out from the city.

She heard them come in. She was in her bedroom. She had regained her composure, but as she entered the kitchen she could feel her heart beating wildly. Truus was preparing lunch.

"Mummy, look at this," Christopher said. He held up a sheet of paper. "Do you see what this is?"

"Yes. It's very nice."

"This is the engine," he said. "These are the wings. These are the guns."

She tried to focus her attention on the scrawled outline with its garish colors, but she was conscious only of the girl at work behind the counter. As Truus brought the plates to the table Gloria tried to look calmly at her face, a face she realized she had not seen before. In it she recognized for the first time depravity, and in Truus's limbs, their smoothness, their volume, she saw brutality and vice. Outside, in the ordinary daylight, were the trees along the side of the property, the roof of a house, the lawn, some scattered toys. It was a landscape that seemed ominous, too idyllic, too still.

"Don't use your fingers, Christopher," Truus said, sitting down with him. "Use your fork."

"It won't reach," he said.

She pushed the plate an inch or two toward him.

"Here, try now," she said.

Later, watching them play outside on the grass, Gloria could not help noticing a wild, almost a bestial, aspect in her son's excitement, as if a crudeness were somehow becoming a part of him, soiling him. A line from the many that lay writhing in her head came forth. *I hope you will be ready to take my big cock when I see you again. P.S. Have you had any big cocks lately? I miss you and think of you and it makes me very hard.*

"Have you ever read anything like that?" Gloria asked.

"Not exactly."

"It's the most disgusting thing. I can't believe it."

"Of course, she didn't write them," Ned said.

"She kept them, that's worse."

He had them all in his hand. *If you came to Europe it would be great,* one said. *We would travel and you could help me. We could work together. I know you would be very good at it. The girls we would be looking for are between thirteen and eighteen years old. Also guys, a little older.*

"You have to go in there and tell her to leave," Gloria said. "Tell her she has to be out of the house."

He looked at the letters again. *Some of them are very well developed, you would be surprised. I think you know the type we are looking for.*

"I don't know . . . Maybe these are just a silly kind of love letter."

"Ned, I'm not kidding," she said.

Of course, there would be a lot of fucking, too.

"I'm going to call the FBI."

"No," he said, "that's all right. Here, take these. I'll go and tell her."

Truus was in the kitchen. As he spoke to her he tried to see in her gray eyes the boldness he had overlooked. There was only confusion. She did not seem to understand him. She went in to Gloria. She was nearly in tears. "But why?" she wanted to know.

"I found the letters" was all Gloria would say.

"What letters?"

They were there on the desk. Gloria held them up.

"They're mine," Truus protested. "They belong to me."

"I've called the FBI," Gloria said.

"Please, give them to me."

"I'm not giving them to you. I'm burning them."

"Please let me have them," Truus insisted.

She was confused and weeping. She passed Ned on her way

upstairs. He noticed attributes praised in the letters — the Saudi letters, as he later called them.

In her room Truus sat on the bed. She did not know what she would do or where she would go. She began to pack her clothes, hoping that somehow things might change if she took long enough. She moved very slowly.

"Where are you going?" Christopher said from the door.

She did not answer him. He asked again, coming into the room.

"I'm going to see my mother," she said.

"She's downstairs."

Truus shook her head.

"Yes, she is," he insisted.

"Go away. Don't bother me right now," she said in a flat voice.

He began kicking at the door with his foot. After a while he sat on the couch. Then he disappeared.

When the taxi came for her, he was hiding behind some trees out near the driveway. She had been looking for him at the end.

"Oh, there you are," she said. She put down her suitcases and knelt to say good-bye. He stood with his head bent. From a distance it seemed a kind of submission.

"Look at that," Gloria said. She was in the house. Ned was standing behind her. "They always love sluts," she said.

Christopher stood beside the road after the taxi had gone. That night he came down to his mother's room. He was crying and she turned on the light.

"What is it?" she said. She tried to comfort him. "Don't cry, darling. Did something frighten you? Here, Mummy will take you upstairs. Don't worry. Everything will be all right."

"Goodnight, Christopher," Ned said.

"Say goodnight, darling."

She went up, climbed into bed with him, and finally got him to sleep, but he kicked so much she came back down, holding her robe closed with one hand. Ned had left her a note: his back was giving him trouble, he had gone home.

Truus's place was taken by a Colombian woman who was very religious and did not drink or smoke. Then by a black girl named Mattie who did both but stayed for a long time.

One night in bed, reading *Town & Country*, Gloria came across something that stunned her. It was a photograph of a garden party in Brussels, only a small photograph but she recognized a face, she was absolutely certain of it, and with a terrible sinking feeling she moved the page closer to the light. She was without makeup and at her most vulnerable. She examined the picture closely. She was no longer talking to Ned, she hadn't seen him for over a year, but she was tempted to call him anyway. Then, reading the caption and looking at the picture again, she decided she was mistaken. It wasn't Truus, just someone who looked like her, and anyway, what did it matter? It all seemed long ago. Christopher had forgotten her. He was in school now, doing very well, on the soccer team already, playing with eight- and nine-year-olds, bigger than them and bright. He would be six three. He would have girlfriends hanging all over him, girls whose families had houses in the Bahamas. He would devastate them.

Still, lying there with the magazine mute on her knees, she could not help thinking of it. What had actually become of Truus? She looked at the photograph again. Had she found her way to Amsterdam or Paris and, making dirty movies or whatever, met someone? It was unbearable to think of her being invited to places, slimmer now, sitting in the brilliance of crowded restaurants with her complexion still bad beneath the makeup and the morals of a housefly. The idea that there is an unearned happiness, that certain people find their way to it, nearly made her sick. Like the girl Ned was marrying, who used to work in the catering shop just off the highway near Bridgehampton. That had been a blow, that had been more than a blow. But then nothing, almost nothing, really made sense anymore.

JEANNE SCHINTO

Caddies' Day

(FROM THE GREENSBORO REVIEW)

THE BOTTLE IS STICKY around the spout. Do not pick it up by its spout. Keep your hands far away from the spout. A caddy's mouth has germs.

Two brown ants run around the rim of it. The caddy who threw it left a sip. Maybe the golfer was calling him to come on along. So he flung it beyond the caddy path, and it would have broken if he hit a rock. Behind those rocks caddies hide their bicycles. Caddies steal from one another.

I don't often walk along this path during the day. I come out here after supper. The golf course is empty of everyone then, but not sounds: the sprinklers tick around. And I take the flag out of its hole and march and sing. Sometimes I drop the flag and run because the darkness falls so soon. I run and climb the chain-link fence behind our house without cutting open my hand. My sneaker toes fit into the fence holes exactly. In a year or two they'll be too big. I do not tear open my hand, because I'm careful.

My mother thinks I am walking home the other way. On the road. I usually do. But today I have dirty paw prints down the front of my new dress, and I'm sneaking. I'd like to sneak into the house the cellar way so my mother won't see me and scream. Maybe I can take my dress off outside and bury it under the leaf pile in the corner of the back yard. If my mother says why don't you wear that little party dress Aunt Rhoda gave you anymore, I'll say I will next time, next time. And then I'll think of it rotting. And if she looks for it in my bedroom closet and doesn't find it and asks me where it is, I will say I don't know, it's not in there? It's not? And I'll start to look for it too.

The path is dusty, the color of a dog. The dust rises up. Over the bunker, on the green, the grass is short. Short as hair. As short as the milkman's. He told my mother: I don't even have to comb it when I get out of bed in the morning. Lucky duck! Sometimes the milkman pinches my cheek. It hurts. I give him a look. Then my mother gives me a slap. What'sa matter? He's saying he likes you.

On the green, a golfer is down on his knees, with his cheek to the grass. He's looking to see which way it's growing. My father said. He doesn't play golf, but he knows the greenskeeper, Mike, and Mike knows plenty. He runs the machines and he's very tall and dark, with a smile like an open tractor shovel. He talks to policemen all the time, and in summer, he has a crew of boys working for him. Members' sons, my father says, and this makes him shake his head and look sorry.

Change falls from the golfer's pocket. Nobody sees it but me. Not the golfer and not the other three with him. If the golfers had caddies, the caddies would see, but they have carts instead. And after they are going up the fairway, I scramble over the bunker. I pick up the coins — there are three — quarters, so big and round and silver. They looked funny lying on the grass. After the coins are in my pocket, the men look back and see me and wag their fingers. These are the two of them who are walking. The other two have driven the carts far up the fairway. And they say no, you better not play here, little girl. A ball could come and knock you on the head. Dangerous. Someone will hurt you, little girl. And don't be walking on that green.

Back on the path, I think, that's what they always say, and a ball hasn't hit me yet. I'd like to see them try and hit me with such a tiny ball. I'd go up on the fairway and stand. And I'd bet them, and I'd win. If I saw the ball coming close, I would duck, and they wouldn't see me. They would be too far away. And God would forgive me. He wouldn't want me to be killed. He loves me and watches out for me and knows the number of hairs on my head. He sees everything. And if I pulled one out by the roots? He'd see, even if he was busy. Even if he was busy saving someone from drowning. I would not be killed. Heaven is scary.

I see the caddy shed. From here it looks like a shoebox. And I hear the caddies' voices. They are swearing, but do not be afraid.

I'm not afraid, but I stop to read each tree. They are carved deep with initials, names, and hearts with arrows through them. My mother says that will kill the poor trees, gouging out bark with knives, and where do those boys get knives anyway? My father says the letters will grow, stretch right along with the bark. I'd like to see that. And I'd like to carve my initials here, but I don't have a knife. Some night after supper, I'll take one from the drawer in the kitchen.

The caddies' voices get louder as I walk along. It sounds like they are having a fight. Maybe they won't see me, and I'll sneak past them like a ghost. They'll be too busy spitting, shouting, shoving each other. On Caddies' Day they play golf themselves, and I hide behind the bunker and watch. They have fights, spit their words, raise their clubs. In the fall the bunkers burn. I used to think the caddies did it, and I cried. Our house would be burned. Then I saw Mike, the greenskeeper, with his torch. Fires burn black right to the path.

Not all of the caddies are young. Some of them are men my father's age, but they do not look like him. They look like his friends, the ones my mother says are vulgar. I do not see them yet. They are on the other side of the caddy shed, but I can hear them and I can picture them. They sit on two long wooden benches, their backs up against the shed. Unless they are play-ing cards, and then the benches face each other. Their shirts have wet marks under the arms. Hair curls around their ears. They smoke, hold their cigarettes between their teeth when they have to throw a card down. Sometimes they take the cigarettes from their mouths and call out to me. Comeer, little girlie. Sit on my lap, little girl. Other times they don't see me at all, and I walk the rest of the way home with my heart beating right out through my shirt.

And today? I think I will be safe! I will crawl past them un-seen! They are all standing, shaking their fists, shouting, point-ing to the benches. Both of the benches have been dragged out from their places up against the shed. One of the benches has been kicked over, legs up. Yes, I think, I will be safe! And I stride along. But then something happens.

A boy holding a card between his fingers swaggers to the center of the crowd. He wears a black T-shirt and his pants are too short and a curl of hair hangs in his eyes. He holds the card up, shows it, each side, as if it's a moth he's caught. He flicks it, watches it flutter down, turns and walks away.

Half of the caddies follow him, walking backwards and swearing at the others, who stay behind. Passing the fallen bench, they lift it high onto their shoulders. They walk with it to the carved trees and are about to set it down. But then the boy in the black T-shirt sees me.

He nudges the others, lifts his chin, looks behind him, smiles. I smile, too, a little. Then he takes the bench up himself, lifts it over his head, walks to the path with it, and sets it down across it.

The fence runs the length of the path. It runs all around the golf course. I could climb it right here and then walk home on the road. I would go in the kitchen-door way, and my mother would see my dirty dress, and I don't care. But the caddies all are watching me. They would watch me climb. They would see my underpants. They would see if I fell. And if I cut my hand on the twists of wire at the top of the fence? I wouldn't want to run to them and ask them to make it stop bleeding.

Besides, on the road there are dogs I'm afraid of. They are not like the dog at the party. One of them bit me, a tiny dog, no bigger than a cat. But its teeth were like a rat's. It was a Chihuahua. My mother told me a dog can smell fear, and I must have had the smell on me that day. My father said next time give it a good kick in the teeth. Should I? A dog that small. God wouldn't like it. One of his creatures. They all have their purpose. What should I do?

I could go around them on the other side, on the golf course grass. The golfers would scream, but I would explain. They would give me time. Then they would come back to the caddy shed and scream at the caddies. I've seen them scream at them before. Men with red faces, red pants, red shirts, potbellies like they're expecting. White belts around them, white shoes, little hats. My father calls them fairies. I ask him what do you mean? He laughs. My mother makes a smirk. Sometimes the golfers hit the caddies. Well, I saw that once. And when it rains, a storm, golfers don't share their umbrellas with the caddies. The golfer

takes the bag and walks ahead and the caddy walks behind —
or runs. Or stands under a tree. My father says that's one way
to get his hair curled but good when the lightning strikes him. I
watch them shivering under the trees. No wonder caddies are
so mean.

One of them comes up to me. His shirt is striped, his pants
cuffs drag, he is holding a bottle. His palm is flat to the bottom
of it, one finger stops up the spout, and he tips the bottle sideways and watches the bright red soda slosh. I watch it too, and
then I see there is something else inside. It is filled with tiny
brown ants riding on the surface of the red. They make a ship
inside the bottle, inch-high, climbing over one another. Below,
some have sunken into the red and are drowning.

I look up into the caddy's sweaty face. He is as tall as a tree
and smiling. One of his front teeth is chipped. All of his teeth
are yellow and must have germs, but you can't see them. Germs
are invisible. He says, "Hey, girlie, you gotta pay the toll," and
he turns and points his chin back over his shoulder at the other
caddies on the bench across the path. The one in the black
T-shirt gets up and starts coming toward me. "Don't walk backwards," he says to me. "You might trip over something. A tree
root. See those roots behind you?" He laughs and the one with
the ants in the bottle laughs too.

And then I laugh. I cannot help it. I cannot stop the laugh. I
try to make my eyes look mad, but they are laughing too. Sometimes when my father's friends tell a joke my mother tries to
frown, but I can see her smiling, laughing behind her frown.
Once, I was kissing my doll and I could not stop it either.

I feel a tickle. The caddy in the black T-shirt is tickling my
neck. Then he tries to brush the dirt from the front of my dress.
And he straightens my bow. If he were my father or my mother
or my aunt, he would tell me to twirl and show him how far the
skirt goes out. Well, that was when I was smaller. But he doesn't
ask me to twirl. He is talking, like the other one did, about the
pay toll ahead.

He asks me if I have any money while the other caddies from
the bench gather around. I tell him no with a shrug. I shrug
and shrug to each question he asks, because that eases the tickle.
His hand is still tickling my neck.

He asks me, "What are you doing walking down the caddy

path anyway? This is for caddies only. Didn't you know that? And nobody should leave the house without at least a couple pieces of change. Didn't your mother even give you a dime for a phone call in case you got lost? And how'd you get your dress front all dirty?"

Sweat.

I sweat from my upper lip, from my forehead, my chest. I like to feel the first sweat of summer. It happened in the school-yard this year. I was playing jump rope: high-water, low. A girl everyone hates was holding the rope, and she tripped me, and everyone sneered at that girl and came to see if I was all right. With all of them standing around me in a circle, I started to cry. I was not hurt very badly, no blood, but I knew they wanted me to cry. I knew. They wanted to see me hurt good enough to cry so they could make the other girl scared, feel bad, worry that we would tell the teacher. And we did. And I cried some more when she came over. I wonder if I should cry now. Wonder if that is what the caddies want me to do.

"Hey, girlie, how 'bout a little kiss?"

I do not look into their faces. I look at their knees spread wide. One of them has his hands out.

After supper my father puts his hand palm up on the table, and I'm supposed to put my hand inside it. And I do. This is an old game. I'm too old now. But he makes me play. And I do. And he says, "How much do you love me?" And I say, "Five hundred." "How much?" He squeezes my hand. "A thousand." "How much?" "Ten thousand!" "How much?" "A million!" "That's better," he says. Then he lets go.

One of them puts a hand on my shoulder. It is heavy as an iron. I used to not be able to pick up my mother's iron. She used to tell me to stay away from the board when she was ironing. Once, I was playing underneath it. That was my house. I was hiding. She was on the phone. When she walked back into the room and found me, she screamed.

They are whispering among themselves. Maybe I can walk away. My feet in my shoes are sweaty — they will squeak. But if my feet were bare they would make little footprints in the dust. And then the caddies would follow them right to the cellar door and up to my room.

Their voices are like low rumbles of thunder. I look up and watch the Adam's apple of the one with the bottle of ants. It looks as if it will soon burst through. It looks as if it hurts him. The hand on my shoulder is squeezing hard. It's the hand of the black T-shirt boy. Then it's lazy — resting, not holding. I start to walk away. Then I run. And a shout goes up. And everything changes.

My ankles hurt me. My nose hits their knees. I am upside down. They hold me by the ankles and laugh, thumbs pressed into my bones. Then money drops. Coins on the ground. They are dropping their money? No. It's the money I found on the green. I forgot about it.

"No money for the toll, huh? What's this? What's this?"

Someone picks up the coins. Snaps my underpants. I try to cover them with my dress. Someone takes my hands.

Sometimes I walk around my room with a mirror under my eyes. Everything is upside down. And I walk in the world upside down. I like to do this best when my room is messy and my mother says clean it up, it's a pigsty, clean it up now! And I take the mirror and instantly it's clean! The ceiling-floor so white and neat makes my room instantly picked up! I want my mother to look into the mirror with me, but she won't. I know without asking. Besides, there's only room for one pair of eyes at a time.

I want to cry. Will my mother hear me? I don't want my father to see. He would come and kill them with steak knives from the kitchen drawer. I would stand behind him and plead: they don't mean any harm. Passing me from one to the other. It's a game. They are laughing. Hear them laugh! My ankles hurt, and my nose. But they don't know it. They think I like it. I am laughing, too. Sometimes when you squeeze my hand, it hurts, and I say nothing. I laugh. And you, mother, nod, and say that's a good girl, and you laugh. Look at their faces! What do you think? Maybe they're saying they like me.

Then they put me down.

My feet feel funny on the ground. I'm dizzy and do not walk away. They are waiting, watching me to see what I will do next. They look a little afraid. That is funny, too. I think they think I'm going to do something back to them. What could it be?

The boy in the black T-shirt whispers something to the one

with the ants in the bottle and gives him a smack on the shoulder to send him on his way. The ant boy throws his bottle down — it doesn't break; it rolls — and he goes back to the caddy shed, hands in his pockets, head down. The rest of the caddies are all around me, watching and waiting still. There is an opening in the circle. I could walk out of it, but I don't — even though I know that they wouldn't stop me if I tried.

When the ant boy returns, he has a new bottle of soda. He hands it to the black T-shirt boy, who hands it to me. It's orange. My favorite. How did he know? The bottle is icy and clean. I want to put it to my cheek, but they are waiting for me to take a sip.

I take a small one. The black T-shirt boy says, "You're okay, right, girlie? Right?" And he's frowning, and I'm scared again, but I know what to do. I nod. And all of the caddies smile. And I smile, too, and sip again.

Two of the caddies sit down on the bench and start to deal the cards. A couple more go get sodas of their own and bring them back to the path and drink them. I am getting full, but I keep drinking, even when a golfer comes over. "Who's this? Who's this?" he asks. "What is going on?" But all of us keep drinking our sodas. We are celebrating something.

Biographical Notes
Other Distinguished Short Stories
  of 1983
Editorial Addresses

Biographical Notes

LEE K. ABBOTT, who has taught since 1977 at Case Western Reserve University, attended New Mexico State University and the University of Arkansas. His first collection of stories, *The Heart Never Fits Its Wanting*, won the St. Lawrence Award for Fiction in 1981. He has published in many literary journals, including *The Missouri Review, The Ohio Review, The Southern Review,* and *North American Review.* In 1984, he won an O. Henry Award.

MADISON SMARTT BELL was born in Tennessee and now lives in Brooklyn. His first novel, *The Washington Square Ensemble,* was published by Viking/Penguin in 1983. He currently teaches a fiction workshop at the New York Ninety-second Street Y.

DIANNE BENEDICT is a native Texan now living in Portland, Maine, with her three daughters. Her collection of short stories, *Shiny Objects,* won the Iowa Short Fiction Award in 1982 and was published by the University of Iowa Press. Her stories have appeared in *MSS, The Atlantic Monthly, fiction international,* and *Intro.* She has taught in the Graduate Writing Program at Syracuse University and the Writers' Workshop at the University of Iowa and is currently teaching at the University of Southern Maine and in the M.F.A. Writing Program at Vermont College.

PAUL BOWLES was born in New York seventy-three years ago. In 1931, he made his first visit to Tangier, which has been his only home since 1959 when he sold his island off Sri Lanka. His most recent volume of short stories is *Midnight Mass.*

MARY WARD BROWN lives near Marion, Alabama, on the farm where she grew up. She is a graduate of Judson College and has studied creative writing at the University of North Carolina and recently at the University of Alabama, Birmingham, under Leonard Michaels.

Her stories have been published in *Ascent, McCall's, Grand Street, Prairie Schooner, U.S. Catholic,* and *The Threepenny Review.* She has two granddaughters.

RICK DeMARINIS lives in Missoula, Montana, with his wife and daughter. He attended the University of Montana and San Diego State University. He is the author of three novels and a collection of short stories. His stories have appeared in *The Atlantic Monthly, Esquire,* and a number of literary quarterlies. He is at work now on a new novel.

ANDRE DUBUS has published a novel and, with David Godine, four collections of short stories. Godine will publish his novella *Voices from the Moon* in the fall of 1984. He has four grown children and a grandson and lives in Haverhill, Massachusetts, with his wife and two-year-old daughter.

MAVIS GALLANT is the author of six collections of short stories, two novels, and a play. Nearly all her short fiction has appeared in *The New Yorker,* to which she has been a contributor since 1950.

MARY HOOD lives near Woodstock, Georgia. A collection of her short stories, *How Far She Went,* is being published this year by the University of Georgia Press. Her writing has appeared in *The Georgia Review, Yankee,* and *North American Review.* New stories are forthcoming in *The Ohio Review* and *Kenyon Review.*

DONALD JUSTICE was born in Miami, Florida, and teaches now at the University of Florida. In 1980, he received the Pulitzer Prize for his *Selected Poems* (Atheneum).

STEPHEN KIRK is a native of Geneva, New York, and a graduate of St. Lawrence University in Canton, New York. He is currently enrolled in the M.F.A. program at the University of North Carolina at Greensboro. "Morrison's Reaction" is his first published short story.

SUSAN MINOT grew up in Manchester-by-the-Sea, Massachusetts. She received an M.F.A. from Columbia University in 1983 and works as an assistant editor at *Grand Street* in New York City. Her stories have appeared in *The New Yorker, Grand Street,* and *The Paris Review.* A book of fiction is forthcoming with Seymour Lawrence at Dutton.

WRIGHT MORRIS's two recent volumes of memoirs, *Will's Boy* and *Solo,* will be followed by *A Cloak of Light,* to be published early in 1985.

JOYCE CAROL OATES has appeared a number of times in *The Best American Short Stories.* Her most recent book is *Last Days,* a story collection published by Dutton; her next novel, due in the spring of 1985, is *Solstice.* She is currently on the faculty at Princeton.

CYNTHIA OZICK is the author of two novels, *The Cannibal Galaxy* and *Trust;* three volumes of short stories, *The Pagan Rabbi, Bloodshed,* and *Levitation;* and *Art & Ardor,* a collection of essays. She was a 1982 Guggenheim Fellow and is a current holder of the American Academy's Strauss Living Award. She is married to Bernard Hallote and is the mother of a college-age daughter, Rachel. This is her fifth appearance in *The Best American Short Stories.*

LOWRY PEI grew up in St. Louis and has been teaching writing at the college level, mostly to freshmen, for the last ten years. He has published several articles of literary criticism, including a study of Eudora Welty's *The Golden Apples* in *Modern Fiction Studies.* His fiction has appeared in *Roadwork, Stories, The Ohio Review,* and *Edges,* an anthology edited by Ursula K. Le Guin and Virginia Kidd. He was a finalist in fiction in the Massachusetts Artists Fellowship competition, 1984, and is nearing completion of a novel.

JONATHAN PENNER is the author of two novels, *Going Blind* and *The Intelligent Traveler's Guide to Chiribosco,* and of a collection of short stories, *Private Parties,* winner of the third annual Drue Heinz Prize. Born in Bridgeport, Connecticut, he attended the University of Bridgeport and the University of Iowa. He lives now in Tucson and teaches fiction writing at the University of Arizona.

NORMAN RUSH has published short fiction in a variety of literary magazines, most recently in *The Paris Review* and *The New Yorker.* His work has been anthologized in *The Best American Short Stories* (1971) and other collections. From 1978 to 1983 he lived in Africa, and he is presently at work on a sequence of stories and a novel based on that experience.

JAMES SALTER is the author of five novels, the best known of which are *Light Years* and *A Sport and a Pastime.* He has also written journalism, essays, and short stories. His stories have appeared mostly in *The Paris Review, Grand Street,* and *Esquire.* He was born in 1926 and lives now in Bridgehampton, New York, amid what remains of the fields there.

JEANNE SCHINTO was born and grew up in Greenwich, Connecticut. She received a B.A. from George Washington University and an M.A. from the fiction program at Johns Hopkins University. Her stories have appeared in *Ascent, Cimarron Review, The Ontario Review, The Greensboro Review,* and elsewhere; her nonfiction has been published in the *Washington Post* and many other places. She lives in Takoma Park, Maryland, with her husband, Bob Frishman, and works as a greenhouse keeper.

100 Other Distinguished Short Stories of the Year 1983

SELECTED BY SHANNON RAVENEL

ABBOTT, LEE K.
When Our Dream World Finds Us, and These Hard Times Are Gone. New Orleans Review, Winter.

ADAMS, ALICE
Waiting for Stella. The New Yorker, May 2.

BARTHELME, DONALD
The Palace at 4 A.M. The New Yorker, October 17.

BARTHELME, FREDERICK
Trick Scenery. Chicago Review, Spring.
Violet. The New Yorker, January 31.

BAXTER, CHARLES
Weights. TriQuarterly 56, Winter.

BENNETT, HAL
Virginia in the Window. The Virginia Quarterly Review, Summer.

BOLLING, DOUG
Farewell, Henry James. Cimarron Review, April.

BOVEY, JOHN
At the Feet of Theodora. New England Review/Breadloaf Quarterly, Spring.

BOYLE, T. CORAGHESSAN
Rara Avis. Antaeus, Winter.

BRODKEY, HAROLD
Ceil. The New Yorker, September 12.

BROWN, SUZANNE HUNTER
Antigone. Carolina Quarterly, Fall.

BUSCH, FREDERICK
A History of Small Ideas. Carolina Quarterly, Spring.
The Settlement of Mars. TriQuarterly 56, Winter.

CAMOIN, FRANÇOIS
The Rescue. Ascent, Vol. 9, No. 1.

CAPONEGRO, MARY
The Star Café. The Mississippi Review, Fall.

CAPOUYA, EMILE
A Dream of Fair Women. The Antioch Review, Spring.

CARLSON, RON
Ferguson Lives. Carolina Quarterly, Winter.
Why We Cry. Western Humanities Review, Autumn.

CARVER, RAYMOND
Careful. The Paris Review, Summer.
The Compartment. The Antioch Review, Spring.
Fever. The North American Review, June.

Editorial Addresses of American and Canadian Magazines Publishing Short Stories

Agni Review, P.O. Box 349, Cambridge, Massachusetts 02138

Akros Review, University of Akron, Akron, Ohio 44325

Analog, 380 Lexington Avenue, New York, New York 10017

Antaeus, 1 West 30th Street, New York, New York 10001

Antietam Review, 33 West Washington Street, Hagerstown, Maryland 21740

Antioch Review, P.O. Box 148, Yellow Springs, Ohio 45387

Apalachee Quarterly, P.O. Box 20106, Tallahassee, Florida 32304

Aphra, RFD, Box 355, Springtown, Pennsylvania 18081

Arizona Quarterly, University of Arizona, Tucson, Arizona 85721

Ascent, English Department, University of Illinois, Urbana, Illinois 61801

Aspen Journal, P.O. Box 3185, Aspen, Colorado 81612

Atlantic, 8 Arlington Street, Boston, Massachusetts 02116

Aura Literary/Arts Review, 117 Campbell Hall, University Station, Birmingham, Alabama 35294

Bennington Review, Bennington College, Bennington, Vermont 05201

Black Warrior Review, P.O. Box 2936, University, Alabama 35486

Bloodroot, P.O. Box 891, Grand Forks, North Dakota 58201

Boston Globe Magazine, The Boston Globe, Boston, Massachusetts 02107

California Quarterly, 100 Sproul Hall, University of California, Davis, California 95616

California Voice, 1782 Pacific Avenue, San Francisco, California 94109

Canadian Fiction, Box 946, Station F, Toronto, Ontario M4Y 2N9, Canada

Capilano Review, Capilano College, 2055 Purcell Way, North Vancouver, British Columbia, Canada

Carolina Quarterly, Greenlaw Hall 066A, University of North Carolina at Chapel Hill, Chapel Hill, North Carolina 27514

Chariton Review, Division of Language & Literature, Northeast Missouri State University, Kirksville, Missouri 63501

Chattahoochee Review, DeKalb Community College, 2101 Womack Road, Dunwoody, Georgia 30338

Chelsea, P.O. Box 5880, Grand Central Station, New York, New York 10163

Chicago, Three Illinois Center, 303 East Wacker Drive, Chicago, Illinois 60601

Chicago Review, 5700 South Ingleside, Box C, University of Chicago, Chicago, Illinois 60637

Cimarron Review, 208 Life Sciences East, Oklahoma State University, Stillwater, Oklahoma 74078

Clockwatch Review, Driftwood Publications, 737 Penbrook Way, Hartland, Wisconsin 53209

Commentary, 165 East 56th Street, New York, New York 10022

Confrontation, English Department, Brooklyn Center for Long Island University, Brooklyn, New York 11201

Cosmopolitan, 224 West 57th Street, New York, New York 10019

Cottonwood Magazine, Box J, Kansas Union, Lawrence, Kansas 66045

Crazyhorse, Department of English, University of Arkansas at Little Rock, Little Rock, Arkansas 72204

Creative Pittsburgh, P.O. Box 7346, Pittsburgh, Pennsylvania 15213

Crescent Review, P.O. Box 15065, Winston-Salem, North Carolina 27103

Crosscurrents, 2200 Glastonbury Road, Westlake Village, California 91361

Cumberlands (formerly Twigs), Pikeville College Press, Pikeville College, Pikeville, Kentucky 41501

CutBank, Department of English, University of Montana, Missoula, Montana 49812

December, December Press, 6232 N. Hoyne, Chicago, Illinois 60659

Denver Quarterly, University of Denver, Denver, Colorado 80208

Descant, P.O. Box 314, Station P, Toronto, Ontario M5S 2S5, Canada

descant, Department of English, Texas Christian University Station, Forth Worth, Texas 76129

Ecology Digest, P.O. Box 60961, Sacramento, California 95860

Epoch, 245 Goldwin Smith Hall, Cornell University, Ithaca, New York 14853

Esquire, 2 Park Avenue, New York, New York 10016

Event, Kwantlen College, P.O. Box 9030, Surrey, British Columbia V3T 5H8, Canada

Expanding Horizons, 93-05 68th Avenue, Forest Hills, New York 11375

Fantasy & Science Fiction, Box 56, Cornwall, Connecticut 06753

Fiction, c/o Department of English, City College of New York, New York, New York 10031

Fiction International, Department of English, Saint Lawrence University, Canton, New York 13617

Fiction-Texas, College of the Mainland, Texas City, Texas 77590

Fiddlehead, The Observatory, University of New Brunswick, Fredericton, New Brunswick E3B 5A3, Canada

Four Quarters, LaSalle College, 20th and Olney Avenues, Philadelphia, Pennsylvania 19141

Gargoyle, P.O. Box 57206, Washington, D.C. 20037

Georgia Review, University of Georgia, Athens, Georgia 30602

Good Housekeeping, 959 Eighth Avenue, New York, New York 10019

Grain, Box 1885, Saskatoon, Saskatchewan S7K 3S2, Canada

Grand Street, 50 Riverside Drive, New York, New York 10024

Great Lakes Review, P.O. Box 122, Anspach Hall, Central Michigan University, Mt. Pleasant, Michigan 48858

Great River Review, P.O. Box 14805, Minneapolis, Minnesota 55414

Greensboro Review, Department of English, University of North Carolina at Greensboro, Greensboro, North Carolina 27412

Harper's Magazine, 2 Park Avenue, New York, New York 10016

Harpoon, P.O. Box 2581, Anchorage, Alaska 99510

Hawaii Review, University of Hawaii, Department of English, 1733 Donaghho Road, Honolulu, Hawaii 96822

Helicon Nine, 6 Petticoat Lane, Kansas City, Missouri 64106

Hoboken Terminal, P.O. Box 841, Hoboken, New Jersey 07030

Hudson Review, 65 East 55th Street, New York, New York 10022

Indiana Review, 316 N. Jordan, Bloomington, Indiana 47405

Indiana Writes, 110 Morgan Hall, Indiana University, Bloomington, Indiana 47401

In Roads, 87-93 College Street, Burlington, Vermont 05401

Iowa Review, EPB 308, University of Iowa, Iowa City, Iowa 52242

Issues, Box 1930, Brown University, Providence, Rhode Island 02912

Kansas Quarterly, Department of English, Denison Hall, Kansas State University, Manhattan, Kansas 66506

Kenyon Review, Kenyon College, Gambier, Ohio 43022

Lilith, The Jewish Women's Magazine, 250 West 57th Street, New York, New York 10019

Literary Review, Fairleigh Dickinson University, Madison, New Jersey 07940

Little Magazine, Dragon Press, P.O. Box 78, Pleasantville, New York 10570

Mademoiselle, 350 Madison Avenue, New York, New York 10017

Malahat Review, University of Victoria, Box 1700, Victoria, British Columbia V8W 2Y2, Canada

Massachusetts Review, Memorial Hall, University of Massachusetts, Amherst, Massachusetts 01002

Matrix, Box 510, Lennoxville, Quebec J1M 1Z7, Canada

Mendocino Review, 18601 North Highwood One, Fort Bragg, California 95437

Michigan Quarterly Review, 3032 Rackham Building, University of Michigan, Ann Arbor, Michigan 48109

Mid-American Review, 106 Hanna Hall, Department of English, Bowling Green State University, Bowling Green, Ohio 43403

Mississippi Review, Center for Writers, Southern Station, Box 5144, Hattiesburg, Mississippi 39406

Missouri Review, Department of English 231 A & S, University of Missouri-Columbia, Columbia, Missouri 65211

Mother Jones, 625 Third Street, San Francisco, California 94107

Ms., 199 West 40th Street, New York, New York 10018

MSS, Department of English, State University of New York, Binghamton, New York 13901

Nantucket Review, P.O. Box 1234, Nantucket, Massachusetts 02554

National Jewish Monthly, 1640 Rhode Island Avenue, N.W., Washington, D.C. 20036

Negative Capability, 6116 Timberly Road North, Mobile, Alabama 36609

New Directions, W.W. Norton Company, 500 Fifth Avenue, New York, New York 10110

New England Review, Box 170, Hanover, New Hampshire 03755

New Laurel Review, 828 Lesseps Street, New Orleans, Louisiana 70117

New Letters, University of Missouri-Kansas City, 5346 Charlotte, Kansas City, Missouri 64110

New Mexico Humanities Review, Box A, New Mexico Tech, Socorro, New Mexico 87801

New Orleans Review, Loyola University, New Orleans, Louisiana 70118

New Renaissance, 9 Heath Road, Arlington, Massachusetts 02174

New Yorker, 25 West 43rd Street, New York, New York 10036

North American Review, 1222 West 27th Street, Cedar Falls, Iowa 50614

Northwest Review, 369 PLC, University of Oregon, Eugene, Oregon 97403

Ohio Journal, Department of English, Ohio State University, 164 West 17th Avenue, Columbus, Ohio 43210

Ohio Review, Ellis Hall, Ohio University, Athens, Ohio 45701
Old Hickory Review, P.O. Box 1178, Jackson, Tennessee 38301
Omni, 909 Third Avenue, New York, New York 10022
Only Prose, 54 East 7th Street, New York, New York 10003
Ontario Review, 9 Honey Brook, Princeton, New Jersey 08540
Paris Review, 45-39 171 Place, Flushing, New York 11358
Partisan Review, 121 Bay State Road, Boston, Massachusetts 02215
Passages North, William Bonifas Fine Arts Center, 7th Street & 1st Avenue South, Escanaba, Michigan 49829
Pequod, 536 Hill Street, San Francisco, California 94114
Piedmont Review, The Piedmont Literary Society, P.O. Box 3656, Danville, Virginia 24540
Playboy, 919 North Michigan Avenue, Chicago, Illinois 60611
Playgirl, 3420 Ocean Park Boulevard, Suite 3000, Santa Monica, California 90405
Ploughshares, P.O. Box 529, Cambridge, Massachusetts 02139
Plum, 1121 First Avenue, #4, Salt Lake City, Utah 84103
Poetry East, Star Route 1, Box 50, Earlysville, Virginia 22936
Prairie Schooner, 201 Andrews Hall, University of Nebraska, Lincoln, Nebraska 68588
Present Tense, 165 East 56th Street, New York, New York 10022
Primavera, Ida Noyes Hall, University of Chicago, 1212 East 59th Street, Chicago, Illinois 60637
Prism International, University of British Columbia, Vancouver, British Columbia V6T 1W5, Canada
Quarry West, Porter College, University of California, Santa Cruz, California 95060
Quarterly West, 312 Olpin Union, University of Utah, Salt Lake City, Utah 84112
RE:AL, Stephen F. Austin State University, Nacogdoches, Texas 75962
Redbook, 230 Park Avenue, New York, New York 10017
Richmond Quarterly, P.O. Box 12263, Richmond, Virginia 23241
Rubicon, McGill University, 853 rue Sherbrooke ouest, Montreal, Quebec H3A 2T6, Canada
Salmagundi Magazine, Skidmore College, Saratoga Springs, New York 12866
San Jose Studies, San Jose State University, San Jose, California 95192
Saturday Night, 70 Bond Street, Suite 500, Toronto, Ontario M5B 2J3, Canada
Seattle Review, Padelford Hall GN-30, University of Washington, Seattle, Washington 98195
Seventeen, 850 Third Avenue, New York, New York 10022
Sewanee Review, University of the South, Sewanee, Tennessee 37375
Shenandoah, Box 722, Lexington, Virginia 24450

Shout in the Street, Queens College of the City University of New York, 63-30 Kissena Boulevard, Flushing, New York 11367

South Carolina Review, Department of English, Clemson University, Clemson, South Carolina 29631

South Dakota Review, University of South Dakota, Vermillion, South Dakota 57069

Southern Humanities Review, 9088 Haley Center, Auburn University, Alabama 36849

Southern Review, Drawer D, University Station, Baton Rouge, Louisiana 70893

Southwest Review, Southern Methodist University, Dallas, Texas 75275

Sou'wester, Department of English, Southern Illinois University, Edwardsville, Illinois 62026

St. Andrews Review, St. Andrews Presbyterian College, Laurinsburg, North Carolina 28352

Stories, 14 Beacon Street, Boston, Massachusetts 02108

StoryQuarterly, P.O. Box 1416, Northbrook, Illinois 60062

Tendril, Box 512, Green Harbor, Massachusetts 02041

Texas Review, English Department, Sam Houston State University, Huntsville, Texas 77341

Threepenny Review, P.O. Box 9131, Berkeley, California 94709

TriQuarterly, 1735 Benson Avenue, Northwestern University, Evanston, Illinois 60201

Twilight Zone Magazine, 800 Second Avenue, New York, New York 10017

U.S. Catholic, 221 West Madison Street, Chicago, Illinois 60606

University of Windsor Review, Department of English, University of Windsor, Windsor, Ontario N9B 3P4, Canada

Vanderbilt Review, 911 West Vanderbilt Street, Stephenville, Texas 76401

Virginia Quarterly Review, 1 West Range, Charlottesville, Virginia 22903

Vision, 3000 Harry Hines Boulevard, Dallas, Texas 75201

Wascana Review, English Department, University of Regina, Regina, Saskatchewan, Canada

Waves, 79 Denham Drive, Thornhill, Ontario L4J 1P2, Canada

Webster Review, Webster College, Webster Groves, Missouri 63119

West Branch, Department of English, Bucknell University, Lewisburg, Pennsylvania 17837

Western Humanities Review, University of Utah, Salt Lake City, Utah 84112

Whispers, 70 Highland Avenue, Binghamton, New York 13905

Wind/Literary Review, RFD Route #1, Box 809K, Pikeville, Kentucky 41501

Wittenberg Review, Box 1, Recitation Hall, Wittenberg University, Springfield, Ohio 45501

Writers Forum, University of Colorado, P.O. Box 7150, Colorado Springs, Colorado 80933

Yale Review, 250 Church Street, 1902A Yale Station, New Haven, Connecticut 06520

Yankee, Yankee, Inc., Dublin, New Hampshire 03444